- Go to **awmi.net/sg426** to download PDFs of the following resources for each lesson in this study guide:
  - o Outlines
  - o Discipleship Questions
  - o Scriptures
- Share as many copies as you'd like.
- These documents are not for resale.

THE WAR IS OVER

God is Not
Mad, So Stop
Struggling With
Sin and Judgment

Study Guide

Andrew Wommack

The War Is Over Study Guide
ISBN: 978-1-59548-119-1

Copyright © 2008 by Andrew Wommack Ministries, Inc.
P.O. Box 3333
Colorado Springs, CO 80934-3333

Contents

Introduction

The War Is Over will either make you glad or mad, but you won't be indifferent any more! Using God's Word, I counter a tremendous amount of religious teaching masquerading as Christianity today, and I establish the truth of the Gospel. Many people have told me they were shocked at first, but as they meditated on these truths, they were set free (John 8:32).

There needs to be some major changes in the way most Christians believe. The Word clearly reveals that if we aren't getting the right results, it's because we aren't believing right.

For as he thinketh in his heart, so is he.

PROVERBS 23:7

I understand that there's a resistance to changing the way we think, but it's the way we think that has caused us to be the way we are. Most Christians I've met feel like there's a lot of room for improvement in the way they're receiving from God.

Therefore, I encourage you not to reject the truths presented in this study just because they sound different. Listen to the Lord, and let Him speak to you. You'll be blessed to know *The War Is Over*!

How to Use Your Study Guide

Whether you are teaching a class, leading a small group, discipling an individual, or studying *The War Is Over* on your own, you'll find that this ***Study Guide*** is designed for you! Here's how it works:

Each study consists of a **Lesson**, **Lesson Outline**, **Teacher's Guide**, **Discipleship Questions**, an **Answer Key**, and **Scriptures**. Some **Lessons** also have **Additional Information**.

The teacher reads the **Lesson** aloud. While the **Lesson** is being read, students follow along with their own copy of the **Lesson Outline**.

Once the **Lesson** is read, the teacher then facilitates a group Bible study using the **Teacher's Guide**. Simply read aloud one numbered section at a time, ask the corresponding questions that follow, and have the group answer them. Repeat the process for the next numbered section. For your convenience, answers are provided in parentheses.

Except for the corresponding questions and answers, the information on the **Teacher's Guide** is the same as the **Lesson Outline**. Therefore, the group should use their **Lesson Outlines** to assist them in answering the questions.

Whenever a question mentions a specific scripture, be sure to have the group look it up in their Bibles and read it together before answering the question. Feel free to interact with the group over the scriptures and points from the **Lesson** as time allows. Don't let any individual dominate the discussion, but try to draw out the quieter ones for participation in the group conversation too. As much as possible, keep the discussion centered on the scriptures and the **Lesson** points at hand. Remember, the goal is understanding (Matt. 13:19).

Discipleship Questions are provided for further study and meditation. They are designed for use as "homework," but—according to the teacher's discretion—may be helpful during the group study as well. Each **Lesson** comes with an **Answer Key**. As a brief review before launching into the current **Lesson**, the teacher may wish to go over with the group the **Answer Key** for the previous study's **Discipleship Questions**.

Some **Lessons** also have **Additional Information**, which is geared toward the teacher. It contains supplementary information, illustrations, and/or resource recommendations for further study.

Scriptures from the *King James Version* of the Bible are included as another tool for reference and meditation.

For personal study, read the **Lesson** and review the **Teacher's Guide**. Then, do the **Discipleship Questions** and check your work with the **Answer Key**. For maximum impact, be sure to utilize the **Additional Information** and **Scriptures**.

Outline for Group Study:

I. Briefly review the previous study by going over the **Answer Key** for the **Discipleship Questions** (homework).

II. Read the current **Lesson** aloud.
   - A. Be sure that each student has a copy of the **Lesson Outline**.
   - B. While the **Lesson** is being read, students should use their **Lesson Outline** to follow along.

III. Once the **Lesson** is read, facilitate a group Bible study using the **Teacher's Guide**.
   - A. Read one entire numbered section (above).
   - B. Ask the corresponding questions (below).
   - C. Group looks up and reads aloud each specifically mentioned scripture before answering the question.
   - D. Discuss the scripture and the answer/point from the **Lesson** as desired.
   - E. Repeat the process by reading the next numbered section (above).

IV. Distribute copies of the **Discipleship Questions** to be worked on as homework.

Materials Needed:

Study guide, Bible, and enough copies of the **Outline, Discipleship Questions**, and **Scriptures** for each student. (PDFs of the **Outlines, Discipleship Questions**, and **Scriptures** can be downloaded via the URL located on the first page of this study guide.)

Outline for Personal Study:

I. Read **Lesson**.
   - A. Read **Additional Information**, if any.
   - B. Meditate on the **Scriptures**, as desired.

II. Review **Teacher's Guide**.

III. Do **Discipleship Questions**.

IV. Check your work with the **Answer Key**.

Materials Needed:

Study guide, Bible, and something to write with.

Good Will toward Men
LESSON 1

There were in the same country shepherds abiding in the field, keeping watch over their flock by night. And, lo, the angel of the Lord came upon them, and the glory of the Lord shone round about them: and they were sore afraid. And the angel said unto them, Fear not: for, behold, I bring you good tidings of great joy, which shall be to all people. For unto you is born this day in the city of David a Saviour, which is Christ the Lord. And this shall be a sign unto you; Ye shall find the babe wrapped in swaddling clothes, lying in a manger. And suddenly there was with the angel a multitude of the heavenly host praising God, and saying, Glory to God in the highest, and on earth peace, good will toward men.

LUKE 2:8-14

This is a familiar passage of Scripture. All too often we use it to create a certain mood and get ourselves into the "Christmas spirit." Therefore, we don't really think about what this is saying.

Instead of **"Glory to God in the highest, and on earth peace, good will toward men,"** many translations actually render Luke 2:14 to say, **"peace among men," "peace toward men of goodwill,"** or something similar. Since this tends to be the dominant interpretation, most people think that the angels were proclaiming that Jesus' arrival would stop division, end strife, and usher in a new era of peace on earth. They believe this announcement means the Lord was coming to bring peace among men. Yet that's not what this verse is saying.

A Sword

Jesus Himself declared:

Think not that I am come to send peace on earth: I came not to send peace, but a sword. For I am come to set a man at variance against his father, and the daughter against her mother, and the daughter in law against her mother in law. And a man's foes shall be they of his own household.

MATTHEW 10:34-36

The Lord also prophesied that one of the signs of the end times would be increased war, division, and strife.

And ye shall hear of wars and rumours of wars: see that ye be not troubled: for all these things must come to pass, but the end is not yet. For nation shall rise against nation, and kingdom against kingdom…all these are the beginning of sorrows.

MATTHEW 24:6-8

You simply cannot defend the position that Jesus came to bring peace among people. Now, it's true that there are benefits available for those who will receive the Prince of Peace into their hearts. By God's grace, you can turn the other cheek, love your enemies, and operate in a different degree of love (Luke 6:27-29 and 1 Cor. 13). I don't doubt that there has been a tremendous amount of peace among men as a byproduct of people receiving salvation. However, that's not the message the angels were singing. That's not what Jesus Himself said He came here to do.

Jesus Ended the War

What were these angels proclaiming?

Glory to God in the highest, and on earth peace, good will toward men.
Luke 2:14

They were announcing, "Peace. Good will toward men from God!"

Prior to the advent of the Lord Jesus Christ, God was at war against man's sins. His wrath came upon people because of the sin in their lives. Many Christians haven't mentally separated this out and really looked at it. They just run everything in the Bible together. However, a closer examination of God's Word reveals there was a wrath and a judgment from God against people in the Old Testament that is totally unjustified and wrong in the New Testament. Why? Jesus ended the war between God and man. He made all the difference!

Yet most people run all of this together. They still think of God as being angry at their sins. They mistakenly believe there is still a war going on between God and man and that every time they sin, somehow or another it's a new affront against Him. You'll hear people say "God is ticked off!" and quote Old Testament scriptures about the wrath of God falling on people. "God is angry today. He's dangling our country over hell by a thin thread that's on fire, and He's just about ready to turn us over to the devil." People are proclaiming that God is the one who sent the hurricanes and tsunamis and that He's going to cause other disasters too. Well-known religious leaders stood up and declared that God was the one who sent the terrorist attacks and that this is the beginning of His judgment on our nation. They're still proclaiming that there is wrath from God toward men.

Good News

Yet this isn't the message of the New Testament. These angels who announced the birth of Jesus understood the Gospel. They understood that He came to pay the price, to redeem us, and to stop God's wrath upon sin. The New Testament church should be proclaiming to people that their sins have been paid for. We ought to be telling people the Gospel.

The Gospel is good news. In fact, this Greek word translated *Gospel* actually means "nearly-too-good-to-be-true news." The Gospel is the nearly-too-good-to-be-true news that God isn't angry with you, that He loves you, and that He wants to extend all of His blessings toward you.

As a whole, the church isn't preaching this. We're still telling people that God is angry with them, and then we wonder why they aren't beating down the doors to get into church. It's the goodness of God that leads people to repentance (Rom. 2:4)!

God is just, but Jesus paid the price. He totally changed the way God deals with mankind. That's what these angels were singing about.

God Isn't Upset

While summarizing the ministry of Jesus, Paul made the same point in 2 Corinthians.

> **Therefore if any man be in Christ, he is a new creature: old things are passed away; behold, all things are become new. And all things are of God, who hath reconciled us to himself by Jesus Christ.**
>
> 2 CORINTHIANS 5:17-18

To *reconcile* is simply to make friendly or to bring back into harmony. God is not upset with you!

Some of the things I'm about to share run so contrary to our Christian culture that you may be tempted to reject them and lay this book aside. However, I'm just going to step out in faith and make some radical statements, trusting that the Holy Spirit will bear witness to you. I pray you'll read the rest of the book and give me a chance to explain. This could be the breakthrough in your relationship with God that you've been believing for.

God is not upset. In fact, He's not only *not* mad at you as a Christian—which many believers really struggle with—but He's also not mad at unbelievers. God is not about to judge us.

Wrath Appeased

I used to preach that if God didn't judge America, He'd have to apologize to Sodom and Gomorrah. Our country is as corrupt—or pretty close—as Sodom and Gomorrah. I used to proclaim that until my mind became renewed to God's Word. Now I know that if God were to judge America, He'd have to apologize to Jesus.

Jesus made a difference in the way God relates to mankind. This is what the angels were praising Him for. "Glory to God in the highest. The war is over!" The anger and wrath of God have been atoned and appeased. God's wrath was placed upon His Son, and He isn't angry with us anymore.

> **And all things are of God, who hath reconciled us to himself by Jesus Christ, and hath given to us the ministry of reconciliation.**
>
> 2 CORINTHIANS 5:18

The Lord made us friendly. He brought us—not only believers, but all of mankind—back into harmony with God. The debt has been paid. Now we must receive it. We must put our faith in the Lord before what He has provided has its full effect in our lives. But God's wrath has been appeased. Man may not be reconciled to God, but God has been reconciled to man. His wrath is over, and He's given us the ministry of reconciliation!

The reason Christianity isn't having a greater impact on our world today is because we aren't preaching this message.

The Power of God

I am not ashamed of the gospel of Christ: for it is the power of God unto salvation to every one that believeth.

ROMANS 1:16

The meaning of the Greek word translated **"salvation"** here isn't limited only to the forgiveness of sins; it's also talking about healing, prosperity, and deliverance—everything Jesus came to do. Therefore, the power of God for you and me to receive salvation—forgiveness of sins, healing, prosperity, and deliverance—is released through the Gospel, the nearly-too-good-to-be-true news, of Jesus Christ.

As a whole, the church isn't preaching this. The church is telling people, "You're going to hell. You're a sinner, and God is angry!" It's true that before a person is born again, they are, by nature, a sinner. Their sin separated them from God. Although this is true, it's not "good news." It's not the Gospel.

The Gospel speaks of how God placed all of the punishment for our sins upon Jesus. In spite of our sins, our relative unworthiness, and need, Christ paid the price for us. Justice demanded our punishment, but Jesus took it for us. Now God's wrath has been forever satisfied. He's not angry with people. Jesus paid the price, and all we must do is receive that payment. That's good news. That's the Gospel!

Since much of the church isn't preaching the Gospel, the nearly-too-good-to-be-true news of Jesus Christ, people aren't coming to the Lord. The power of the Gospel isn't in manifestation much today, and that's why people are turning away from it.

"Not Imputing"

Now, I'm not against the church. I love God's people everywhere. However, very few of them recognize the Gospel—as recorded and expressed in the Word—when they hear it. That's why I usually prefer to hold citywide meetings in a hotel or convention center, rather than in a building called a "church." I've been run out of town, kicked off radio stations, and removed from television stations for preaching that God isn't mad anymore. Yet this is the same message the angels proclaimed at Jesus' birth!

Glory to God in the highest, and on earth peace, good will toward men.

LUKE 2:14

"God's not angry! There's peace! He's not upset with you!" Yet somehow or another, people today just love to let others know just how "angry" God is, thinking this will drive them away from hell. That's simply not the way it works!

The Lord has given us the ministry of reconciliation.

> **God was in Christ**, reconciling the world unto himself, **not imputing their trespasses unto them**; and hath committed unto us the word of reconciliation.
>
> 2 CORINTHIANS 5:19, EMPHASIS MINE

God was in Christ not imputing! This word *impute* means "to hold against." It's actually an accounting term. If you bought something and said "Put that on my account," the company would write it down. Then, at the end of the month, you'd have to pay up. **"Not imputing"** would be like using a credit card to purchase something and it never being charged to your bill. That amount isn't held against you. This verse says that God was in Christ not holding man's sins against them.

"Hush Money"

This was the reason Jesus was so radical. It's why the religious leaders of His day came out against Him. They stayed in power and kept people under their thumbs by holding the wrath of God over their heads. They said, "We're the ones who have the truth. If you don't come to our synagogue, give us your tithe, and all these other things, then God will get you!"

It's like the mafia. Guido comes and knocks on your door. He says, "There sure is a lot of arson in this area, and many stores have been broken into. Your business stands a good chance of getting robbed or burned to the ground. But if you pay me, the boys and I will keep that from happening." Of course, Guido and the boys are the ones doing all this, but he wants you to pay them "hush money."

In a sense, this is what many churches are preaching. "God is angry with you, and He's fixing to get you. But if you will come to church, pay your tithes, read the Bible an hour a day, do this, and do that, then you can appease the wrath of God. Then He won't send your children to the hospital, wreck your marriage, or otherwise destroy your life." To a large degree, the church is like the mafia, saying, "If you'll pay up, if you'll do all the things on our list, then God will stay off your case for one more week." That's how they're trying to motivate people to serve the Lord.

But the Word reveals that God was in Christ not imputing man's sins unto them. Jesus—both by His life and His message—declared, "God isn't mad at you anymore. Your sins aren't a problem!"

Most people will stone you for saying, "Your sin isn't a problem with God." They'll ask, "How could you say such a thing? You're making light of sin. You're acting as though there is nothing wrong with sin." No, that's not what I'm saying. I'm not encouraging anyone to sin. If you just stick with me, I'll be putting all of this into perspective.

Sin Isn't the Issue

Anyone who takes what I'm sharing and says "This is awesome. I love it! Now I can go live in sin" needs to be born again. The Word declares that…

Every man that hath this hope in him purifieth himself, even as he is pure.

1 JOHN 3:3

If you are truly born again and have the hope of being like Jesus, then you're looking for a way to overcome sin—not indulge in it! If you take what I'm saying and tell people, "Andrew is encouraging people to sin," you're either lying or you've misunderstood what I'm communicating.

When people accuse me of making light of sin, I respond, "You're making light of Jesus!" I'm not saying that sin isn't bad and that you can just go live in it. Sin is terrible, but it's not as big as Jesus. The Lord paid for our sins. The payment He made is infinitely greater than the sins of the entire world. One drop of Jesus' blood was more holy, more righteous, more pure than all of the impurity and ungodliness of this entire world put together. When the Lord Jesus Christ died for our sins, His sacrifice forever satisfied the wrath of God. Sin isn't the issue!

Good Will toward Men
LESSON 1 – OUTLINE

I. Luke 2 is a familiar passage of Scripture.

> **There were in the same country shepherds abiding in the field, keeping watch over their flock by night. And, lo, the angel of the Lord came upon them, and the glory of the Lord shone round about them: and they were sore afraid. And the angel said unto them, Fear not: for, behold, I bring you good tidings of great joy, which shall be to all people. For unto you is born this day in the city of David a Saviour, which is Christ the Lord. And this shall be a sign unto you; Ye shall find the babe wrapped in swaddling clothes, lying in a manger.**
>
> LUKE 2:8-12

> **And suddenly there was with the angel a multitude of the heavenly host praising God, and saying, Glory to God in the highest, and on earth peace, good will toward men.**
>
> LUKE 2:13-14

A. Most people think that the angels were proclaiming that Jesus' arrival would stop division, end strife, and usher in a new era of peace on earth.

B. That's not what Luke 2:13-14 is saying.

C. You simply cannot defend the position that Jesus came to bring peace among people.

> **Think not that I am come to send peace on earth: I came not to send peace, but a sword. For I am come to set a man at variance against his father, and the daughter against her mother, and the daughter in law against her mother in law. And a man's foes shall be they of his own household.**
>
> MATTHEW 10:34-36

> **And ye shall hear of wars and rumours of wars: see that ye be not troubled: for all these things must come to pass, but the end is not yet. For nation shall rise against nation, and kingdom against kingdom…all these are the beginning of sorrows.**
>
> MATTHEW 24:6-8

II. The angels were announcing, "Peace. Good will toward men from God!"

> **Glory to God in the highest, and on earth peace, good will toward men.**
>
> LUKE 2:14

A. Prior to the advent of the Lord Jesus Christ, God was at war against man's sins.

B. His wrath came upon people because of the sin in their lives.

C. Jesus ended the war between God and man—He made all the difference!

D. Yet most people still think of God as being angry at their sins.

III. The Gospel is the nearly-too-good-to-be-true news that God isn't angry with you, that He loves you, and that He wants to extend all of His blessings toward you.

A. It's the goodness of God that leads people to repentance (Rom. 2:4).

B. God is just, but Jesus paid the price.

C. Jesus totally changed the way God deals with mankind.

IV. The anger and wrath of God have been atoned and appeased.

> **Therefore if any man be in Christ, he is a new creature: old things are passed away; behold, all things are become new. And all things are of God, who hath reconciled us to himself by Jesus Christ, and hath given to us the ministry of reconciliation.**
>
> 2 CORINTHIANS 5:17-18

A. *Reconcile* simply means "to make friendly" or "to bring back into harmony."

B. God's wrath was placed upon His Son, and He isn't angry with us anymore!

C. The reason Christianity isn't having a greater impact on our world today is because we aren't preaching this message.

D. The power of God for you and me to receive salvation—forgiveness of sins, healing, prosperity, and deliverance—is released through the Gospel, the nearly-too-good-to-be-true news, of Jesus Christ.

> **I am not ashamed of the gospel of Christ: for it is the power of God unto salvation to every one that believeth.**
>
> ROMANS 1:16

V. God was in Christ not holding man's sins against them.

> **God was in Christ, reconciling the world unto himself, not imputing their trespasses unto them; and hath committed unto us the word of reconciliation.**
>
> 2 Corinthians 5:19, emphasis mine

A. Jesus—both by His life and message—declared, "God isn't mad at you anymore. Your sins aren't a problem!"

B. Anyone who takes what I'm sharing and says "This is awesome. I love it! Now I can go live in sin" needs to be born again.

Every man that hath this hope in him purifieth himself, even as he is pure.

1 JOHN 3:3

C. If you are truly born again and have the hope of being like Jesus, then you're looking for a way to overcome sin—not indulge it!

D. When the Lord Jesus Christ died for our sins, His sacrifice forever satisfied the wrath of God.

E. Sin isn't the issue!

Good Will toward Men
LESSON 1 – TEACHER'S GUIDE

1. Luke 2:8-14 is a familiar passage of Scripture. Most people think that the angels were proclaiming that Jesus' arrival would stop division, end strife, and usher in a new era of peace on earth. That's not what this passage is saying. The position that Jesus came to bring peace among people simply cannot be defended (Matt. 10:34-36 and 24:6-8).

2. The angels were announcing, "Peace. Good will toward men from God!" (Luke 2:14). Prior to the advent of the Lord Jesus Christ, God was at war against man's sins. His wrath came upon people because of the sin in their lives. Jesus ended the war between God and man—He made all the difference! Yet most people still think of God as being angry at our sins.

3. The Gospel is the nearly-too-good-to-be-true news that God isn't angry with us, that He loves us, and that He wants to extend all of His blessings toward us. It's the goodness of God that leads people to repentance (Rom. 2:4). God is just, but Jesus paid the price. He totally changed the way God deals with mankind.

4. The anger and wrath of God has been atoned and appeased (2 Cor. 5:17-18). *Reconcile* simply means "to make friendly" or "to bring back into harmony." God's wrath was placed upon His Son, and He isn't angry with us anymore! The reason Christianity isn't having a greater impact on our world today is because we aren't preaching this message. The power of God for us to receive salvation—forgiveness of sins, healing, prosperity, and deliverance—is released through the Gospel, the nearly-too-good-to-be-true news, of Jesus Christ (Rom. 1:16).

5. God was in Christ not holding man's sins against them (2 Cor. 5:19). Jesus—both by His life and message—declared, "God isn't mad at man anymore. Your sins aren't a problem!" Anyone who takes what I'm sharing and says "This is awesome. I love it! Now I can go live in sin" needs to be born again. If we are truly born again and have the hope of being like Jesus, then we're looking for a way to overcome sin—not indulge in it (1 John 3:3). When the Lord Jesus Christ died for our sins, His sacrifice forever satisfied the wrath of God. Sin isn't the issue!

1. A. Read Luke 2:8-14. What do most people think that the angels were proclaiming? (That Jesus' arrival would stop division, end strife, and usher in a new era of peace on earth)
   B. In light of Matthew 10:34-36 and 24:6-8, can the position that Jesus came to bring peace among people be defended? (No)
2. A. What were the angels announcing in Luke 2:14? ("Peace. Good will toward men from God!")
   B. What did Jesus end? (The war between God and man)
3. A. What is the Gospel? (The nearly-too-good-to-be-true news that God isn't angry with us, that He loves us, and that He wants to extend all of His blessings toward us)
   B. According to Romans 2:4, what is it that leads people to repentance? (The goodness of God)

4. A. Read 2 Corinthians 5:17-18. What has been atoned and appeased? (The anger and wrath of God)
   B. Read Romans 1:16. How is the power of God for us to receive salvation—forgiveness of sins, healing, prosperity, and deliverance—released? (Through the Gospel, the nearly-too-good-to-be-true news, of Jesus Christ)
5. A. According to 2 Corinthians 5:19, what was God doing in Christ? (Not holding man's sins against him)
   B. According to 1 John 3:3, what are people who are truly born again looking for? (A way to overcome sin)

Good Will toward Men
LESSON 1 – DISCIPLESHIP QUESTIONS

1. In Luke 2:8-12, to whom did the angel of the Lord come?

2. How did they react when the glory of the Lord shone round about them?

3. What did the angel say to them?

4. Whose birth was being announced?

5. How shall they find the Baby?

6. In Luke 2:13-14, who joined the angel?

7. What were they doing?

8. What were they saying?

9. According to Matthew 10:34-36, did Jesus come to send peace on earth?

10. What did He come to send instead?

11. Who did He say a man's foes would be?

12. In Matthew 24:6-8, Jesus said that all these things must come to pass, but…
    A. You will not hear of them.
    B. The end is not yet.
    C. The end is now.

13. What are all these bad things the beginning of?

14. Which of these best summarizes Luke 6:27-29?
    A. Bless them who do good to you.
    B. Curse them who hate you.
    C. Love your enemies.
    D. All of the above.
    E. None of the above.

15. Which of these are included in what 1 Corinthians 13 reveals about God's kind of love?
    A. Charity never fails.
    B. Charity seeks not her own.
    C. Charity believes all things.
    D. Charity is not puffed up.
    E. All of the above.
    F. None of the above.

16. According to Romans 2:4, what leads people to repentance?

17. Who is a new creature in 2 Corinthians 5:17-19?

18. What ministry has Jesus given to us?

19. Who was in Christ, reconciling the world to Himself?

20. What was He doing with people's trespasses?

21. According to Romans 1:16, Paul was not ashamed of what?

22. It is the power of God unto what?

23. To whom?

24. According to 1 John 3:3, what does everyone who has this hope in them do?

25. Even as who is pure?

Good Will toward Men
LESSON 1 – ANSWER KEY

1. Shepherds abiding in the field, keeping watch over their flock by night.

2. They were sore afraid.

3. Fear not, I bring you good tidings of great joy.

4. The Savior, which is Christ the Lord.

5. Wrapped in swaddling clothes, lying in a manger.

6. A multitude of the heavenly host.

7. Praising God.

8. Glory to God in the highest, and on earth peace, good will toward men.

9. No.

10. A sword.

11. They of his own household.

12. B. The end is not yet.

13. Sorrows.

14. C. Love your enemies.

15. A. Charity never fails.
    B. Charity seeks not her own.
    C. Charity believes all things.
    D. Charity is not puffed up.
    E. All of the above.

16. The goodness of God.

17. Anyone in Christ.

18. The ministry of reconciliation.

19. God.

20. He was not imputing their trespasses unto them.

21. The Gospel of Christ.

22. Salvation.

23. Everyone that believes.

24. They purify themselves.

25. Jesus.

Good Will toward Men
LESSON 1 - SCRIPTURES

And there were in the same country shepherds abiding in the field, keeping watch over their flock by night. And, lo, the angel of the Lord came upon them, and the glory of the Lord shone round about them: and they were sore afraid. And the angel said unto them, Fear not: for, behold, I bring you good tidings of great joy, which shall be to all people. For unto you is born this day in the city of David a Saviour, which is Christ the Lord. And this shall be a sign unto you; Ye shall find the babe wrapped in swaddling clothes, lying in a manger. And suddenly there was with the angel a multitude of the heavenly host praising God, and saying, Glory to God in the highest, and on earth peace, good will toward men.

Luke 2:8-14

Think not that I am come to send peace on earth: I came not to send peace, but a sword. For I am come to set a man at variance against his father, and the daughter against her mother, and the daughter in law against her mother in law. And a man's foes shall be they of his own household.

Matthew 10:34-36

And ye shall hear of wars and rumours of wars: see that ye be not troubled: for all these things must come to pass, but the end is not yet. For nation shall rise against nation, and kingdom against kingdom: and there shall be famines, and pestilences, and earthquakes, in divers places. All these are the beginning of sorrows.

Matthew 24:6-8

But I say unto you which hear, Love your enemies, do good to them which hate you, Bless them that curse you, and pray for them which despitefully use you. And unto him that smiteth thee on the one cheek offer also the other; and him that taketh away thy cloke forbid not to take thy coat also.

Luke 6:27-29

Though I speak with the tongues of men and of angels, and have not charity, I am become as sounding brass, or a tinkling cymbal. And though I have the gift of prophecy, and understand all mysteries, and all knowledge; and though I have all faith, so that I could remove mountains, and have not charity, I am nothing. And though I bestow all my goods to feed the poor, and though I give my body to be burned, and have not charity, it profiteth me nothing. Charity suffereth long, and is kind; charity envieth not; charity vaunteth not itself, is not puffed up, Doth not behave itself unseemly, seeketh not her own, is not easily provoked, thinketh no evil; Rejoiceth not in iniquity, but rejoiceth in the truth; Beareth all things, believeth all things, hopeth all things, endureth all things. Charity never faileth: but whether there be prophecies, they shall fail; whether there be tongues, they shall cease; whether there be knowledge, it shall vanish away. For we know in part, and we prophesy in part. But when that which is perfect is come, then that which is in part shall be done away. When I was a child, I spake as a child, I understood as a child, I thought as a child: but when I became a man, I put away childish things. For now we see through a glass, darkly; but then face to face: now I know in part; but then shall I know even as also I am known. And now abideth faith, hope, charity, these three; but the greatest of these is charity.

1 CORINTHIANS 13

Or despisest thou the riches of his goodness and forbearance and longsuffering; not knowing that the goodness of God leadeth thee to repentance?

ROMANS 2:4

Therefore if any man be in Christ, he is a new creature: old things are passed away; behold, all things are become new. And all things are of God, who hath reconciled us to himself by Jesus Christ, and hath given to us the ministry of reconciliation; To wit, that God was in Christ, reconciling the world unto himself, not imputing their trespasses unto them; and hath committed unto us the word of reconciliation.

2 CORINTHIANS 5:17-19

For I am not ashamed of the gospel of Christ: for it is the power of God unto salvation to every one that believeth; to the Jew first, and also to the Greek.

ROMANS 1:16

And every man that hath this hope in him purifieth himself, even as he is pure.

1 JOHN 3:3

Be Reconciled to God
LESSON 2

Contrary to popular opinion, people don't go to hell because of their sins. They go to hell because they rejected the payment for their sins. They go to hell because they refused to receive the Savior. When Christians proclaim "If you don't quit dipping, cussing, chewing, and doing this and that, God won't accept you," they're imputing people's sins unto them. They are also demeaning and decreasing the value of Jesus' sacrifice. In reality, they're saying, "Your sin is bigger and more important than what Jesus did on the cross."

But God was in Jesus, not imputing man's sins unto him. Sin isn't the issue. It's all a matter of what people are doing with Jesus. Have they made a commitment of their lives to Him, or are they rejecting Him? If people don't receive Jesus, they reject the only payment available for their sins. There's no other way to the Father except through His Son.

Jesus saith unto him, I am the way, the truth, and the life: no man cometh unto the Father, but by me.

JOHN 14:6

If they don't accept the payment for their sins—the Lord Jesus Christ—they'll be rejected and cast into hell—not because of their sins—but because they rejected Jesus. In hell, they'll be held accountable and have to pay for those sins. But the truth is, all their sins have been paid for by Jesus. Therefore, sin really isn't the issue. The issue is, what are you going to do with Jesus?

Receive God's Love

If you have already received the Lord Jesus Christ, then you've been born again. Sin isn't an issue. God isn't angry with you over your sin. The Lord wants you to stop focusing on sin and start receiving His love. God loves you even though you don't deserve it. He's pleased with you even though you're not pleased with yourself. If you could ever get a picture of the price Jesus paid for your sins, you'd fall head over heels in love with Him. And since faith works by love (Gal. 5:6), your faith would shoot through the roof!

When you read the Word with this proper mindset, 1 John makes much more sense. It's not saying, "Keep the commandments to get God to love you"; it's saying, "If you understood the love of God, you'd keep His commandments. If you truly comprehended just how much Jesus loves you and the price He paid to reconcile you to God the Father, you'd serve Him more accidentally than you ever have on purpose. You'd live holier accidentally, motivated by love, than you ever have on purpose due to fear and dread. You'd experience a whole new joy and peace in your relationship with God that you've never had before."

God was in Christ, reconciling the world unto himself, not imputing their trespasses unto them; and hath committed unto us the word of reconciliation.

2 CORINTHIANS 5:19

This is the word that the church should be preaching. God's not angry. He's not even in a bad mood. He loves you and has paid the price for you. Receive Him. Receive His love! We shouldn't be proclaiming, "If our country doesn't repent, God's going to judge us. The wrath of God is coming!" It's simply not true. God didn't send the terrorists to kill all those people. He didn't send those hurricanes and tsunamis that ruined those cities and swept all those folks away. That wasn't God.

However, a time is coming when this current age of grace—the church age—will come to an end. The book of Revelation makes it very clear that there will come a time when the Lord says, "All right, that's it." At that time, those who have accepted Him will be received into joy and peace, but those who have rejected Him will suffer the wrath of God. And when God's judgment is poured out as revealed in Revelation, nobody will wonder, *Is this the wrath of God?* They'll all know beyond a shadow of a doubt exactly what's happening. It'll make these recent hurricanes look like spring showers in comparison. Nobody will be debating or guessing, "Was this the wrath of God?" They'll know it.

Right now, though, the grace of God is extended toward all people. We should be telling people, "God loves you!" We ought to be saying the same thing the angels sang at the announcement of Christ's arrival on earth: "Glory to God in the highest! Peace on earth from God toward men. God's not angry with you!" Isn't that good news?

An Accurate Representation

Now then we are ambassadors for Christ.

2 Corinthians 5:20

Ambassadors don't just proclaim whatever they want; ambassadors must be in touch with their home country so they can accurately represent it. For instance, the United States ambassador represents the president and the people of the United States of America. Ambassadors aren't free to make up their own message. Their job is to accurately represent those who have sent them. As believers, we are supposed to be doing the same thing. We're supposed to be representing God.

We are supposed to have the same ministry Jesus had—and God, in Christ, did not impute man's sins unto him. He ate with publicans, harlots, and other sinners who wouldn't have anything to do with God anymore because the religious system had condemned them so much. These are the ones Jesus built relationships with and extended love toward. We are His ambassadors. We are supposed to be ministering His message, saying what He's told us to say.

Most Christians today aren't proclaiming that message. They've adopted a religious system that has been entrenched for hundreds of years. They're saying, "God is angry. If you don't do this and that, He's going to pour out His wrath on you. If you don't do this and that, God won't answer your prayers. If you aren't holy, God won't move!" And they're imputing people's sins unto them. Satan uses that to keep people beat down and discouraged.

I recently received an email from a partner couple thanking me. This couple has been listening to me for four or five years. A few days ago, the husband died of a blood clot, or something similar, in the middle of the night. The wife wrote, saying, "Because I've been listening to you, I knew what to do." She raised him from the dead. He got up, went to the bathroom, and came back to bed. Everything is fine and she was praising God that she knew what to do.

Faith Works by Love

Let's say you were attending one of my meetings when someone came forward and fell over dead. If I said, "We're going to pray for this person, and I believe God is going to raise them from the dead," you'd probably say, "Go for it, brother!" Then you'd eagerly join me up front because you'd want to see it. You'd think, *This is awesome! I'll have a great story to tell everybody.* You'd be excited until I said, "All right, I want *you* to pray for them." Then, instead of excitement and faith, fear would hit you. Do you know why? It's not because you doubt God's ability. It's because you doubt God's willingness to use His ability through you, because you know you aren't worthy.

Most of us believe that God only moves in our lives when we're worthy. We've tied His ability to our goodness. The moment we do that, Satan will defeat us, because our own hearts will condemn us and let us know we don't deserve God moving in our lives. But that's not the message Jesus brought. He wasn't imputing man's sins unto him. He told us to preach a message that tells people, "The war is over. God isn't mad anymore!"

Now, this doesn't mean that it's all up to God. If it were, you would receive from Him because He is a good God. He has nothing but good things in store for you. However, you must believe God in order to receive from Him. You don't have to be holy and do everything just right, but you do have to believe. If you feel so unworthy and feel you've messed up so badly that God doesn't love you, that's unbelief. That is not the message of the Gospel, and it's the very thing that's keeping your faith from working.

Again, faith works by love (Gal. 5:6). If you understand how much God loves you—that He carries your picture around in His wallet; that He isn't angry, disappointed, or ashamed of you; and that He's proud of you—your faith would go through the roof. You'd say, "Any God who could love me and overlook all the stupid things I've done is an awesome God. If He'll do that, He'll do anything!"

Gone and Forgotten

Now then we are ambassadors for Christ, as though God did beseech you by us; we pray you in Christ's stead, be ye reconciled to God.

2 Corinthians 5:20

That's my purpose in writing this book. I want to help you become reconciled to God. God has reconciled Himself to you. He has forgiven your sins and taken them away. He's not angry with you. God is now friendly and harmonized with you. Will you reconcile yourself to God? Will you now accept what He has said? This is the message we're supposed to be sharing.

We pray you in Christ's stead, be ye reconciled to God. For he [God the Father] **hath made him** [Jesus] **to be sin for us, who knew no sin; that we might be made the righteousness of God in him.**

2 CORINTHIANS 5:20-21, BRACKETS MINE

The Lord didn't just ignore your sins. He didn't just somehow or another say, "All right, I'm not going to hold your sins against you." He paid for your sins. Your sins are paid for through the Lord Jesus. He not only took your sins away, but then He made you the righteousness of God. Jesus took your sin into Himself and suffered for your sins on the tree. He paid the penalty for your sins and then gave you His righteousness. You aren't just forgiven. You aren't just an "old sinner" who's been saved by grace. You were an "old sinner," but you were saved by grace and are now the righteousness of God in Christ Jesus. God sees you righteous, holy, and pure. He's not angry with you. It's not a matter of Him just turning the other way and somehow "overlooking" your sins. They've been paid for! They're gone! Your sins have been obliterated.

Your sins have been cast into the sea of forgetfulness. He has forgotten them (Heb. 8:12 and 10:17).

As far as the east is from the west, so far hath he removed our transgressions from us.

PSALM 103:12

God isn't looking at your sins. He's not dealing with you based on the way you deal with yourself.

Be Reconciled to God
LESSON 2 – OUTLINE

I. When people don't receive Jesus, they reject the only payment available for their sins.

    A. There's no other way to the Father except through His Son.

> **Jesus saith unto him, I am the way, the truth, and the life: no man cometh unto the Father, but by me.**
>
> JOHN 14:6

    B. If they don't accept the payment for their sins—the Lord Jesus Christ—they'll be rejected and cast into hell, not because of their sins, but because of rejecting Jesus.

    C. Since all their sins have already been paid for by Jesus, sin really isn't the issue.

    D. The issue is, what are you going to do with Jesus?

II. If you have already received the Lord Jesus Christ, then you've been born again.

    A. The Lord wants you to stop focusing on sin and start receiving His love.

    B. If you could ever get a picture of the price Jesus paid for your sins, you'd fall head over heels in love with Him.

    C. Since faith works by love (Gal. 5:6), your faith would shoot through the roof!

    D. If you truly comprehended just how much Jesus loves you and the price He paid to reconcile you to God the Father, you'd serve Him more accidentally than you ever have on purpose.

> **God was in Christ, reconciling the world unto himself, not imputing their trespasses unto them; and hath committed unto us the word of reconciliation.**
>
> 2 CORINTHIANS 5:19

III. We should be telling people, "God loves you. He isn't angry with you."

    A. A time is coming when this current age of grace—the church age—will come to an end.

    B. But right now, the grace of God is extended toward all people.

    C. As His ambassadors, we are supposed to be ministering His message, saying what He's told us to say.

> **Now then we are ambassadors for Christ, as though God did beseech you by us; we pray you in Christ's stead, be ye reconciled to God.**
>
> 2 CORINTHIANS 5:20

IV. Most of us believe that God only moves in our lives when we're worthy.

    A. We've tied His ability to our goodness.

    B. You must believe to receive.

    C. You don't have to be holy and do everything just right, but you do have to believe.

    D. If you understand how much God loves you—that He carries your picture around in His wallet; that He isn't angry, disappointed, or ashamed of you; and that He's proud of you—your faith would go through the roof.

V. Jesus paid the penalty for your sins and then gave you His righteousness.

> **We pray you in Christ's stead, be ye reconciled to God. For he** [God the Father] **hath made him** [Jesus] **to be sin for us, who knew no sin; that we might be made the righteousness of God in him.**
>
> 2 CORINTHIANS 5:20-21, BRACKETS MINE

    A. You were an "old sinner," but you were saved by grace and are now the righteousness of God in Christ Jesus.

    B. God sees you righteous, holy, and pure—He's not angry with you.

    C. Your sins have been obliterated, and He's forgotten them (Heb. 8:12 and 10:17).

> **As far as the east is from the west, so far hath he remove our transgressions from us.**
>
> PSALM 103:12

    D. God isn't looking at your sins.

    E. He's not dealing with you based on the way you deal with yourself.

Be Reconciled to God
LESSON 2 – TEACHER'S GUIDE

1.   When people don't receive Jesus, they reject the only payment available for their sins. There's no other way to the Father except through His Son (John 14:6). If they don't accept the payment for their sins—the Lord Jesus Christ—they'll be rejected and cast into hell, not because of their sins, but because they rejected Jesus. Since all our sins have already been paid for by Jesus, sin really isn't the issue. The issue is, what are we going to do with Jesus?

2.   If we have already received the Lord Jesus Christ, then we've been born again. The Lord wants us to stop focusing on sin and start receiving His love. If we could ever get a picture of the price Jesus paid for our sins, we'd fall head over heels in love with Him. Since faith works by love (Gal. 5:6), our faith would shoot through the roof! If we truly comprehended just how much Jesus loves us and the price He paid to reconcile us to God the Father, we'd serve Him more accidentally than we ever have on purpose (2 Cor. 5:19).

3.   We should be telling people, "God loves you. He isn't angry with you." A time is coming when this current age of grace—the church age—will come to an end. But right now, the grace of God is extended toward all people. As His ambassadors, we are supposed to be ministering His message, saying what He's told us to say (2 Cor. 5:20).

1. A. According to John 14:6, is there any other way to the Father besides Jesus? (No)
   B. Since all of our sins have already been paid for by Jesus, what is the real issue? (What are we going to do with Jesus—receive Him or reject Him?)
2. A. If we've been born again, what does the Lord want us to stop focusing on and start receiving? (Sin; His love)
   B. Read Galatians 5:6 and 2 Corinthians 5:19. What does faith work by? (Love)
3. A. Right now, the grace of God is extended toward whom? (All people)
   B. According to 2 Corinthians 5:20, as His ambassadors, what are we supposed to be ministering and saying? (His message, what He's told us to say)

4.   Most of us believe that God only moves in our lives when we're worthy; i.e., we've tied His ability to our goodness. But the truth is, we must believe God in order to receive from Him. We don't have to be holy and do everything just right, but we do have to believe. If we understand how much God loves us—that He carries our picture around in His wallet; that He isn't angry, disappointed, or ashamed of us; and that He's proud of us—our faith would go through the roof.

5.   Jesus paid the penalty for our sins and then gave us His righteousness (2 Cor. 5:20-21). We were "old sinners," but we were saved by grace and are now the righteousness of God in Christ Jesus. God sees us righteous, holy, and pure—He's not angry with us. Our sins have been obliterated—and He's forgotten them (Heb. 8:12, 10:17; and Ps. 103:12). God isn't looking at our sins. He's not dealing with us based on the way we deal with ourselves.

4. A. Most of us believe that God only moves in our lives when we're what? (Worthy)
   B. Do we have to be holy and do everything just right in order to receive from God? (No, we just have to believe Him)
5. A. Read 2 Corinthians 5:20-21; Hebrews 8:12, 10:17; and Psalm 103:12. Jesus paid the penalty for our sins and gave us what? (His righteousness)
   B. How does God see us? (Righteous, holy, and pure)

Be Reconciled to God
LESSON 2 – DISCIPLESHIP QUESTIONS

1. Who was speaking in John 14:6?

2. What did He say?
    A. I am the truth.
    B. I am the life.
    C. I am the way.
    D. All of the above.
    E. None of the above.

3. Is there any other way someone can come to God the Father besides through Jesus Christ, His Son?

4. According to 2 Corinthians 5:19, God was in whom?

5. Whom was He reconciling to Himself?

6. What was He not imputing unto them?

7. What has He committed unto us?

8. According to 2 Corinthians 5:20, when are we ambassadors for Christ?

9. What do we pray you in Christ's stead?

10. According to 2 Corinthians 5:21, what did God make Christ to be for us?

11. Had He known sin before that?

12. Why did He do this?

13. According to Galatians 5:6, what does not avail anything in Jesus Christ?

14. In Christ Jesus, what does avail something?

15. How does it work?

16. According to Hebrews 8:12, what is God toward our unrighteousness?

17. What does He do with our sins and iniquities?

18. According to Hebrews 10:17, what does God remember no more?

19. According to Psalm 103:12, what has God removed from us?

20. How far?
    A. One mile.
    B. One hundred miles.
    C. One thousand miles.
    D. One million miles.
    E. As far as the east is from the west.

Be Reconciled to God
LESSON 2 – ANSWER KEY

1. Jesus.

2. A. I am the truth.
   B. I am the life.
   C. I am the way.
   D. All of the above.

3. No.

4. Christ.

5. The world.

6. Their trespasses.

7. The word of reconciliation.

8. Now.

9. Be reconciled to God.

10. Sin.

11. No.

12. That we might be made the righteousness of God in Christ.

13. Neither circumcision nor uncircumcision.

14. Faith.

15. By love.

16. Merciful.

17. He remembers them no more.

18. Our sins and iniquities.

19. Our transgressions.

20. E. As far as the east is from the west.

Be Reconciled to God
LESSON 2 – SCRIPTURES

Jesus saith unto him, I am the way, the truth, and the life: no man cometh unto the Father, but by me.

JOHN 14:6

For in Jesus Christ neither circumcision availeth any thing, nor uncircumcision; but faith which worketh by love.

GALATIANS 5:6

To wit, that God was in Christ, reconciling the world unto himself, not imputing their trespasses unto them; and hath committed unto us the word of reconciliation. Now then we are ambassadors for Christ, as though God did beseech you by us; we pray you in Christ's stead, be ye reconciled to God. For he hath made him to be sin for us, who knew no sin; that we might be made the righteousness of God in him.

2 CORINTHIANS 5:19-21

For I will be merciful to their unrighteousness, and their sins and their iniquities will I remember no more.

HEBREWS 8:12

And their sins and iniquities will I remember no more.

HEBREWS 10:17

As far as the east is from the west, so far hath he remove our transgressions from us.

PSALM 103:12

Jesus Took it All
LESSON 3

Comfort ye, comfort ye my people, saith your God.

ISAIAH 40:1

God was actually speaking to John the Baptist in this verse. It was meant to be John's message that he was to proclaim. (Compare Is. 40:3 with John 1:23.) Here's what he was supposed to say:

Speak ye comfortably to Jerusalem, and cry unto her, that her warfare is accomplished, that her iniquity is pardoned: for she hath received of the LORD'S hand double for all her sins.

ISAIAH 40:2

Even though the nation of Israel suffered and was led into captivity, no amount of physical suffering—losing their nation, going into captivity, all the terrible things that happened—can pay for all of their sins. You can't pay for spiritual transgressions and sins in the natural.

People who wonder *How can a loving God ever send anyone to hell?* don't have a revelation of what sin is all about. Sin is such a terrible transgression against God that spending eternity in a place of torment will still never fully pay for the sins people have committed. Sin is a terrible thing!

"Woe Is Me!"

I was born again at age eight, but the Lord revealed Himself to me in a powerful way at age eighteen. This was the first time I really saw Him, and instantly I had a revelation of His holiness. Even though I was a good person by religious and moral standards, I immediately recognized my relative un-holiness and unworthiness. I've never said a word of profanity, never taken a drink of liquor, never smoked a cigarette, and never tasted coffee in all my life. Now, I understand that coffee and booze aren't the same thing. You have Scripture to stand on for drinking coffee.

If they drink any deadly thing, it shall not hurt them.

MARK 16:18

I'm just saying that I've lived a super holy life. However, even though I was holier than most people by man's standards, once I saw the glory of God, I realized my relative unworthiness and instantly knew in my heart that I deserved to be destroyed.

When Isaiah saw the Lord in all His splendor and glory, he, too, fell on his face and cried out:

Woe is me! for I am undone; because I am a man of unclean lips, and I dwell in the midst of a people of unclean lips.

ISAIAH 6:5

There's no one, after seeing the glory of God, who didn't expect to be destroyed. That's God's justice. It's what we all deserve. Anyone who says "I can't believe that a loving God would ever send someone to hell" has never seen imperfect man in the light of God's perfection. They haven't seen the transgressions and total mess of things man has made. Even so-called "good people" have seriously transgressed against the Lord. There's just no way people can pay for their sins' transgressions in just this physical life.

"Her Warfare Is Accomplished"

Isaiah 40:2 is a prophetic scripture speaking about the Lord Jesus Christ. It's not talking about how, in the natural, Jerusalem had suffered enough and now God says, "Her warfare is accomplished." This verse is referring to the war God had toward mankind for his sins. It's saying, "When the Messiah comes, He's going to bear your sins. The warfare will be over because your sins have been paid for. God the Father put twice as much wrath upon His Son, the Lord Jesus Christ, as the entire human race was worthy of receiving." Jesus bore our sins, and now the warfare is over.

If you continued through the rest of Isaiah 40, you'd see that the whole chapter is prophetically speaking of Jesus and what He would accomplish when He came. It's saying that John the Baptist was to proclaim to the people that the wrath of God had now been satisfied. The war is over. God's not angry with you anymore. Sin isn't an issue. Jesus has paid for your sins!

Starting with chapter 40 and continuing on through the rest of Isaiah, these are all prophetic scriptures about the Lord Jesus. They are verses and passages that John the Baptist quoted. These scriptures made it clear that Jesus understood this was God's instructions to Him.

"Marred More Than Any Man"

Behold, my servant shall deal prudently, he shall be exalted and extolled, and be very high. As many were astonied [astonished] at thee; his visage [face] was so marred more than any man.

ISAIAH 52:13-14, BRACKETS MINE

Jesus' face was marred more than any person who has ever lived. A man came to one of my meetings in Kansas City who had cancer all over his face. His whole face was a cancer! Another fellow came who had lost his nose. It had been eaten away by cancer. He came forward for prayer with a big towel over his face. Not knowing the situation, I asked him, "Well, what am I praying for?" He took the towel off, and I could see right up into his head where his nose used to be. Yet, this scripture says that Jesus was marred more than that.

His visage [face] was so marred more than any man, and his form more than the sons of men.

ISAIAH 52:14, BRACKETS MINE

If you study all this out in Hebrew, it means that Jesus didn't even look human! How could this happen?

People said Mel Gibson was too graphic in his portrayal of Jesus' beating and crucifixion in the movie *The Passion of the Christ*. However, Mel himself freely admits that he had to tone those scenes down significantly from what Scripture describes, because nobody would have ever viewed them.

According to these scriptures, Jesus' face looked worse than any person who has ever lived. His body was so marred, it didn't even look human. He wasn't recognizable as a human being. It doesn't matter how bad of a physical beating someone endures, a whip with small pieces of metal or bone at the tips can't accomplish that.

He Became Sin

Jesus took our sins into His own body on the cross.

Who his own self bare our sins in his own body on the tree.

1 PETER 2:24

He was wounded for our transgressions, he was bruised for our iniquities: the chastisement of our peace was upon him.

ISAIAH 53:5

Every sin, sickness, and disease of the entire human race—every deformity, tumor, and perversion—entered into the physical body of the Lord Jesus Christ. That's why His face looked worse than any other person who has ever lived, and His form became so distorted that He didn't even look human. God did this to His Son.

The Passion of the Christ only showed the physical beating. There's no way it could fully depict our Lord's emotional and spiritual suffering too. Who can imagine the agony that came upon Jesus in the Garden of Gethsemane as He thought about becoming sin—the very thing He hated and the very thing He came to set us free from? He had to become that sin so that we could become the righteousness of God.

In a sense, our religious system today has diminished the atonement of the Lord Jesus Christ. It says, "Even if you're born again and have made Jesus your Lord, God is still mad at you every time you sin. He won't answer your prayer if there's un-confessed (therefore, un-forgiven) sin in your life." Basically, we've made Jesus just a part of the solution, but not the total solution. We've said, "Yes, you have to have the atonement of Christ. But you also have to repent, feel terrible over your sin, grovel in the dirt, and do all of these things." People who say these kinds of things don't understand the totality of the price Jesus paid for us.

Forsaken by His Father

While hanging on the cross, Jesus said:

My God, my God, why hast thou forsaken me?

PSALM 22:1 AND MARK 15:34

After putting all of the sin, sickness, disease, and suffering of the entire world upon His Son, the Father turned His back on Him. God forsook His only Son because that was the price that you and I deserved.

By the Spirit of God, I have had just a tiny glimpse of what it's like to be God-forsaken. I tell you, that'll be hell! Scripture reveals that hell will include physical things like suffering in flames (Luke 16:24). There will be emotional torment too. But the worst part of hell will be the absence of anything good. Everything good—everything God—is gone. Nothing but darkness, hatred, and strife will remain. Nothing good!

Some of us think we live in a bad world. Sure, there's plenty of corruption in this world, but we don't even have a clue. There is still so much good that is here. There are still people who are going out of their way to make this world a better place to live. As bad as things are, it's nothing like hell. Whether there's any physical suffering or not, total separation from God is hell itself. There's no hope, nothing!

Jesus bore that. He was forsaken by His Father. The Father forsook His own Son so that you and I wouldn't be forsaken. He totally rejected Him so that you and I wouldn't be rejected. All this, and people say that Jesus only paid for sin up to a point. "When you sin, God is still upset with you. He turns away from you and won't answer your prayers because of the sin in your life." Wrong!

If you think I'm making light of sin, the truth is, you're making light of the sacrifice of Christ. Jesus paid such a great and awesome price for you that it forever satisfied the wrath of God. He's not angry with you, regardless of what you've done. Now, that's good news!

Nothing Special

Who hath believed our report? and to whom is the arm of the LORD revealed?

ISAIAH 53:1

In other words, this is nearly too good to be true. Who would believe this? Who can believe that God isn't angry with you anymore and that He never will be? Who would believe that all of your sins—past, present, and even future tense sins—have been paid for? Not everyone believes this report.

For he shall grow up before him as a tender plant, and as a root out of a dry ground: he hath no form nor comeliness; and when we shall see him, there is no beauty that we should desire him.

ISAIAH 53:2

Did you know that Jesus wasn't one of these "beautiful" people? This doesn't necessarily mean that He was ugly, but He definitely wasn't special. Jesus wasn't one of these people who everybody wants to be close to, seen with, and receive attention from. He was just plain and ordinary. If you had seen Jesus when He walked here on the earth as a man, you wouldn't have been impressed. There was simply nothing physically special about Him.

Sometimes people say, "Oh, I wish I could have been one of the twelve disciples walking around with Jesus. Wouldn't that have been awesome?" No, it would've been hard—hard to believe this was God! Jesus walked twenty or thirty miles a day in the hot Judean weather. He didn't have a Holiday Inn to check into. He didn't take a shower each night before His message. Do you know what? Jesus stunk. He got dirty. His hair was matted. The Lord didn't carry a suitcase full of clothes to change into. He'd wear the same clothes day after day, and probably week after week if He was a typical person living in those times. That means you could smell Him coming. You had to look past all that. Jesus became like we are.

We portray Him as walking around with a halo over His head, but I guarantee you that people didn't see a halo over His head. He was just as plain and normal as any one of us. Jesus did that for those of you who don't feel special. He felt what you feel. Jesus was looked over, passed over, taken for granted, and unappreciated. Anything you've ever suffered, He suffered those things for you.

By His Stripes

He is despised and rejected of men; a man of sorrows, and acquainted with grief: and we hid as it were our faces from him; he was despised, and we esteemed him not. Surely he hath borne our griefs, and carried our sorrows.

ISAIAH 53:3-4

Jesus didn't have any grief of His own to bear. He had never done anything that caused Himself misery. The Lord took all of our sorrow, grief, and misery upon Himself.

Yet we did esteem him stricken, smitten of God, and afflicted. But he was wounded for our transgressions, he was bruised for our iniquities: the chastisement of our peace was upon him; and with his stripes we are healed.

ISAIAH 53:4-5

People try to limit the application of this verse to only emotional and/or spiritual things. But this verse was quoted in Matthew 8 after Jesus healed Peter's mother-in-law and many others (Matt. 8:14-17). It says this was done…

That it might be fulfilled which was spoken by Esaias [Isaiah] **the prophet, saying, Himself took our infirmities, and bare our sicknesses.**

MATTHEW 8:17, BRACKETS MINE

Therefore, the New Testament comments on Isaiah 53:5, showing that healing isn't just limited to spiritual and/or emotional things. Jesus suffered so that we could receive healing— spirit, soul, and body—by His stripes.

"The Iniquity of Us All"

All we like sheep have gone astray; we have turned every one to his own way; and the LORD hath laid on him [Jesus] the iniquity of us all.

ISAIAH 53:6, BRACKETS MINE

Jesus didn't just suffer in principle for sin. It's not like God gave Him a tiny taste, a sampling, of sin for all mankind. Jesus took all of your iniquity—all the iniquity of the entire world—upon Himself. He literally had the corruption of every sin that has ever been committed on the face of the earth—murder, sexual immorality, etc.—enter into His physical flesh. Truly, the iniquity of us all was laid upon Him.

Jesus Took it All
LESSON 3 – OUTLINE

I. This is God speaking to John the Baptist.

> **Comfort ye, comfort ye my people, saith your God. Speak ye comfortably to Jerusalem, and cry unto her, that her warfare is accomplished, that her iniquity is pardoned: for she hath received of the LORD'S hand double for all her sins.**
>
> ISAIAH 40:1-2

A. Even though the nation of Israel suffered and was led into captivity, no amount of physical suffering—losing their nation, going into captivity, all the terrible things that happened—can pay for all of their sins.

B. Anyone who says "I can't believe that a loving God would ever send someone to hell" has never seen imperfect man in the light of God's perfection.

> **Woe is me! for I am undone; because I am a man of unclean lips, and I dwell in the midst of a people of unclean lips.**
>
> ISAIAH 6:5

C. Isaiah 40:2 is a prophetic scripture speaking about the Lord Jesus Christ.

D. Jesus bore our sins, and now the warfare is over.

II. Jesus took our sins into His own body on the cross.

> **Behold, my servant shall deal prudently, he shall be exalted and extolled, and be very high. As many were astonied** [astonished] **at thee; his visage** [face] **was so marred more than any man, and his form more than the sons of men.**
>
> ISAIAH 52:13-14, BRACKETS MINE

> **Who his own self bare our sins in his own body on the tree.**
>
> 1 PETER 2:24

> **He was wounded for our transgressions, he was bruised for our iniquities: the chastisement of our peace was upon him.**
>
> ISAIAH 53:5

A. Every sin, sickness, and disease of the entire human race—every deformity, tumor, and perversion—entered into the physical body of the Lord Jesus Christ.

B. That's why His face looked worse than any other person who has ever lived, and His form became so distorted that He didn't even look human.

C. He had to become that sin so that we could become the righteousness of God.

D. After putting all of the sin, sickness, disease, and suffering of the entire world upon His Son, the Father turned His back on Him.

> **My God, my God, why hast thou forsaken me?**
>
> PSALM 22:1 AND MARK 15:34

E. Jesus paid such a great and awesome price for us that it forever satisfied the wrath of God.

III. This is nearly-too-good-to-be-true news!

> **Who hath believed our report? and to whom is the arm of the LORD revealed? For he shall grow up before him as a tender plant, and as a root out of a dry ground: he hath no form nor comeliness; and when we shall see him, there is no beauty that we should desire him.**
>
> ISAIAH 53:1-2

A. Jesus was just as plain and normal as any one of us.

B. The Lord took all of our sorrow, grief, and misery upon Himself.

> **He is despised and rejected of men; a man of sorrows, and acquainted with grief: and we hid as it were our faces from him; he was despised, and we esteemed him not. Surely he hath borne our griefs, and carried our sorrows. Yet we did esteem him stricken, smitten of God, and afflicted. But he was wounded for our transgressions, he was bruised for our iniquities: the chastisement of our peace was upon him; and with his stripes we are healed.**
>
> ISAIAH 53:3-5

C. Jesus suffered so that we could receive healing—spirit, soul, and body—by His stripes.

> **That it might be fulfilled which was spoken by Esaias [Isaiah] the prophet, saying, Himself took our infirmities, and bare our sicknesses.**
>
> MATTHEW 8:17, BRACKETS MINE

D. Jesus took all of your iniquity—all the iniquity of the entire world—upon Himself.

> **All we like sheep have gone astray; we have turned every one to his own way; and the LORD hath laid on him [Jesus] the iniquity of us all.**
>
> ISAIAH 53:6, BRACKETS MINE

E. Truly, the iniquity of us all was laid upon Him.

Jesus Took it All
LESSON 3 – TEACHER'S GUIDE

1.   Isaiah 40:1-2 is God speaking to John the Baptist. Even though the nation of Israel suffered and was led into captivity, no amount of physical suffering—losing their nation, going into captivity, all the terrible things that happened—can pay for all of their sins. Anyone who says "I can't believe that a loving God would ever send someone to hell" has never seen imperfect man in the light of God's perfection (Is. 6:5). Isaiah 40:2 is a prophetic scripture speaking about the Lord Jesus Christ. Jesus bore our sins, and now the warfare is over.

2.   Jesus took our sins into His own body on the cross (Is. 52:13-14, 53:5; and 1 Pet. 2:24). Every sin, sickness, and disease of the entire human race—every deformity, tumor, and perversion—entered into the physical body of the Lord Jesus Christ. That's why His face looked worse than any other person who has ever lived, and His form became so distorted that He didn't even look human. He had to become that sin so that we could become the righteousness of God. After putting all of the sin, sickness, disease, and suffering of the entire world upon His Son, the Father turned His back on Him (Ps. 22:1 and Mark 15:34). Jesus paid such a great and awesome price for us that it forever satisfied the wrath of God.

3.   This is nearly-too-good-to-be-true news! (Is. 53:1-2). Jesus was just as plain and normal as any one of us. The Lord took all of our sorrow, grief, and misery upon Himself (Is. 53:3-5). Jesus suffered so that we could receive healing—spirit, soul, and body—by His stripes (Matt. 8:17). Jesus took all of our iniquity—all the iniquity of the entire world—upon Himself (Is. 53:6). Truly, the iniquity of us all was laid upon Him.

1. A. In Isaiah 40:1-2, who was speaking to whom about whom? (God was speaking to John the Baptist about the Lord Jesus Christ)
   B. Read Isaiah 6:5. Anyone who says, "I can't believe that a loving God would ever send someone to hell," has never seen what? (Imperfect man in the light of God's perfection)
2. A. Read Isaiah 52:13-14, 53:5; 1 Peter 2:24; Psalm 22:1; and Mark 15:34. What entered into the physical body of the Lord Jesus Christ on the cross? (Every sin, sickness, and disease of the entire human race—every deformity, tumor, and perversion)
   B. What forever satisfied the wrath of God? (The great and awesome price Jesus paid for us)
3. A. Read Isaiah 53:1-6 and Matthew 8:17. Why did Jesus suffer and receive stripes upon His body? (So that we could receive healing—spirit, soul, and body)
   B. What did Jesus take upon Himself? (All our iniquity—all the iniquity of the entire world)

Jesus Took it All
LESSON 3 – DISCIPLESHIP QUESTIONS

1. In Isaiah 40:1-2, what two things are the messenger supposed to speak comfortably to Jerusalem about?

2. According to Mark 16:18, what are believers able to do?
   A. Lay hands on the sick, and they shall recover.
   B. Drink any deadly thing, and it shall not hurt them.
   C. Take up serpents.
   D. All of the above.
   E. None of the above.

3. According to Isaiah 6:5, what were Isaiah's first words when he saw the splendor and glory of the Lord?
   A. "I'm so glad to see You!"
   B. "Woe is me!"
   C. "You're bigger than I thought!"
   D. "Get me out of here!"

4. What does Isaiah 52:13-14 prophesy would happen to Jesus' face and body?

5. What does 1 Peter 2:24 tell us that Jesus bore in His own body on the tree (cross)?

6. Now that we are dead to sins, how should we live?

7. How were we healed?

8. Fill in the blank: According to 1 Peter 2:24, with His "stripes ye _____ healed."
   A. Were (past tense).
   B. Are (present tense).
   C. Will be (future tense).

9. What does Isaiah 53:5 prophesy that Jesus would be wounded for?

10. Why was He bruised?

11. What else was upon Him?

12. Fill in the blank: According to Isaiah 53:5, "with His stripes we _____ healed."
    A. Were (past tense)
    B. Are (present tense)
    C. Will be (future tense)

13. Who was looking ahead to what Jesus would do on the cross and the provision for healing that would be made continuously available thereafter?
    A. Isaiah.
    B. Peter.

14. Who was looking back to what Jesus had already done on the cross and the provision made for healing that's been available ever since?
    A. Isaiah.
    B. Peter.

15. As Jesus quoted Psalm 22:1 while on the cross in Mark 15:34, what did He say?

16. In Luke 16:24, how did the man in hell describe his condition?

17. According to Isaiah 53:1-6, how was Jesus described by the prophet?
    A. Despised and rejected of men.
    B. A man of sorrows and acquainted with grief.
    C. No form, comeliness, nor beauty that we should desire Him.
    D. All of the above.
    E. None of the above.

18. All of us have gone astray like what?

19. What has every one of us turned to?

20. What has the Lord laid upon Him?

21. According to Matthew 8:14-17, who did Jesus see sick with a fever in Peter's house?

22. What happened to the fever after Jesus touched her hand?

23. What happened later when many sick and demonized people were brought to Him?

24. Which words of Isaiah the prophet was Jesus fulfilling through these deliverances and healings?

1. That her warfare is accomplished and that her iniquity is pardoned.

2. A. Lay hands on the sick, and they shall recover.
   B. Drink any deadly thing, and it shall not hurt them.
   C. Take up serpents.
   D. All of the above.

3. B. "Woe is me!"

4. His visage and form would be marred more than any man.

5. Our sins.

6. Unto righteousness.

7. By His stripes.

8. A. Were (past tense).

9. Our transgressions.

10. For our iniquities.

11. The chastisement of our peace.

12. B. Are (present tense)

13. A. Isaiah.

14. B. Peter.

15. "My God, my God, why hast thou forsaken me?"

16. I am tormented in this flame.

17. A. Despised and rejected of men.
    B. A man of sorrows and acquainted with grief.
    C. No form, comeliness, nor beauty that we should desire Him.
    D. All of the above.

18. Sheep.

19. Our own way.

20. The iniquity of us all.

21. Peter's mother-in-law.

22. It left.

23. Jesus cast out the spirits and healed all that were sick.

24. Himself took our infirmities, and bare our sicknesses.

Jesus Took it All

Comfort ye, comfort ye my people, saith your God. Speak ye comfortably to Jerusalem, and cry unto her, that her warfare is accomplished, that her iniquity is pardoned: for she hath received of the LORD'S hand double for all her sins.

ISAIAH 40:1-2

They shall take up serpents; and if they drink any deadly thing, it shall not hurt them; they shall lay hands on the sick, and they shall recover.

MARK 16:18

Then said I, Woe is me! for I am undone; because I am a man of unclean lips, and I dwell in the midst of a people of unclean lips: for mine eyes have seen the King, the LORD of hosts.

ISAIAH 6:5

Behold, my servant shall deal prudently, he shall be exalted and extolled, and be very high. As many were astonied at thee; his visage was so marred more than any man, and his form more than the sons of men.

ISAIAH 52:13-14

Who his own self bare our sins in his own body on the tree, that we, being dead to sins, should live unto righteousness: by whose stripes ye were healed.

1 PETER 2:24

But he was wounded for our transgressions, he was bruised for our iniquities: the chastisement of our peace was upon him; and with his stripes we are healed.

ISAIAH 53:5

My God, my God, why hast thou forsaken me? why art thou so far from helping me, and from the words of my roaring?

PSALM 22:1

And at the ninth hour Jesus cried with a loud voice, saying, Eloi, Eloi, lama sabachthani? which is, being interpreted, My God, my God, why hast thou forsaken me?

MARK 15:34

And he cried and said, Father Abraham, have mercy on me, and send Lazarus, that he may dip the tip of his finger in water, and cool my tongue; for I am tormented in this flame.

LUKE 16:24

Who hath believed our report? and to whom is the arm of the LORD revealed? For he shall grow up before him as a tender plant, and as a root out of a dry ground: he hath no form nor comeliness; and when we shall see him, there is no beauty that we should desire him. He is despised and rejected of men; a man of sorrows, and acquainted with grief: and we hid as it were our faces from him; he was despised, and we esteemed him not. Surely he hath borne our griefs, and carried our sorrows: yet we did esteem him stricken, smitten of God, and afflicted. But he was wounded for our transgressions, he was bruised for our iniquities: the chastisement of our peace was upon him; and with his stripes we are healed. All we like sheep have gone astray; we have turned every one to his own way; and the LORD hath laid on him the iniquity of us all.

ISAIAH 53:1-6

And when Jesus was come into Peter's house, he saw his wife's mother laid, and sick of a fever. And he touched her hand, and the fever left her: and she arose, and ministered unto them. When the even was come, they brought unto him many that were possessed with devils: and he cast out the spirits with his word, and healed all that were sick: That it might be fulfilled which was spoken by Esaias the prophet, saying, Himself took our infirmities, and bare our sicknesses.

MATTHEW 8:14-17

Pleased to Bruise Him
LESSON 4

He [Jesus] was oppressed, and he was afflicted, yet he opened not his mouth: he is brought as a lamb to the slaughter, and as a sheep before her shearers is dumb, so he openeth not his mouth. He was taken from prison and from judgment.

ISAIAH 53:7-8, BRACKETS MINE

This means Jesus never even had a chance to go to prison or have a fair trial. He missed those things.

And who shall declare his generation?

ISAIAH 53:8

Jesus didn't have any physical descendants—regardless of what the *Da Vinci Code* says!

For he was cut off out of the land of the living: for the transgression of my people was he stricken. And he made his grave with the wicked, and with the rich in his death; because he had done no violence, neither was any deceit in his mouth. Yet it pleased the LORD to bruise him.

ISAIAH 53:8-10

God was pleased to bruise, hurt, and forsake His Son. He made His Son suffer to the point that His face looked worse than anyone else's ever has throughout all of history. He made Him suffer so much that Jesus didn't even look human anymore. God was pleased to do that. It's not because He's a masochist or a mean God. It's because He knew that by putting all of your sin upon His Son that He would break Satan's dominion and set the entire human race free.

We Are His Seed!

God was pleased to do this because He knew it would totally solve the problem. By His Son's suffering, the sin issue would be forever settled, and the war would be over. The wrath of God was fully satisfied by the suffering of His Son. If you think that God is still upset with you, won't answer your prayers, or move because you have some sin in your life, then you don't have a clue what God did to His own Son.

If somehow or another I could transfer your sin to my son and punish him so that I wouldn't be angry with you, I wouldn't do it unless it was sufficient. I wouldn't do it unless it was more than enough. Why in the world would I make my own son suffer if it wasn't going to solve the problem? Yet, by and large, the church has been saying, "Oh, yes, Jesus died for your sins. But if you have un-confessed sin in your life, He won't answer your prayer. God can't use a dirty vessel. He can't fellowship with someone who has sin in their life." Basically, they've just diminished the sacrifice of Jesus.

Yet it pleased the LORD to bruise him; he hath put him to grief: when thou shalt make his soul an offering for sin, he shall see his seed.

ISAIAH 53:10

This isn't just talking about Jews; it's everyone who places their faith in the Lord Jesus Christ.

Satisfied

He shall see his seed, he shall prolong his days, and the pleasure of the LORD shall prosper in his hand.

ISAIAH 53:10

He made His soul an offering for sin because when He sees the people whom He has set free, that will please Him. The Lord did all of this because of the benefit it had for us—the body of Christ.

He shall see of the travail of his soul, and shall be satisfied.

ISAIAH 53:11

This scripture says that God the Father was satisfied with what Jesus paid for your sins. You can't satisfy Him with anything additional. Your repentance, groveling in the dirt, feeling unworthy and separated from God, and all these other things cannot add anything to the way God the Father views you. He is satisfied with you through Jesus, not through your great goodness. The only thing you had to contribute was your sin. Sin qualified you. Then God paid the whole price. The only thing you can do is either believe and receive or doubt and do without. If you've made Jesus your Savior, God is satisfied with your payment—not because you've repented and done all these things, but because Jesus has borne all of your sin. That's awesome!

Just as if I'd Never Sinned

He shall see the travail of his soul [Jesus' soul, not yours]**, and shall be satisfied: by his knowledge shall my righteous servant justify many.**

ISAIAH 53:11, BRACKETS MINE

"Justify" means "just as if I had never sinned." I'm justified, just as if I had never sinned. God saw the travail of Jesus and imputed that justification to me just as if I had suffered and paid for my own sins throughout all eternity. He's satisfied! The payment has been made. Sin has been paid for, and now I'm justified—just as if I'd never sinned.

God doesn't see me as a sinner. I'm not an "old sinner saved by grace." I am now the righteousness of God (2 Cor. 5:21).

My righteous servant [shall] **justify many; for he shall bear their iniquities.**

ISAIAH 53:11, BRACKETS MINE

All my sin was placed on Jesus, and all His righteousness was given to me. He made me just as if I'd never sinned!

Fruitful

Therefore will I divide him a portion with the great, and he shall divide the spoil with the strong; because he hath poured out his soul unto death: and he was numbered with the transgressors; and he bare the sin of many, and made intercession for the transgressors.

ISAIAH 53:12

Here's the result of this:

Sing, O barren, thou that didst not bear.

ISAIAH 54:1

This isn't talking about just being unable to have children physically. This is saying that if it seems you're spiritually barren and you can't see victory or the blessing of God come to pass. It just seems like you aren't flowing in the things of God. Because of what Jesus did—as recorded in chapters 52 and 53—you can sing, because you aren't going to be barren anymore. You're going to…

Break forth into singing, and cry aloud, thou that didst not travail with child: for more are the children of the desolate than the children of the married wife, saith the LORD.

ISAIAH 54:1

Through the Lord, we can prosper more. We can have more joy, more victory, more power, and more success than if we would've had all of these things in the natural. Nobody with natural ability and talent alone can even begin to be as fruitful and successful as a person who is doing it through trusting in the Lord and what He's done for us.

We're Blessed!

Enlarge the place of thy tent, and let them stretch forth the curtains of thine habitations: spare not, lengthen thy cords, and strengthen thy stakes; For thou shalt break forth on the right hand and on the left; and thy seed shall inherit the Gentiles and make the desolate cities to be inhabited.

ISAIAH 54:2-3

This is talking about growth, success, and prosperity, not only physically and materially, but emotionally and in every other area too. Through Jesus, you should be expecting nothing but blessings. You ought to be saying, "God loves me! How can anybody be against me?" Instead of saying "Nothing ever works for me!" it ought to be just the opposite: "I'm so blessed, I can't lose for winning!"

You wouldn't be depressed or discouraged if you understood how much God loves you and has forgiven you. It doesn't matter if the doctor has told you that you're going to die. God loves you, and you're going to live forever with Him. You've missed hell. Sure, God can heal you, and you can live. But if worse comes to worse and you die, you go directly to be with the Lord. We sing, "When we all get to heaven, what a day that'll be!" Then the doctor tells you you're going, and you start crying and falling apart like a two-dollar suitcase. If you just understood that you're forgiven, you win! If you lose, you win. You can't lose for winning! You're blessed! It's impossible to be fearful and depressed thinking about things like that.

God Is for You!

This is why Paul was fearless. He had this revelation and knew all of these things. People would tell him, "Quit preaching the Gospel or we'll kill you!" He'd just kiss them and say, "This is wonderful!"

For to me to live is Christ, and to die is gain.

PHILIPPIANS 1:21

"Well, then, we're going to throw you in jail!" So they put him in stocks in the deepest, darkest cell of the prison, and he worshiped God. While listening to him sing, the Lord started tapping His foot, and it caused an earthquake. All of the cell doors in the prison opened up, including Paul's, but he didn't leave. He wasn't just praising God so that he could get out of trouble; he was genuinely worshiping the Lord! It didn't matter to him that his back was beaten and he was locked in stocks. He didn't care, because he knew that God loved him and he was forgiven.

Before then, Paul had been persecuting and killing Christians. He was so grateful that Jesus had made him just as if he'd never sinned, he just praised God. "Now I don't have to worry about what my next sermon is. I can just worship God all night long!" He got the jailer saved! The presence of God was so thick, none of the other prisoners escaped (Acts 16:16-40).

Tell Paul you're going to kill him—he loved it! Persecute him, stick him in the stocks—he thrived! The brand of Christianity most of us have today pales in comparison. We whine if we don't have a brand-new car. Very few Christians have understood what we deserve on our own. Even fewer comprehend what a great price Jesus paid for us.

If you know these things, you have no reason whatsoever to gripe or complain about anything. If your husband or wife left you, so what? God said He'd never leave you nor forsake you (Heb. 13:5). You ought to be rejoicing over that! If nothing else, say, "Father, I thank You that in heaven, we neither marry nor are given in marriage. Thank You, Jesus" (Matt. 22:30)! It's only temporary.

You don't have a right to gripe or complain about anything. Almighty God loves you. He's taken your sins. The war is over. Glory to God in the highest! Peace on earth. Good will toward men. You ought to be planning to break forth on the right and the left, because you're going to prosper, prosper, prosper. Enlarge your tent because God is for you!

Pleased to Bruise Him
LESSON 4 – OUTLINE

I. God was pleased to bruise, hurt, and forsake His Son.

    A. Jesus never even had a chance to go to prison or have a fair trial.

> He [Jesus] **was oppressed, and he was afflicted, yet he opened not his mouth: he is brought as a lamb to the slaughter, and as a sheep before her shearers is dumb, so he openeth not his mouth. He was taken from prison and from judgment: and who shall declare his generation?**
>
> ISAIAH 53:7-8, BRACKETS MINE

    B. Jesus didn't have any physical descendants.

> **For he was cut off out of the land of the living: for the transgression of my people was he stricken. And he made his grave with the wicked, and with the rich in his death; because he had done no violence, neither was any deceit in his mouth. Yet it pleased the LORD to bruise him; he hath put him to grief: when thou shalt make his soul an offering for sin, he shall see his seed, he shall prolong his days, and the pleasure of the LORD shall prosper in his hand.**
>
> ISAIAH 53:8-10

    C. God was pleased to do this because He knew it would totally solve the problem.

    D. By His Son's suffering, the sin issue would be forever settled, and the war would be over.

    E. His seed is everyone who places their faith in the Lord Jesus Christ.

> **And if ye be Christ's, then are ye Abraham's seed, and heirs according to the promise.**
>
> GALATIANS 3:29

II. The Scripture says that God the Father was satisfied with what Jesus paid for your sins.

> **He shall see the travail of his soul** [Jesus' soul, not yours], **and shall be satisfied: by his knowledge shall my righteous servant justify many; for he shall bear their iniquities.**
>
> ISAIAH 53:11, BRACKETS MINE

    A. **"Justify"** means "just as if I had never sinned."

    B. God saw the travail of Jesus and imputed that justification to me just as if I had suffered and paid for my own sins throughout eternity.

C. All my sin was placed on Jesus, and all His righteousness was given to me (2 Cor. 5:21).

D. He made me just as if I'd never sinned!

> **Therefore will I divide him a portion with the great, and he shall divide the spoil with the strong; because he hath poured out his soul unto death: and he was numbered with the transgressors; and he bare the sin of many, and made intercession for the transgressors.**
>
> ISAIAH 53:12

III. Because of what Jesus did—as recorded in Isaiah 52 and 53—you can sing, because you aren't going to be barren anymore.

> **Sing, O barren, thou that didst not bear; break forth into singing, and cry aloud, thou that didst not travail with child: for more are the children of the desolate than the children of the married wife, saith the LORD.**
>
> ISAIAH 54:1

A. Through Jesus, you should be expecting nothing but blessings.

> **Enlarge the place of thy tent, and let them stretch forth the curtains of thine habitations: spare not, lengthen thy cords, and strengthen thy stakes; For thou shalt break forth on the right hand and on the left; and thy seed shall inherit the Gentiles and make the desolate cities to be inhabited.**
>
> ISAIAH 54:2-3

B. You wouldn't be depressed or discouraged if you understood how much God loves you and has forgiven you.

> **For to me to live is Christ, and to die is gain.**
>
> PHILIPPIANS 1:21

C. You don't have a right to gripe or complain about anything!

D. You ought to be planning to break forth on the right and the left, because you're going to prosper, prosper, prosper.

E. Enlarge your tent because God is for you!

Pleased to Bruise Him
LESSON 4 – TEACHER'S GUIDE

1.   God was pleased to bruise, hurt, and forsake His Son. Jesus never even had a chance to go to prison or have a fair trial (Is. 53:7-8). Jesus didn't have any physical descendants (Is. 53:8-10). God was pleased to do this because He knew it would totally solve the problem. By His Son's suffering, the sin issue would be forever settled, and the war would be over. His seed is everyone who places their faith in the Lord Jesus Christ (Gal. 3:29).

2.   The Scripture says that God the Father was satisfied with what Jesus paid for our sins (Is. 53:11-12). **"Justify"** means "just as if I had never sinned." God saw the travail of Jesus and imputed that justification to us just as if we had suffered and paid for our own sins throughout eternity. All our sin was placed on Jesus, and all His righteousness was given to us (2 Cor. 5:21). He made us just as if we'd never sinned!

3.   Because of what Jesus did—as recorded in Isaiah 52 and 53—we can sing because we aren't going to be barren anymore (Is. 54:1). Through Jesus, we should be expecting nothing but blessings (Is. 54:2-3). We wouldn't be depressed or discouraged if we understood how much God loves us and has forgiven us (Phil. 1:21). We don't have a right to gripe or complain about anything! We ought to be planning to break forth on the right and the left, because we're going to prosper, prosper, prosper. Let's enlarge our tents because God is for us!

1. A. Read Isaiah 53:7-10. Why was God pleased to bruise, hurt, and forsake His Son? (Because He knew it would totally solve the problem. By His Son's suffering, the sin issue would be forever settled, and the war would be over)
   B. According to Galatians 3:29, who is His seed? (Everyone who places their faith in the Lord Jesus Christ)
2. A. Read Isaiah 53:11-12. What does **"justify"** mean? (Just as if I had never sinned)
   B. According to 2 Corinthians 5:21, all our sin was placed on Jesus, and all His _____ was given to us. (Righteousness)
3. A. Read Isaiah 54:1-3. Through Jesus, what should we be expecting? (Nothing but blessings)
   B. Read Philippians 1:21. What must we understand in order to be free of discouragement and depression? (How much God loves us and has forgiven us)

Pleased to Bruise Him
LESSON 4 – DISCIPLESHIP QUESTIONS

1. Who is Isaiah 53:7-9 speaking of?

2. Even though He was oppressed and afflicted, He did not what?

3. For this, to what animal was He immediately compared?

4. Why was He stricken?

5. Had He done any violence?

6. Was there any deceit in IIis mouth?

7. According to Isaiah 53:10, who did it please to bruise Him?

8. What was His soul made?

9. What shall He see?

10. According to Galatians 3:29, who are Abraham's seed and heirs according to the promise?

11. Who was made sin for us in 2 Corinthians 5:21?

12. That we might be made what in Him?

13. According to Isaiah 53:11-12, what happened when God the Father saw the travail of Jesus' soul?

14. Why can the knowledge of God's righteous servant enable Him to justify many?

15. For what reasons will God the Father divide Him a portion with the great and the spoil with the strong?
    A. Because He bore the sin of many.
    B. Because He made intercession for the transgressors.
    C. Because He poured out His soul to death.
    D. Because He was numbered with the transgressors.
    E. All of the above.
    F. None of the above.

16. In light of this, Isaiah 54:1-3 says to _____.
    A. Enlarge the place of thy tent.
    B. Cry aloud.
    C. Break forth into singing.
    D. All of the above.
    E. None of the above.

17. According to Philippians 1:21, to live is Christ and to die is what?

18. How did Paul exemplify this attitude in Acts 16:16-40?

19. What did Jesus promise in Hebrews 13:5?

20. According to Matthew 22:30, will people marry or be given in marriage in the resurrection?

Pleased to Bruise Him
LESSON 4 – ANSWER KEY

1. Jesus.

2. Open His mouth.

3. A lamb and a sheep.

4. For people's transgression.

5. No.

6. No.

7. The LORD.

8. An offering for sin.

9. His seed.

10. All those in Christ.

11. Jesus—Him who knew no sin.

12. The righteousness of God.

13. He was satisfied.

14. Because He bore their iniquities.

15. A. Because He bore the sin of many.
    B. Because He made intercession for the transgressors.
    C. Because He poured out His soul to death.
    D. Because He was numbered with the transgressors.
    E. All of the above.

16. A. Enlarge the place of thy tent.
    B. Cry aloud.
    C. Break forth into singing.
    D. All of the above.

17. Gain.

18. No matter what his circumstances were, Paul was always either worshiping Jesus or sharing Him with others.

19. I will never leave thee, nor forsake thee.

20. No.

Pleased to Bruise Him
LESSON 4 – SCRIPTURES

He was oppressed, and he was afflicted, yet he opened not his mouth: he is brought as a lamb to the slaughter, and as a sheep before her shearers is dumb, so he openeth not his mouth. He was taken from prison and from judgment: and who shall declare his generation? for he was cut off out of the land of the living: for the transgression of my people was he stricken. And he made his grave with the wicked, and with the rich in his death; because he had done no violence, neither was any deceit in his mouth.

Isaiah 53:7-9

Yet it pleased the LORD to bruise him; he hath put him to grief: when thou shalt make his soul an offering for sin, he shall see his seed, he shall prolong his days, and the pleasure of the LORD shall prosper in his hand. He shall see of the travail of his soul, and shall be satisfied: by his knowledge shall my righteous servant justify many; for he shall bear their iniquities. Therefore will I divide him a portion with the great, and he shall divide the spoil with the strong; because he hath poured out his soul unto death: and he was numbered with the transgressors; and he bare the sin of many, and made intercession for the transgressors.

Isaiah 53:10-12

And if ye be Christ's, then are ye Abraham's seed, and heirs according to the promise.

Galatians 3:29

For he hath made him to be sin for us, who knew no sin; that we might be made the righteousness of God in him.

2 Corinthians 5:21

Sing, O barren, thou that didst not bear; break forth into singing, and cry aloud, thou that didst not travail with child: for more are the children of the desolate than the children of the married wife, saith the LORD. Enlarge the place of thy tent, and let them stretch forth the curtains of thine habitations: spare not, lengthen thy cords, and strengthen thy stakes; For thou shalt break forth on the right hand and on the left; and thy seed shall inherit the Gentiles and make the desolate cities to be inhabited.

Isaiah 54:1-3

For to me to live is Christ, and to die is gain.

Philippians 1:21

And it came to pass, as we went to prayer, a certain damsel possessed with a spirit of divination met us, which brought her masters much gain by soothsaying: The same followed Paul and us, and cried, saying, These men are the servants of the most high God, which shew unto us the way of salvation. And this did she many days. But Paul, being grieved, turned and said to the spirit, I command thee in the name of Jesus Christ to come out of her. And he came out the same hour.

ACTS 16:16-18

And when her masters saw that the hope of their gains was gone, they caught Paul and Silas, and drew them into the marketplace unto the rulers, And brought them to the magistrates, saying, These men, being Jews, do exceedingly trouble our city, And teach customs, which are not lawful for us to receive, neither to observe, being Romans. And the multitude rose up together against them: and the magistrates rent off their clothes, and commanded to beat them. And when they had laid many stripes upon them, they cast them into prison, charging the jailer to keep them safely: Who, having received such a charge, thrust them into the inner prison, and made their feet fast in the stocks.

ACTS 16:19-24

And at midnight Paul and Silas prayed, and sang praises unto God: and the prisoners heard them. And suddenly there was a great earthquake, so that the foundations of the prison were shaken: and immediately all the doors were opened, and every one's bands were loosed. And the keeper of the prison awaking out of his sleep, and seeing the prison doors open, he drew out his sword, and would have killed himself, supposing that the prisoners had been fled. But Paul cried with a loud voice, saying, Do thyself no harm: for we are all here. Then he called for a light, and sprang in, and came trembling, and fell down before Paul and Silas. And brought them out, and said, Sirs, what must I do to be saved? And they said, Believe on the Lord Jesus Christ, and thou shalt be saved, and thy house. And they spake unto him the word of the Lord, and to all that were in his house. And he took them the same hour of the night, and washed their stripes; and was baptized, he and all his, straightway. And when he had brought them into his house, he set meat before them, and rejoiced, believing in God with all his house.

ACTS 16:25-34

And when it was day, the magistrates sent the serjeants, saying, Let those men go. And the keeper of the prison told this saying to Paul, The magistrates have sent to let you go: now therefore depart, and go in peace. But Paul said unto them, They have beaten us openly uncondemned, being Romans, and have cast us into prison; and now do they thrust us out privily? nay verily; but let them come themselves and fetch us out. And the serjeants told these words unto the magistrates: and they feared, when they heard that they were Romans. And they came and besought them, and brought them out, and desired them to depart out of the city. And they went out of the prison, and entered into the house of Lydia: and when they had seen the brethren, they comforted them, and departed.

ACTS 16:35-40

Let your conversation be without covetousness; and be content with such things as ye have: for he hath said, I will never leave thee, nor forsake thee.

HEBREWS 13:5

For in the resurrection they neither marry, nor are given in marriage, but are as the angels of God in heaven.

MATTHEW 22:30

Established in Righteousness
LESSON 5

O thou afflicted, tossed with tempest, and not comforted, behold, I will lay thy stones with fair colours, and lay thy foundations with sapphires. And I will make thy windows of agates, and thy gates of carbuncles, and all thy borders of pleasant stones. And all thy children shall be taught of the LORD; and great shall be the peace of thy children. In righteousness shalt thou be established.

Isaiah 54:11-14

Do you know why most Christians aren't established? We don't understand that we're righteous. We think we're unrighteous. Since we aren't hearing the true Gospel, we still think that God is imputing sin unto us. That's the reason we aren't established—strong, steady, and secure.

In righteousness shalt thou be established: thou shalt be far from oppression.

Isaiah 54:14

If you are oppressed, do you know why? You don't know that you're righteous! You don't know that your sins are forgiven. You may say you're forgiven, but with the next breath, you'll say something like, "God didn't answer my prayer, because I have a sin that I just haven't been able to overcome." If you understood righteousness, you'd be far from oppression.

For thou shalt not fear.

Isaiah 54:14

If you understood righteousness, you wouldn't have fear. Who or what can you fear if God is for you?

And from terror; for it shall not come near thee.

Isaiah 54:14

An Unconditional Covenant

Let's back up to verse 9, which says:

For this is as the waters of Noah unto me: for as I have sworn that the waters of Noah should no more go over the earth; so have I sworn that I would not be wroth with thee, nor rebuke thee.

Isaiah 54:9

This covenant that God made with Noah had no qualifications.

And I will establish my covenant with you [Noah]; neither shall all flesh be cut off any more by the waters of a flood; neither shall there any more be a flood to destroy the earth.

GENESIS 9:11, BRACKETS MINE

God didn't say, "If you do this, I'll do that." He didn't stipulate, "If the people never provoke Me again, if they never return to the degree of sinfulness that they were before the Flood, then I'll never destroy the earth again with water." That's not the kind of covenant it was. Noah's covenant was unconditional—no strings attached. It's just a promise that no matter what the world does, God will never destroy the earth with a flood again.

Your Own Conscience

In Isaiah 54, God was saying this New Covenant that Jesus has put into effect is like that covenant with Noah. It's an unconditional, unqualified covenant. In the same way that He swore to never again destroy the earth with a flood…

So have I sworn that I would not be wroth with thee, nor rebuke thee.

ISAIAH 54:9

For those who enter into this covenant, God is never, ever, ever angry with you. He has never, ever, ever rebuked you. Now, the Lord will show you when you do something wrong. It's not because it isn't paid for. He's already paid for your sins. But God knows that when you yield to sin, you are opening up a door to the devil in your life. If you do that, the Enemy will come in, eat your lunch, and pop the bag! Out of love, the Lord will tell you not to do that, not because He's going to hold it against you or withhold His blessings, but because He doesn't want Satan to have an inroad into your life.

God will reveal things to you and say "Quit doing this," but the guilt, condemnation, and unworthiness you feel isn't coming from Him. Religion is what makes you think that God is angry with you, has forsaken you, and put you on the shelf. That's religion—working through your own conscience—condemning you. God is not the author of condemnation.

Covenant of Peace

There is therefore now no condemnation to them which are in Christ Jesus, who walk not after the flesh, but after the Spirit.

ROMANS 8:1

God isn't angry with you. He has sworn an unconditional covenant. Regardless of what you do, God isn't angry with you. He's never going to rebuke you. All of those times that you've heard people stand up and testify "I did something wrong and God has just been on my case" aren't true. The Holy Spirit may have shown them that they were wrong, but it was their own consciences condemning them and making them feel miserable. Those times you've said "Well, I sinned against God and now He's left me," it's your own conscience that condemned you and cut you off.

Think about all of those times you sang David's prayer:

Create in me a clean heart, O God; and renew a right spirit within me. Cast me not away from thy presence; and take not thy holy spirit from me.

PSALM 51:10-11

It's wrong. David prayed this because he was an Old Testament saint. But as a New Testament believer, God created a clean heart in you the very moment you were born again (Eph. 4:24). He promised to never leave you nor forsake you (Matt. 28:20 and Heb. 13:5). Every time you feel like God is ticked off at you and has left—you're wrong!

For the mountains shall depart, and the hills be removed; but <u>my kindness shall not depart from thee, neither shall the covenant of my peace be removed, saith the LORD</u> that hath mercy on thee.

ISAIAH 54:10, EMPHASIS MINE

The Gospel of Peace

Which brings us back to:

Glory to God in the highest, and on earth peace, good will toward men.

LUKE 2:14

God is now at peace with mankind. The war is over. He has made a covenant and signed a treaty. He'll never be angry with us nor rebuke us ever again.

Put on the whole armour of God, that ye may be able to stand against the wiles of the devil…stand therefore, having your…feet shod with the preparation of the <u>gospel of peace</u>.

EPHESIANS 6:11-15, EMPHASIS MINE

The Gospel of peace! Preaching "There's war. God is angry and upset. If you don't repent, He won't bless you or move in your life" isn't the Gospel of peace. The reason people aren't responding better is because they haven't heard the true Gospel. They aren't hearing the same message Jesus proclaimed.

Christ had read these scriptures in Isaiah. He wasn't imputing people's sins unto them. He knew what was happening. Jesus understood that He was the Lamb of God who would pay the price and bear all the sins of the entire world (John 1:29). Because of that, He was able to turn around and extend mercy toward sinners.

Blinded by Religion

We've allowed religion to blind us to the truth that Jesus has paid for all sin—not only for the sins of believers—but also for the sins of the whole world.

And he [Jesus] is the propitiation for our sins: and not for ours only, but also for the sins of the whole world.

1 JOHN 2:2, BRACKETS MINE

Everybody's sins are paid for. Sin isn't the issue. People aren't going to hell because of their sin; they're going to hell because they haven't accepted the payment for their sin. They haven't received the Lord Jesus Christ. They don't know Him. They haven't made Jesus their personal Lord and Savior.

You Can't Do Enough

Are you still trying to pay for your sins? Are you doing "penance"? I've actually met a man with grotesque, ugly scars on his hands, knees, and elbows. He had crawled over glass for three miles, doing penance. Another guy told me how he had allowed himself to be crucified during the Lent season because he thought it would help atone for his sins. That's an affront against God! It's saying, "Jesus didn't pay it all, and I still have to do something."

Jesus was crucified so that I don't have to be crucified. Now, most of us wouldn't allow ourselves to be crucified, but many of us still feel separated from God. We'll go through a week of being miserable because we feel like we have to do that in order for God to accept us. That's the exact same mindset. It's just a different standard and different type of "penance."

You may think that by going to church, giving extra in the offering, or trying to be good that you're "appeasing" God. You might be appeasing your own conscience, but have you ever truly personally trusted in Jesus? Have you received Him, or are you still trying somehow to barter with God? Are you trusting in the payment Christ made, or are you trusting in your own good works, hoping they'll be enough for you to be saved? Be honest with yourself because eternity is forever.

You can't do enough! There's nothing you can offer that will ever supersede what Jesus has done. Jesus plus nothing equals everything. But Jesus plus anything—especially your own effort—equals nothing! Either you have to trust the Lord one hundred percent or you have to trust yourself, but there cannot be a combination of the two. You either have a Savior who earned your salvation by what He did, or you must earn salvation on your own merit, which cannot be done.

Established in Righteousness
LESSON 5 – OUTLINE

I. Most Christians aren't established—strong, steady, and secure—because they don't understand that they're righteous.

> **O thou afflicted, tossed with tempest, and not comforted, behold, I will lay thy stones with fair colours, and lay thy foundations with sapphires. And I will make thy windows of agates, and thy gates of carbuncles, and all thy borders of pleasant stones. And all thy children shall be taught of the LORD; and great shall be the peace of thy children. In righteousness shalt thou be established: thou shalt be far from oppression; for thou shalt not fear: and from terror; for it shall not come near thee.**
>
> ISAIAH 54:11-14

A. If you understood righteousness, you'd be far from oppression.

B. If you understood righteousness, you wouldn't have fear.

II. This covenant that God made with Noah had no qualifications.

> **For this is as the waters of Noah unto me: for as I have sworn that the waters of Noah should no more go over the earth; so have I sworn that I would not be wroth with thee, nor rebuke thee.**
>
> ISAIAH 54:9

> **And I will establish my covenant with you [Noah]; neither shall all flesh be cut off any more by the waters of a flood; neither shall there any more be a flood to destroy the earth.**
>
> GENESIS 9:11, BRACKETS MINE

A. In Isaiah 54, God was saying this New Covenant that Jesus has put into effect is like that covenant with Noah—an unconditional, unqualified covenant.

B. For those who enter into this covenant, God is never, ever, ever angry with you.

C. God is not the author of condemnation.

> **There is therefore now no condemnation to them which are in Christ Jesus, who walk not after the flesh, but after the Spirit.**
>
> ROMANS 8:1

D. David prayed Psalm 51:10-11 because he was an Old Testament saint, but as a New Testament believer, God created a clean heart in you the very moment you were born again (Eph. 4:24).

Create in me a clean heart, O God; and renew a right spirit within me. Cast me not away from thy presence; and take not thy holy spirit from me.

PSALM 51:10-11

E. Every time you feel like God is ticked off at you and has left—you're wrong! (Matt. 28:20 and Heb. 13:5)

For the mountains shall depart, and the hills be removed; <u>but my kindness shall not depart from thee, neither shall the covenant of my peace be removed, saith the LORD</u> that hath mercy on thee.

ISAIAH 54:10, EMPHASIS MINE

III. God is now at peace with mankind.

Glory to God in the highest, and on earth peace, good will toward men.

LUKE 2:14

A. The war is over—He has made a covenant and signed a treaty.

B. He'll never be angry with us nor rebuke us ever again.

Put on the whole armour of God, that ye may be able to stand against the wiles of the devil…stand therefore, having your…feet shod with the preparation of the <u>gospel of peace</u>.

EPHESIANS 6:11-15, EMPHASIS MINE

C. The reason people aren't responding better is because they haven't heard the true Gospel—the same message Jesus proclaimed.

IV. We've allowed religion to blind us to the truth that Jesus has paid for all sin—not only for the sins of believers—but also for the sins of the whole world.

And he [Jesus] is the propitiation for our sins: and not for ours only, but also for the sins of the whole world.

1 JOHN 2:2, BRACKETS MINE

A. Everybody's sins are paid for—sin isn't the issue.

B. People are going to hell because they haven't accepted the payment for their sin—they haven't received the Lord Jesus Christ.

C. Are you trusting in the payment Christ made, or are you trusting in your own good works, hoping they'll be enough for you to be saved?

V. You can't do enough!

A. There's nothing you can offer that will ever supersede what Jesus has done.

B. Jesus plus nothing equals everything.

C. But Jesus plus anything—especially your own effort—equals nothing!

D. Either you have to trust the Lord one hundred percent or you have to trust yourself, but there cannot be a combination of the two.

E. You either have a Savior who earned your salvation by what He did, or you must earn salvation on your own merit, which cannot be done.

Established in Righteousness
LESSON 5 – TEACHER'S GUIDE

1. Most of us, as Christians, aren't established—strong, steady, and secure—because we don't understand that we're righteous (Is. 54:11-14). If we understood righteousness, we'd be far from oppression. If we understood righteousness, we wouldn't fear.

2. This covenant that God made with Noah had no qualifications (Is. 54:9 and 11). In Isaiah 54, God was saying this New Covenant that Jesus has put into effect is like that covenant with Noah—an unconditional, unqualified covenant. If we've entered into this covenant, God is never, ever, ever angry with us. God is not the author of condemnation (Rom. 8:1). David prayed Psalm 51:10-11 because he was an Old Testament saint, but as New Testament believers, God created a clean heart in us the very moment we were born again (Eph. 4:24). Every time we feel like God is ticked off at us and has left—we're wrong! (Matt. 28:20, Heb. 13:5, and Is. 54:10)

3. God is now at peace with mankind (Luke 2:14). The war is over—He has made a covenant and signed a treaty. He'll never be angry with us nor rebuke us ever again (Eph. 6:11 and 15).

    The reason people aren't responding better is because they haven't heard the true Gospel—the same message Jesus proclaimed.

1. A. Read Isaiah 54:11-14. Why aren't we as Christians established—strong, steady, and secure? (Because we don't understand that we're righteous)
    B. What would be far from us if we understood righteousness? (Oppression and fear)
2. A. Read Isaiah 54:9-11. This New Covenant that Jesus has put into effect is like that covenant God made with Noah in what way? (It's an unconditional, unqualified covenant)
    B. Read Romans 8:1, Psalm 51:10-11, and Ephesians 4:24. As New Testament believers, what did God create in us the very moment we were born again? (A clean heart)
    C. According to Matthew 28:20, Hebrews 13:5, and Isaiah 54:10, what should we recognize whenever we feel like God is ticked off at us and has left? (That we're wrong!)
3. A. Read Luke 2:14; Ephesians 6:11, and 15. Since God is now at peace with mankind, will He ever be angry with us or rebuke us ever again? (No)
    B. Why aren't people responding better? (Because they haven't heard the true Gospel—the same message Jesus proclaimed)

4. We've allowed religion to blind us to the truth that Jesus has paid for all sin—not only for the sins of believers, but also for the sins of the whole world (1 John 2:2). Everybody's sins are paid for—sin isn't the issue. People are going to hell because they haven't accepted the payment for their sin—they haven't received the Lord Jesus Christ. Are we trusting in the payment Christ made, or are we trusting in our own good works, hoping they'll be enough for us to be saved?

5. We can't do enough! There's nothing we can offer that will ever supersede what Jesus has done. Jesus plus nothing equals everything. But Jesus plus anything—especially our own effort—equals nothing! Either we have to trust the Lord one hundred percent or we have to trust ourselves, but there cannot be a combination of the two. We either have a Savior who earned us salvation by what He did, or we must earn salvation on our own merit, which cannot be done.

4. A. Read 1 John 2:2. What truth have we allowed religion to blind us to? (The truth that Jesus has paid for all sin—not only for the sins of believers, but also for the sins of the whole world)
   B. Why are people going to hell? (Because they haven't accepted the payment for their sin—they haven't received the Lord Jesus Christ)
5. A. Jesus plus _____ equals everything. (Nothing)
   B. Is it possible to earn salvation on our own merit? (No)
   C. Who must we trust in one hundred percent? (The Lord—our Savior who earned salvation for us by what He did)

Established in Righteousness
LESSON 5 – ADDITIONAL INFORMATION

My teachings entitled *The Positive Ministry of the Holy Spirit*, "No More Sin Consciousness," and "A Good Conscience" all go into much more detail than I'm able to here. I encourage you to get them.

Established in Righteousness
LESSON 5 – DISCIPLESHIP QUESTIONS

1. What two promises concerning our children does God give us in Isaiah 54:11-14?

2. How shall we be established?

3. Which of the following are benefits of being established in this way?
   A. Fear shall not come near you.
   B. Terror shall not come near you.
   C. Oppression shall be far from you.
   D. All of the above.
   E. None of the above.

4. As the waters of Noah should no more go over the earth, what has God sworn in Isaiah 54:9?

5. According to Genesis 9:11, was the covenant God made with Noah conditional or unconditional?

6. Romans 8:1 says that there is now no _____ to them who are in Christ Jesus.

7. We should not walk after the flesh, but how?

8. Match the aspects of David's Old Testament prayer in Psalm 51:10-11 with the proper corresponding New Testament reality from Ephesians 4:24, Matthew 28:20, and Hebrews 13:5.

   David's Prayer
   A. Create in me a clean heart, O God.
   B. Renew a right spirit within me.
   C. Cast me not away from Your presence.
   D. Take not Your Holy Spirit from me.

   New Testament Reality
   I. I am with you always, even unto the end of the world.
   II. I will never leave you, nor forsake you.
   III. Our born-again spirits were created in true holiness.
   IV. Our new man was created—after God—in righteousness.

9. According to Ephesians 4:24, how was the new man—our born-again spirits—created?

10. In Matthew 28:20, what did the Lord commission us to teach people?

11. How long will Jesus be with us?

12. According to Hebrews 13:5, what should our conversation—behavior—be without?

13. What should we be content with?

14. To explain why, what did Jesus say?

15. According to Luke 2:14, what was God announcing toward mankind at the birth of Jesus?
    A. Wrath and anger.
    B. Hatred and strife.
    C. Judgment and condemnation.
    D. Peace and good will.

16. According to Ephesians 6:11-15, what do we need to put on the whole armor of God to stand against?

17. In order to stand, what must we have our feet shod with?

18. In John 1:29, who did John the Baptist say to behold?

19. What does John continue saying that Jesus came to do?

20. According to 1 John 2:2, Jesus was the propitiation—atoning sacrifice—both for our sins and also for the sins of whom?

Established in Righteousness
LESSON 5 – ANSWER KEY

1. They shall all be taught of the Lord and great shall be their peace.

2. In righteousness.

3. A. Fear shall not come near you.
   B. Terror shall not come near you.
   C. Oppression shall be far from you.
   D. All of the above.

4. To not be wroth with or rebuke us.

5. Unconditional.

6. Condemnation.

7. After the Spirit.

8. David's Prayer   New Testament Reality
   A. Create in me a clean heart, O God.   IV. Our new man was created—after God—in righteousness.
   B. Renew a right spirit within me.   III. Our born-again spirits were created in true holiness.
   C. Cast me not away from Your presence.   II. I will never leave you, nor forsake you.
   D. Take not Your Holy Spirit from me.   I. I am with you always, even unto the end of the world.

9. After God, in righteousness and true holiness.

10. To observe all things whatsoever Jesus has commanded us.

11. Always—even unto the end of the world.

12. Covetousness.

13. Such things as we have.

14. I will never leave you nor forsake you.

15. D. Peace and good will.

16. The wiles of the devil.

17. The preparation of the Gospel of peace.

18. Jesus, the Lamb of God.

19. Take away the sin of the world.

20. The whole world.

Established in Righteousness
LESSON 5 – SCRIPTURES

For this is as the waters of Noah unto me: for as I have sworn that the waters of Noah should no more go over the earth; so have I sworn that I would not be wroth with thee, nor rebuke thee. For the mountains shall depart, and the hills be removed; but my kindness shall not depart from thee, neither shall the covenant of my peace be removed, saith the LORD that hath mercy on thee. O thou afflicted, tossed with tempest, and not comforted, behold, I will lay thy stones with fair colours, and lay thy foundations with sapphires. And I will make thy windows of agates, and thy gates of carbuncles, and all thy borders of pleasant stones. And all thy children shall be taught of the LORD; and great shall be the peace of thy children. In righteousness shalt thou be established: thou shalt be far from oppression; for thou shalt not fear: and from terror; for it shall not come near thee.

ISAIAH 54:9-14

And I will establish my covenant with you; neither shall all flesh be cut off any more by the waters of a flood; neither shall there any more be a flood to destroy the earth.

GENESIS 9:11

There is therefore now no condemnation to them which are in Christ Jesus, who walk not after the flesh, but after the Spirit.

ROMANS 8:1

Create in me a clean heart, O God; and renew a right spirit within me. Cast me not away from thy presence; and take not thy holy spirit from me.

PSALM 51:10-11

And that ye put on the new man, which after God is created in righteousness and true holiness.

EPHESIANS 4:24

Teaching them to observe all things whatsoever I have commanded you: and, lo, I am with you alway, even unto the end of the world. Amen.

MATTHEW 28:20

Let your conversation be without covetousness; and be content with such things as ye have: for he hath said, I will never leave thee, nor forsake thee.

HEBREWS 13:5

Glory to God in the highest, and on earth peace, good will toward men.

LUKE 2:14

Put on the whole armour of God, that ye may be able to stand against the wiles of the devil. For we wrestle not against flesh and blood, but against principalities, against powers, against the rulers of the darkness of this world, against spiritual wickedness in high places. Wherefore take unto you the whole armour of God, that ye may be able to withstand in the evil day, and having done all, to stand. Stand therefore, having your loins girt about with truth, and having on the breastplate of righteousness; And your feet shod with the preparation of the gospel of peace.

Ephesians 6:11-15

The next day John seeth Jesus coming unto him, and saith, Behold the Lamb of God, which taketh away the sin of the world.

John 1:29

And he is the propitiation for our sins: and not for ours only, but also for the sins of the whole world.

1 John 2:2

All Judgment
LESSON 6

God isn't mad anymore! Sin has been atoned for, and He's not imputing man's sins unto him. When **"a Saviour, which is Christ the Lord"** was born (Luke 2:11), a multitude of angels praised God singing:

Glory to God in the highest, and on earth peace, good will toward men.

LUKE 2:14

This wasn't talking about peace "among" men but rather peace from God toward men. Many people haven't understood the difference between the Old Testament and the New. Under the Old Covenant, there was a wrath and punishment from God toward man that was severe. Yet the Lord doesn't operate that same way under the New Covenant. However, many people have missed this truth, and they just mix the Old and New together, thinking that God is still dealing with mankind the same way as before. This isn't so.

If you don't understand this truth, it'll negatively affect your relationship with God. How can you, with love, draw near to God if you think He's striking people down with sickness and disease, withdrawing His presence from you when you sin, and sending the death angel to kill people today? You need to realize we now have a better covenant based upon better promises (Heb. 8:6). Under the New Covenant, the relationship between God and man is totally different.

The war is over! God placed the punishment we deserved upon His Son (Is. 53:4-6). Christ suffered and totally paid the price for our sins. When God the Father saw the travail of Jesus' soul, He was satisfied (Is. 53:11). Now you don't have to suffer separation from God. He's promised never to be angry with you or rebuke you ever again (Is. 54:9). These are tremendous truths!

This is a radically different message than the typical church is giving today. Because of this, many people don't understand how much God loves them. Their faith is hindered, and they're having trouble receiving from God (Gal. 5:6).

Spirit to Born-again Spirit

Most people don't doubt God's ability. What they doubt is His willingness to use His ability on their behalf. Why? They don't feel worthy. The truth is, you aren't worthy in yourself if you just look at your actions. But God doesn't just look at your actions. The punishment for your sin was placed upon Jesus at the cross. Now He's not only taken your sin away, but He's also given you the righteousness of Christ. In your born-again spirit, you are as righteous, holy, and pure as the Lord Jesus Himself.

And that ye put on the new man [your born-again spirit], **which after God is created in righteousness and true holiness.**

EPHESIANS 4:24, BRACKETS MINE

God is a Spirit.

God is a Spirit: and they that worship him must worship him in spirit and in truth.

JOHN 4:24

God looks at you in the spirit realm—Spirit to spirit. He doesn't see you the way you see yourself.

The LORD seeth not as man seeth; for man looketh on the outward appearance, but the LORD looketh on the heart.

1 SAMUEL 16:7

God isn't looking at your actions, sins, and failures. He's not angry with you the way you're angry with yourself. He's not disappointed with you the way you're disappointed with yourself. God sees you in the spirit, and in the spirit you are a brand-new creation (2 Cor. 5:17). God is in love with you. He wants to move in your life, but it takes your cooperation. You don't have to live holy and earn it, but you do have to believe God.

Most of us can't trust that God is really going to move in our lives, because we know we don't deserve it. That's because we've been under a ministry that's been preaching sin-consciousness to us. "If you have sin in your life, God won't answer your prayer. You need to do this and that and all of these things!"

The war is over. God isn't imputing your sins unto you. He's not angry with you. God loves you. If you could just receive this good news, your faith would shoot through the roof. You'd start receiving from God, and His supernatural power would operate in your life much, much greater.

Thunder?

As Jesus was getting ready to lay His life down for us, He headed to Jerusalem. While there, He prayed…

Father, glorify thy name. Then came there a voice from heaven, saying, I have both glorified it, and will glorify it again. The people therefore, that stood by, and heard it, said that it thundered: others said, An angel spake to him.

JOHN 12:28-29

These people heard an audible voice from God out of heaven say, "I have glorified My name, and I will glorify it again." Some of them couldn't believe that it was really God speaking. People pray today, "O Lord, speak to me. Give me a sign!" If you heard an audible voice from

God out of heaven but your heart was hard, you'd explain it away and think, *Oh, that's just thunder.* These people aren't any different than people today. You need to get to where you hear God in your heart.

God isn't going to speak in a booming voice from heaven very often. Even if He did, if your heart was wrong, you'd misinterpret it. You wouldn't believe it. God spoke from heaven in an audible voice, and these people refused to believe it, saying, "Oh, it's just thunder!"

Jesus answered and said, This voice came not because of me, but for your sakes.

JOHN 12:30

In other words, Jesus didn't need to hear God say this; He was already in communion with and listening to His Father. This came for the unbelievers' sake, yet most of them couldn't even receive it.

"Come Across Their Paths in Some Carnal Way"

Now is the judgment of this world: now shall the prince of this world be cast out. And I, if I be lifted up from the earth, will draw all men unto me.

JOHN 12:31-32

This is often interpreted as, "If we worship Jesus and preach Him properly, God will draw the people and everybody will come. You'll just instantly have a large church." That's not what this is saying.

I travel a lot and see many different churches. I don't mean to be critical, but some of the largest churches I've been to have also been some of the worst. They are "seeker-friendly," which means they compromise. They get to where they have a little twenty-minute message. They have all these lights and flashes but very little Word. Those are the churches that are really growing today—the ones built around entertainment rather than proclaiming the Word. They're making Christianity so easy that a person can attend church an hour a week and feel like they're fulfilling the Scripture's requirements concerning church life. They get their consciences salved, but there's no committal, nothing asked of them.

One time, I told the pastor of the 10,000-plus church that I attend, "If you turned this church over to me, I could whittle it down to a thousand in thirty days. If you gave it to me for two months, I could have it down to five hundred. A large portion of these people aren't even baptized in the Holy Spirit!" It's simply not true that the churches preaching the best messages and lifting Jesus up are having the most people come to them. That's not what I observe happening in the body of Christ. It's not true that if you'll just preach the right message, God will draw all men to it.

That's the reason I first went on radio. I went to Childress, Texas, and held some meetings there. At the time, I was under the impression that if I just ministered the Word of God, He would draw all men unto me. We started with six people, and by the third or fourth day, we wound up with about twenty. After the meetings, I was scheduled to go somewhere else. But the night before I left, God woke me up and said, "Andrew, you're assuming that if you're just doing what's right and trusting Me, that I would speak to people and bring them to your meeting. If the people were spiritual enough to hear Me say 'Go hear Andrew Wommack,' I wouldn't need you to minister to them. They aren't listening to the Spirit. They're carnal. Therefore, you need to come across their paths in some carnal way." I woke up early that morning and prayed about it. I started on radio the next day.

The Lord said that I had to come across people's paths. So I've been on radio and television ministering God's Word. I send out cards advertising our conferences and citywide meetings, inviting people to come. Most folks just aren't sensitive enough to the Holy Spirit to hear about these meetings and show up on their own. They need us to cross their paths in some carnal way.

I've heard stories of believers in countries where they're persecuted for their faith. They just pray and God tells them when and where the church meetings are. Every Christian has the capability to hear the Holy Spirit this strongly, but most of us aren't flowing that way. We use carnal means—like radio, television, and letters—to come across people's paths with the Word.

"When I Am Lifted Up"

Getting back to John 12:32, notice that the word **"men"** is italicized in the King James Version. That means this word was not in the original Greek translation. It's a word that the translators supplied to help make the phrase in English grammatically correct. But at least the translators had enough integrity to use italics to identify these words. They are the translators' additions and/or interpretations.

What, then, is John 12:32 really saying?

> **And I [Jesus], if I be lifted up from the earth, will draw all...unto me.**
> JOHN 12:32, BRACKETS MINE

Even though the Lord didn't specify in that particular sentence the **"all"** that would be drawn unto Him, the context makes it clear. Let's consider verse 32 in light of verses 31 and 33.

> **Now is the judgment of this world: now shall the prince of this world be cast out. And I, if I be lifted up from the earth, will draw all [judgment] unto me. This he said, signifying what death he should die.**
> JOHN 12:31-33, BRACKETS MINE

"Judgment" was the topic of verse 31. In verse 33, we see that Jesus said verse 32 signified **"what death he should die."** He wasn't talking about, "If you preach the right message, everyone will come"; He was referring to His upcoming death on the cross. In light of this, we see that the topic of verse 31—judgment—carries over into verse 32. Therefore, Jesus was saying, "When I am lifted up upon the cross, I will draw all of God's judgment, toward the entire human race, to Myself."

"No Condemnation"

All of God's judgment for the entire human race was placed upon Jesus at the cross. God punished Jesus with the punishment we deserved. If God the Father judged His Son with our judgment—punished His Son with our punishment—then it would be double jeopardy for Him to judge us today. In a sense, it would be undoing and discounting what His Son, the Lord Jesus Christ, has done. God has already judged our sin in the flesh of His Son.

> **There is therefore now no condemnation to them which are in Christ Jesus, who walk not after the flesh, but after the Spirit. For the law of the Spirit of life in Christ Jesus hath made me free from the law of sin and death. For what the law could not do, in that it was weak through the flesh, God sending his own Son in the likeness of sinful flesh, and for sin, condemned sin in the flesh.**
>
> ROMANS 8:1-3

The word **"condemned"** here means "judged." God the Father judged sin in the flesh of the Lord Jesus Christ.

> **That the righteousness of the law might be fulfilled in us, who walk not after the flesh, but after the Spirit.**
>
> ROMANS 8:4

Romans 8:3 says that God judged sin in the flesh of His own Son. He put your sin on His Son and judged Him. In our court system here in the United States, if someone has been judged, sent to prison, suffered, and completed their sentence, you can't retry them. They've already paid the debt. You can't drag them back into court, judge them, and punish them again for something they've already suffered for. That would be what's called "double jeopardy."

Well, Jesus suffered for my sin. He suffered the punishment and separation from the heavenly Father that I deserved.

> **My God, my God, why hast thou forsaken me?**
>
> MARK 15:34

I am never going to be forsaken by God, because Jesus was forsaken for me. I will never be separated from God, because Jesus was separated for me. I am never going to be punished by God for my sin, because Jesus was punished by God for me. This is so simple, yet most of the body of Christ today is imputing man's sins unto them and saying, "Well, you did this. God would never heal you, because you did this. Until you repent of this sin, God can't move in your life." They're making you accountable for your own individual sin. They're saying you have to suffer for your own individual sin.

God Loves You, Stupid!

"But, Andrew, are you saying that there are no consequences to my sin?" *No!* That's ***not*** what I'm saying. There are plenty of consequences. If you live in sin, you're stupid! Why? Because God isn't the only person you're dealing with.

God's judgment upon your sin is over. He placed your punishment, rejection, and rebuke upon the Lord Jesus Christ. Therefore, God will never punish, reject, or rebuke you. God's punishment upon sin is over. But sin is also an inroad of the devil into your life. The vertical effect of your sin—God's wrath and judgment coming upon you—has been taken care of. However, the horizontal effect of your sin is great.

> **Know ye not, that to whom ye yield yourselves servants to obey, his servants ye are to whom ye obey; whether of sin unto death, or of obedience unto righteousness?**
>
> ROMANS 6:16

When you yield yourself to sin, you are yielding yourself to the author of that sin. It's absolutely stupid to live in sin, because you're giving the devil an inroad into your life to cause havoc. But God loves you, stupid!

You may be stupid, but God loves you. He's not mad at you, and He certainly isn't punishing you. Does that mean you can just live in sin? You can sin and God will still love you because He's already placed all of your sin upon Jesus, but it's stupid to give Satan an inroad into your life.

There's Nothing You Can Do

Anyone who would take what I'm sharing and say "God loves me and my sins have been paid for, so I can go commit adultery" is playing Russian roulette. Sexual immorality opens the door for all kinds of sexually transmitted diseases. You'll condemn yourself and defile your conscience. You'll lose confidence and your own heart will convict you. You'll hurt the person you're married to, the one you commit adultery with, your children, and their children—lots of people. You'll shame yourself and hurt the kingdom of God. How dumb can you get and still breathe?

But God loves you, stupid! I'm not advocating living in sin, but I am saying that your sin has been paid for. Jesus drew all judgment unto Himself and suffered your iniquity, shame, and rejection. He felt whatever you could imagine a person feeling if they murder, lie, cheat, steal, and hurt other people. Jesus suffered the shame, embarrassment, and rejection. He suffered the separation from God. He's already done it for you, and for you to bear it is totally unnecessary. For you to feel that you have to do "penance" and somehow or another add to what Jesus has already done is a disgrace. It's dishonoring Jesus. It's arrogance on your part to think that what Jesus did wasn't enough and that you have to add something to it to make it complete. There's nothing you can do.

> **Not by works of righteousness which we have done, but according to his mercy he saved us.**
>
> TITUS 3:5

We aren't saved by any worth, value, or merits of our own. We have nothing to claim. There's nothing you can do to add to Jesus!

All Judgment
LESSON 6 – OUTLINE

I. Many people haven't understood the difference between the Old Testament and the New.

   A. If you don't understand this truth, it'll negatively affect your relationship with God.

   B. You need to realize that we have a better covenant based upon better promises today (Heb. 8:6).

   C. Under the New Covenant, the relationship between God and man is totally different.

II. In your born-again spirit, you are as righteous, holy, and pure as the Lord Jesus Himself.

> **And that ye put on the new man** [your born-again spirit]**, which after God is created in righteousness and true holiness.**
>
> EPHESIANS 4:24, BRACKETS MINE

   A. God is a Spirit, and He looks at you in the spirit realm—Spirit to spirit:

> **God is a Spirit: and they that worship him must worship him in spirit and in truth.**
>
> JOHN 4:24

   B. He doesn't see you the way you see yourself.

> **The LORD seeth not as man seeth; for man looketh on the outward appearance, but the LORD looketh on the heart.**
>
> 1 SAMUEL 16:7

   C. God isn't looking at your actions, sins, and failures.

   D. If you could just receive this good news, your faith would shoot through the roof, you'd start receiving from God, and His supernatural power would operate in your life much, much greater.

III. As Jesus was in Jerusalem getting ready to lay His life down for us, He prayed:

> **Father, glorify thy name. Then came there a voice from heaven, saying, I have both glorified it, and will glorify it again. The people therefore, that stood by, and heard it, said that it thundered: others said, An angel spake to him.**
>
> JOHN 12:28-29

   A. If you heard an audible voice from God out of heaven, but your heart was hard, you'd explain it away and think, *Oh, that's just thunder.*

B. This came for the unbelievers' sake, and yet most of those unbelievers couldn't even receive it.

Jesus answered and said, This voice came not because of me, but for your sakes.
JOHN 12:30

IV. In the King James Version, the word **"men"** is italicized in John 12:32, which means it wasn't in the original Greek.

Now is the judgment of this world: now shall the prince of this world be cast out. And I, if I be lifted up from the earth, will draw all men unto me.
JOHN 12:31-32

A. What, then, is John 12:32 really saying?

And I [Jesus], if I be lifted up from the earth, will draw all…unto me.
JOHN 12:32, BRACKETS MINE

B. Even though the Lord didn't specify in that particular sentence the **"all"** that would be drawn unto Him, the context makes it clear.

Now is the judgment of this world: now shall the prince of this world be cast out. And I, if I be lifted up from the earth, will draw all [judgment] unto me. This he said, signifying what death he should die.
JOHN 12:31-33, BRACKETS MINE

C. The topic of verse 31—judgment—carries over into verse 32.

D. Therefore, Jesus was saying, "When I am lifted up upon the cross, I will draw all of God's judgment toward the entire human race to Myself."

V. God has already judged our sin in the flesh of His Son.

There is therefore now no condemnation to them which are in Christ Jesus, who walk not after the flesh, but after the Spirit. For the law of the Spirit of life in Christ Jesus hath made me free from the law of sin and death. For what the law could not do, in that it was weak through the flesh, God sending his own Son in the likeness of sinful flesh, and for sin, condemned sin in the flesh.
ROMANS 8:1-3

A. The word **"condemned"** here means "judged."

B. God the Father judged sin in the flesh of the Lord Jesus Christ.

That the righteousness of the law might be fulfilled in us, who walk not after the flesh, but after the Spirit.
ROMANS 8:4

C. Jesus suffered the punishment and separation from the heavenly Father that I deserved.

My God, my God, why hast thou forsaken me?

MARK 15:34

D. I am never going to be forsaken by God, separated from God, or punished by God for my sin, because Jesus was forsaken, separated, and punished by God for me.

VI. "Are you saying that there are no consequences to my sin?"

A. No, there are plenty of consequences, because God isn't the only person you're dealing with.

Know ye not, that to whom ye yield yourselves servants to obey, his servants ye are to whom ye obey; whether of sin unto death, or of obedience unto righteousness?

ROMANS 6:16

B. When you yield yourself to sin, you are yielding yourself to the author of that sin—the devil.

C. You can sin and God will still love you because He's already placed all of your sin upon Jesus, but it's stupid to give Satan an inroad into your life.

D. I'm not advocating living in sin, but I am saying that your sin has been paid for.

VII. Jesus drew all judgment unto Himself and suffered your iniquity, shame, and rejection.

A. He's already done it for you, and for you to bear it is totally unnecessary.

B. For you to feel that you have to do "penance" and somehow or another add to what Jesus has already done is a disgrace, and it dishonors Christ.

C. It's arrogance on our part to think that what Jesus did wasn't enough and that we have to add something to it to make it complete.

Not by works of righteousness which we have done, but according to his mercy he saved us.

TITUS 3:5

D. There's nothing you can do to add to Jesus!

All Judgment
LESSON 6 – TEACHER'S GUIDE

1. Many people haven't understood the difference between the Old Testament and the New. If we don't understand this truth, it'll negatively affect our relationship with God. We need to realize that we have a better covenant based upon better promises today (Heb. 8:6). Under the New Covenant, the relationship between God and man is totally different.

2. In our born-again spirits, we are as righteous, holy, and pure as the Lord Jesus Himself (Eph. 4:24). God is a Spirit, and He looks at us in the spirit realm—Spirit to spirit (John 4:24). He doesn't see us the way we see ourselves (1 Sam. 16:7). God isn't looking at our actions, sins, and failures. If we could just receive this good news, our faith would shoot through the roof, we'd start receiving from God, and His supernatural power would operate in our lives much, much greater.

3. As Jesus was in Jerusalem getting ready to lay His life down for us, He prayed (John 12:28-29). If we heard an audible voice from God out of heaven but our hearts were hard, we'd explain it away and think, *Oh, that's just thunder.* This came for the unbelievers' sake, and yet most of those unbelievers couldn't even receive it (John 12:30).

4. In the King James Version, the word **"men"** is italicized in John 12:32, which means it wasn't in the original Greek. What, then, is John 12:32 really saying? Even though the Lord didn't specify in that particular sentence the **"all"** that would be drawn unto Him, the context makes it clear (John 12:31-33). The topic of verse 31—judgment—carries over into verse 32. Therefore, Jesus was saying, "When I am lifted up upon the cross, I will draw all of God's judgment toward the entire human race to Myself."

1. A. What happens when we don't understand the difference between the Old Testament and the New? (It negatively affects our relationship with God)
    B. According to Hebrews 8:6, what must we realize? (That we have a better covenant based upon better promises today)
2. A. Read Ephesians 4:24, John 4:24, and 1 Samuel 16:7. In what part of our beings—spirit, soul, or body—are we as righteous, holy, and pure as the Lord Jesus Himself? (Our born-again spirits)
    B. What would happen if we understood the way God sees us? (Our faith would shoot through the roof, we'd start receiving from God, and His supernatural power would operate in our lives much, much greater)
3. A. Read John 12:28-30. Why couldn't these unbelievers receive the audible voice of God? (Their hearts were hard)
    B. If our hearts were hard, and we heard an audible voice from God out of heaven, what would we do? (Explain it away)
4. A. Read John 12:31-33. What is the topic of verse 31, which carries over into verse 32? (Judgment)
    B. What, then, was Jesus really saying in John 12:32? ("When I am lifted up upon the cross, I will draw all of God's judgment toward the entire human race to Myself")

5.   God has already judged our sin in the flesh of His Son (Rom. 8:1-3). The word **"condemned"** in Romans 8:3 means "judged." God the Father judged sin in the flesh of the Lord Jesus Christ (Rom. 8:4). Jesus suffered the punishment and separation from the heavenly Father that we deserved (Mark 15:34). We are never going to be forsaken by God, separated from God, or punished by God for our sin, because Jesus was forsaken, separated, and punished by God for us.

6.   Am I saying that there are no consequences to our sin? No, there are plenty of consequences, because God isn't the only person we're dealing with (Rom. 6:16). When we yield ourselves to sin, we are yielding ourselves to the author of that sin—the devil. We can sin and God will still love us because He's already placed all of our sin upon Jesus, but it's stupid to give Satan an inroad into our lives. I'm not advocating living in sin, but I am saying that our sin has been paid for.

7.   Jesus drew all judgment unto Himself and suffered our iniquity, shame, and rejection. He's already done it for us, and for us to bear it is totally unnecessary. For us to feel that we have to do "penance" and somehow or another add to what Jesus has already done is a disgrace, and it dishonors Christ. It's arrogance on our part to think that what Jesus did wasn't enough and that we have to add something to it to make it complete (Titus 3:5). There's nothing we can do to add to Jesus!

5. A. Read Romans 8:1-4 and Mark 15:34. Has God already judged our sin? (Yes, in the flesh of His Son—the Lord Jesus Christ)
   B. Why are we never going to be forsaken by God, separated from God, or punished by God for our sin? (Because Jesus was forsaken, separated, and punished by God for us)
6. A. According to Romans 6:16, who are we yielding ourselves to when we sin? (The author of that sin—the devil)
   B. Does God still love us when we sin? (Yes, because He's already placed all of our sin upon Jesus)
7. A. What did Jesus draw unto Himself when He suffered our iniquity, shame, and rejection? (All judgment)
   B. Read Titus 3:5. For us to feel that we have to do "penance" and somehow or another add to what Jesus has already done is what? (A disgrace, and it dishonors Christ—it's arrogance on our part to think that what Jesus did wasn't enough and that we have to add something to it to make it complete)

All Judgment
LESSON 6 – DISCIPLESHIP QUESTIONS

1. According to Luke 2:11, where was Christ the Lord born?

2. In Luke 2:14, what are the angels giving God?

3. According to Hebrews 8:6, what has Jesus obtained?

4. What is He the mediator of?

5. What is this better covenant established upon?

6. According to Isaiah 53:4-6, whose griefs and sorrows did Jesus bear?

7. Whose transgressions was He wounded for, and whose iniquities was He bruised for?

8. What does Isaiah 53:11 say that God the Father saw and caused Him to be satisfied?

9. What kind of servant is Jesus?

10. In Isaiah 54:9, who has the Lord sworn not to be wroth with nor rebuke?

11. According to Galatians 5:6, what works by love?

12. In Ephesians 4:24, what are we admonished to put on?

13. Who was he created after?

14. How was he created?

15. According to John 4:24, what is God?

16. How must those who worship Him do so?

17. In 1 Samuel 16:7, why did the Lord tell Samuel not to look on Eliab's countenance or the height of his stature?

18. What does man look upon?

19. What does God look upon?

20. According to 2 Corinthians 5:17, what two things are true about someone who has become a new creature in Christ?

21. In John 12:28-33, who was this voice from heaven for?

22. When was Jesus going to draw all judgment unto Himself?

23. According to Romans 8:1-4, what has made me free from the law of sin and death?

24. How was sin condemned in the flesh?

25. When does Mark 15:34 reveal Jesus cried with a loud voice, "My God, my God, why hast thou forsaken me?"

26. According to Romans 6:16, what does yielding ourselves to sin produce?

27. How do we produce righteous actions—in this verse, righteousness—which is the fruit of our righteous born-again spirits?

28. According to Titus 3:5, are we saved by the righteous works we have done?

29. What motivated God to save us?

30. How did He save us?

All Judgment
LESSON 6 – ANSWER KEY

1. In the city of David.

2. Glory in the highest.

3. A more excellent ministry.

4. A better covenant.

5. Better promises.

6. Ours.

7. Ours.

8. The travail of Jesus' soul.

9. Righteous.

10. Thee—you.

11. Faith.

12. The new man.

13. God.

14. In righteousness and true holiness.

15. A Spirit.

16. In spirit and in truth.

17. Because He had refused him.

18. The outward appearance.

19. The heart.

20. Old things are passed away and all things are become new.

21. The people that stood by.

22. When He was lifted up from the earth (put on the cross).

23. The law of the Spirit of life in Christ Jesus.

24. God sent His own Son in the likeness of sinful flesh, and for sin, condemned sin in the flesh.

25. The ninth hour.

26. Death.

27. By yielding to obedience—obeying God.

28. No.

29. His mercy.

30. By the washing of regeneration and the renewing of the Holy Spirit.

All Judgment

For unto you is born this day in the city of David a Saviour, which is Christ the Lord.

LUKE 2:11

Glory to God in the highest, and on earth peace, good will toward men.

LUKE 2:14

But now hath he obtained a more excellent ministry, by how much also he is the mediator of a better covenant, which was established upon better promises.

HEBREWS 8:6

Surely he hath borne our griefs, and carried our sorrows: yet we did esteem him stricken, smitten of God, and afflicted. But he was wounded for our transgressions, he was bruised for our iniquities: the chastisement of our peace was upon him; and with his stripes we are healed. All we like sheep have gone astray; we have turned every one to his own way; and the LORD hath laid on him the iniquity of us all.

ISAIAH 53:4-6

He shall see of the travail of his soul, and shall be satisfied: by his knowledge shall my righteous servant justify many; for he shall bear their iniquities.

ISAIAH 53:11

For this is as the waters of Noah unto me: for as I have sworn that the waters of Noah should no more go over the earth; so have I sworn that I would not be wroth with thee, nor rebuke thee.

ISAIAH 54:9

For in Jesus Christ neither circumcision availeth any thing, nor uncircumcision; but faith which worketh by love.

GALATIANS 5:6

And that ye put on the new man, which after God is created in righteousness and true holiness.

EPHESIANS 4:24

God is a Spirit: and they that worship him must worship him in spirit and in truth.

JOHN 4:24

But the LORD said unto Samuel, Look not on his countenance, or on the height of his stature; because I have refused him: for the LORD seeth not as man seeth; for man looketh on the outward appearance, but the LORD looketh on the heart.

1 SAMUEL 16:7

Therefore if any man be in Christ, he is a new creature: old things are passed away; behold, all things are become new.

2 CORINTHIANS 5:17

Father, glorify thy name. Then came there a voice from heaven, saying, I have both glorified it, and will glorify it again. The people therefore, that stood by, and heard it, said that it thundered: others said, An angel spake to him. Jesus answered and said, This voice came not because of me, but for your sakes. Now is the judgment of this world: now shall the prince of this world be cast out. And I, if I be lifted up from the earth, will draw all men unto me. This he said, signifying what death he should die.

JOHN 12:28-33

There is therefore now no condemnation to them which are in Christ Jesus, who walk not after the flesh, but after the Spirit. For the law of the Spirit of life in Christ Jesus hath made me free from the law of sin and death. For what the law could not do, in that it was weak through the flesh, God sending his own Son in the likeness of sinful flesh, and for sin, condemned sin in the flesh: That the righteousness of the law might be fulfilled in us, who walk not after the flesh, but after the Spirit.

ROMANS 8:1-4

And at the ninth hour Jesus cried with a loud voice, saying, Eloi, Eloi, lama sabachthani? which is, being interpreted, My God, my God, why hast thou forsaken me?

MARK 15:34

Know ye not, that to whom ye yield yourselves servants to obey, his servants ye are to whom ye obey; whether of sin unto death, or of obedience unto righteousness?

ROMANS 6:16

Not by works of righteousness which we have done, but according to his mercy he saved us, by the washing of regeneration, and renewing of the Holy Ghost.

TITUS 3:5

Understand the Gospel
LESSON 7

Basically, the way the "Gospel" has been presented today is, "Jesus has paid a price, but it's not a full price. And until you repent and live up to some standard, God can't work in your life. Until you quit dipping, cussing, chewing, and going with those who do, He can't answer your prayers." We're adding our own goodness, holiness, and works to what Jesus has done. That's the message most of the church is preaching today.

Every last one of us has been exposed to this and has thought that we must do things in order to earn God's favor. We are accepted by God because of what Jesus did—plus zero. All we have to do is receive it by faith. If we're thinking *Well, I know that Jesus died for me and He did all these things, but I also have to be holy*, that's undoing what Jesus has done.

And if by grace, then is it no more of works: otherwise grace is no more grace. But if it be of works, then is it no more grace: otherwise work is no more work.

ROMANS 11:6

That's just Old English for "You're either saved by grace or by works, but not by a combination of the two." Either you're saved by the grace of God and all you must do is receive it by faith, or you must be saved by your own goodness and merit (which cannot be done). It's not a combination of the two. It's not Jesus providing the minimum payment and then you have to add to it. Jesus paid it all, and it's just a matter of you believing and receiving, or doubting and doing without. That's the way it works.

Yet most of us have fallen under a "works" mentality. Satan is the accuser of the brethren. He can't accuse God, so he focuses his efforts on us. In fact, the devil isn't even trying to tell most of us that "God can't do miracles. God can't set you free, heal you, or bless you." If we believe in God, then—by definition—He can do anything. We don't doubt that God has the power and can do it; Satan is primarily fighting us by saying, "Sure, God can do things. But what makes you think He would do it for you—you sorry thing!" Then he'll show us that we've gotten mad at someone, that we haven't studied the Word, that we haven't prayed, and so forth. The reason we're missing it is because we tie God's movement in our lives to our performance.

Nearly-Too-Good-to-Be-True News

For I am not ashamed of the gospel of Christ: for it is the power of God unto salvation to every one that believeth; to the Jew first, and also to the Greek. For therein is the righteousness of God revealed from faith to faith: as it is written. The just shall live by faith.

ROMANS 1:16-17

The word *Gospel* today is a religious cliché to us. Most of us don't know what it's talking about. We use "Gospel" to refer to anything having to do with church or Christianity. People say they're ministers of the Gospel. Yet many of these folks don't ever preach anything that's "good news," which is what "Gospel" means. They're saying, "You're a sinner on your way to hell. Repent or else! Turn or burn! I'm preaching the Gospel." That's not the Gospel. It's true that there is a God and a devil, a heaven and a hell, and if a person doesn't repent they're going to hell. Those things are true, but that's not good news. That's not the Gospel.

There are only two examples in all of Greek literature of this word translated "Gospel" being used outside of the Bible. That's because *Gospel* means more than just "good news." It's a superlative that literally means "nearly-too-good-to-be-true news." Outside of the Gospel, there isn't anything that's nearly-too-good-to-be-true news. This was a word that existed outside of the Bible before the Bible was written, but it was very seldom used, because there wasn't much in life that was nearly-too-good-to-be-true news.

Outside of God and the good things He's done through Jesus, life is bad. Life is a terminal experience. We're all in various stages of dying. If you were to look at life critically—apart from God's goodness, His promises, and the hope of heaven—there are lots of reasons to be upset. If you aren't having a problem right now, just hold on. You'll have one soon. Life is bad. But Jesus came along and took all of God's wrath and judgment for our sin upon Himself. Now, that's amazing love!

God Almighty died for us! The whole universe fits within the span of His hand (Is. 40:12). We need to think how big that is. God's hand is bigger than the universe. Yet He came and lived inside a physical human being. And now He lives in us. He bore our sins and died for us. That's nearly-too-good-to-be-true news!

Religious People

Who would die for an ant or a flea? It's so insignificant. Yet God is infinitely greater than us, and He loved us enough to die for us. That's nearly-too-good-to-be-true news. He bore our sins. So when Paul used this word *Gospel*, it wasn't a religious cliché. Nobody just passed over this. He was saying, "I'm not ashamed of telling people that God has paid for their sins, that everything has already been done, and that God isn't angry anymore." The religious system of Paul's day just screamed and yelled at this, because they were preaching a bad news "Gospel" that wasn't even Gospel. It was just bad news that God is angry and you have to appease Him by doing all of these rituals. You have to measure how many steps you take on a Sabbath, because if you took too many, God would be angry with you.

John the Baptist was raised by the Essenes. They were a group of Jews who lived by the Dead Sea and wrote the Dead Sea Scrolls. In these scrolls, researchers have discovered documents that reveal how legalistic and ritualistic these people were. The Essenes actually taught that it was against the Law to have a bowel movement on the Sabbath day. They wouldn't allow you to have a bowel movement on the Sabbath day, because it could be considered work! That's the kind of religious system Jesus came into and that Paul was addressing. The Essenes were people who were so ritualistic and legalistic that if you didn't do all of these things, God would be angry with you and reject you.

Paul just boldly proclaimed, "I'm not ashamed of telling people that God loves them and that their sins are paid for." We've come full circle today. I've been persecuted for telling people God loves them. I've received much criticism for preaching that Jesus bore their sins and that God isn't mad at them anymore.

Who was it that persecuted Jesus? Religious people. Who was it that persecuted Paul? Religious people. Can you guess who it is that persecutes the Gospel today? That's right—religious people! It's because they've been taught that God is angry with you and won't move in your life unless you do this and that, and this and that. We have a religious pharisaical system in place today, just like in biblical times. But the Gospel is good news!

Salvation Includes Healing

The Gospel is the power of God unto salvation (Rom. 1:16). *Sozo*, the Greek word translated **"salvation"** here, doesn't only mean "forgiveness of sins"; it also includes healing, deliverance, and prosperity.

> **Is any sick among you? let him call for the elders of the church; and let them pray over him, anointing him with oil in the name of the Lord: and the prayer of faith shall save** [SOZO] **the sick.**
>
> JAMES 5:14-15, BRACKETS MINE

Healing is part of salvation. So when the Word says that the Gospel is the power of God unto salvation, this also means that the Gospel is the power of God unto your healing. The Gospel is the power of God unto your financial prosperity. The Gospel is the power of God unto your deliverance and emotional stability. If you aren't experiencing peace, joy, and victory, and if you aren't healthy in your body, it's because you don't have a full revelation of the Gospel. If you really knew the Gospel—the nearly-too-good-to-be-true news of how much God loves you—your body would be healed.

Many Christians today are promoting all kinds of natural health products. They're saying you should go on a vegetarian diet, eat barley grain, and so forth. It's not unusual to watch Christian television or visit a Christian bookstore and see more information available about health, diet, and exercise than the preaching of the Gospel. Now, there's a balance here. But let me say that I don't believe that what you eat and the way you exercise determines 90 or 99 percent of your health issues. The Bible doesn't teach that.

You might say, "Oh, yes it does!" It talks about these dietary laws. However, the only time these dietary laws are explained is in Colossians.

> **Let no man therefore judge you in meat, or in drink…which are a shadow of things to come; but the body is of Christ.**
>
> COLOSSIANS 2:16-17

Biblical Health

All of these Old Testament dietary laws were shadows and types of New Testament realities that are now fulfilled. For someone to say "God told me not to eat pork because it's bad for me" is incorrect. It's a doctrine of the devil.

> **Now the Spirit speaketh expressly, that in the latter times some shall depart from the faith, giving heed to seducing spirits, and doctrines of devils...commanding to abstain from meats, which God hath created to be received with thanksgiving of them which believe and know the truth.**
>
> 1 TIMOTHY 4:1 AND 3

If someone commands you to abstain from eating meats, it's a doctrine of the devil. I'm not saying you shouldn't use wisdom, but realize that conventional wisdom about what you should eat changes every ten years or so. I heard a report recently that said a really low fat diet is detrimental to you. It keeps your brain from working. I've suspected that all along. Your brain has to have a certain amount of fat to work. They change the "standards" all the time.

What does the Bible say about health? It speaks of operating in honor and joy.

> **A merry heart doeth good like a medicine: but a broken spirit drieth the bones.**
>
> PROVERBS 17:22

> **Honour thy father and thy mother: that thy days may be long upon the land which the LORD thy God giveth thee.**
>
> EXODUS 20:12

If you understood how forgiven and loved you are, you'd start rejoicing and praising God. Once you understand the Gospel, your natural realm—your body and soul—would improve. Your immune system would work better if you weren't beaten down feeling unworthy, defiled, and condemned all of the time. You'd have health in the natural realm, whether you received a supernatural healing from Jesus or not.

Perfect Peace

Food and exercise are a part of it, but it's much less than people think. I can't prove this, but I believe about 20 percent of your health comes from food you eat and exercise. Most people would say it's 90 percent or higher. I believe that your joy in the Lord, honoring your parents, and so forth is more important than these natural things. As Christians, we have—in a sense—become so humanistic. We're ignoring the spiritual roots of things and trying to find a physical, organic reason for everything.

"You're depressed because you don't have certain chemicals." Not true. The reason you don't have certain chemicals is because you're depressed. So you can either deal with depression by doing what the Word says—choosing to rejoice in the Lord and encourage yourself in Him—or you can take a pill and have someone dope you up so you can function. But that's not the right way to do it.

> **Thou wilt keep him in perfect peace, whose mind is stayed on thee: because he trusteth in thee.**
>
> Isaiah 26:3

"That's true for everyone except those who have had traumatic experiences, were raised in dysfunctional families, or have chemical imbalances." No, that's not what the Bible says. There are no exceptions. If you would keep your mind stayed on the Lord, you would be in perfect peace. If you aren't in perfect peace, your mind isn't stayed on the Lord, or it's stayed on religion. If you understood the Gospel, it would produce health, joy, peace, and prosperity. This is awesome!

Intuitive Knowledge

People say, "Well, people need to know that they're sinners. They need to know that God is angry with them." In Romans 1:18-20, Paul basically said, "People already know that they're sinners. It's intuitive knowledge. God has revealed Himself from heaven against all sin and unrighteousness of man." You don't need to condemn people. They already have an intuitive knowledge.

Now, they may get into mind games and try to talk themselves out of it. While I was an American soldier in Vietnam, many people told me they were atheists. One guy, a Princeton-educated atheist, made me look like an absolute fool, because he was a better talker than I was. But when the bombs started dropping and the bullets began to fly, he cried out to the God he said he didn't believe in with all of his heart, saying, "O God, save me!" It's all just a mind game. Put a gun to their heads, and they'll say, "O God, help me!" They know there's a God. It's just a lie. You don't have to try to convince people of their need for God. Everybody already knows it in their hearts. Everybody!

"But, Andrew, I know someone who doesn't know it." No, you don't. You know someone who says they don't believe in God, but they know in their heart. Don't even argue with their head. Just go straight to their heart and talk to them like they know the truth. You'll find out that people will respond.

For the rest of Romans 1, Paul was showing that you don't have to convince people of their sin; they are condemned in their own hearts. They know there's right and wrong. Everybody knows there's only one God and that they are not Him. That's intuitive within every person.

Understand the Gospel
LESSON 7 – OUTLINE

I. You are accepted by God because of what Jesus did—plus zero.

   A. All you have to do is receive it by faith.

      And if by grace, then is it no more of works: otherwise grace is no more grace. But if it be of works, then is it no more grace: otherwise work is no more work.
      ROMANS 11:6

   B. That's just Old English for "You're either saved by grace or by works, but not a combination of the two."

   C. Yet most of us have fallen under a "works" mentality.

   D. The reason you're missing it is because you tie God's movement in your life to your performance.

II. The word translated "Gospel" means more than just "good news"; it's a superlative that literally means "nearly-too-good-to-be-true news."

      For I am not ashamed of the gospel of Christ: for it is the power of God unto salvation to every one that believeth; to the Jew first, and also to the Greek. For therein is the righteousness of God revealed from faith to faith: as it is written, The just shall live by faith.
      ROMANS 1:16-17

   A. Outside of God and the good things He's done through Jesus, life is bad.

   B. Jesus came along and took all of God's wrath and judgment for our sin upon Himself. Now, that's amazing love!

   C. The religious system of Paul's day just screamed and yelled at this, because they were preaching a bad news "Gospel" that wasn't even Gospel.

   D. They were people who were so ritualistic and legalistic that if you didn't do all of these things, God would be angry with you and reject you.

   E. Paul just boldly proclaimed, "I'm not ashamed of telling people that God loves them and that their sins are paid for."

III. *Sozo*, the Greek word translated **"salvation"** in Romans 1:16, doesn't only mean "forgiveness of sins," but also includes healing, deliverance, and prosperity.

Is any sick among you? let him call for the elders of the church; and let them pray over him, anointing him with oil in the name of the Lord: and the prayer of faith shall save [sozo] the sick.

JAMES 5:14-15, BRACKETS MINE

A. When the Word says that the Gospel is the power of God unto salvation, this also means that the Gospel is the power of God unto your healing, deliverance, and prosperity.

B. If you really knew the Gospel—the nearly-too-good-to-be-true news of how much God loves you—your body would be healed.

C. All of these Old Testament dietary laws were shadows and types of New Testament realities that are now fulfilled.

Let no man therefore judge you in meat, or in drink...which are a shadow of things to come; but the body is of Christ.

COLOSSIANS 2:16-17

D. If someone commands you to abstain from eating meats, it's a doctrine of the devil.

Now the Spirit speaketh expressly, that in the latter times some shall depart from the faith, giving heed to seducing spirits, and doctrines of devils...commanding to abstain from meats, which God hath created to be received with thanksgiving of them which believe and know the truth.

1 TIMOTHY 4:1 AND 3

IV. Once you understand the Gospel, your natural realm—your body and soul—would improve.

A. Concerning health, the Bible speaks of operating in honor and joy.

A merry heart doeth good like a medicine: but a broken spirit drieth the bones.

PROVERBS 17:22

Honour thy father and thy mother: that thy days may be long upon the land which the LORD thy God giveth thee.

EXODUS 20:12

B. If you understood how forgiven and loved you are, you'd start rejoicing and praising God.

C. Your immune system would work better if you weren't beaten down feeling unworthy, defiled, and condemned all the time.

D. Food and exercise are a part of it, but it's much less than people think.

E. If you would keep your mind stayed on the Lord, you would be in perfect peace.

Thou wilt keep him in perfect peace, whose mind is stayed on thee: because he trusteth in thee.

ISAIAH 26:3

    F. If you understood the Gospel, it would produce health, joy, peace, and prosperity.

V. In Romans 1:18-20, Paul basically says, "People already know that they're sinners. It's intuitive knowledge. God has revealed Himself from heaven against all sin and unrighteousness of man."

    A. You might know people who say they don't believe in God, but in their hearts they really do.

    B. Go straight to their hearts, and talk to them like they know the truth.

    C. You'll find out that people will respond.

    D. Everybody knows there's only one God and that they are not Him.

Understand the Gospel
LESSON 7 – TEACHER'S GUIDE

1.   We are accepted by God because of what Jesus did—plus zero. All we have to do is receive it by faith. We're either saved by grace or by works, but not a combination of the two (Rom. 11:6). Yet most of us have fallen under a "works" mentality. The reason we're missing it is because we tie God's movement in our lives to our performance.

2.   The word translated "Gospel" means more than just "good news"; it's a superlative that literally means "nearly-too-good-to-be-true news" (Rom. 1:16-17). Outside of God and the good things He's done through Jesus, life is bad. Jesus came along and took all of God's wrath and judgment for our sin upon Himself. Now, that's amazing love! The religious system of Paul's day just screamed and yelled at this, because they were preaching a bad news "Gospel" that wasn't even Gospel. They were people who were so ritualistic and legalistic that if they didn't do all of these things, God would be angry with them and reject them. Paul just boldly proclaimed, "I'm not ashamed of telling people that God loves them and that their sins are paid for."

3.   *Sozo*, the Greek word translated **"salvation"** in Romans 1:16, doesn't only mean "forgiveness of sins," but also includes healing, deliverance, and prosperity (e.g., James 5:14-15). When the Word says that the Gospel is the power of God unto salvation, this also means that the Gospel is the power of God unto our healing, deliverance, and prosperity. If we really knew the Gospel—the nearly-too-good-to-be-true news of how much God loves us—our bodies would be healed. All of these Old Testament dietary laws were shadows and types of New Testament realities that are now fulfilled (Col. 2:16-17). If someone commands us to abstain from eating meats, it's a doctrine of the devil (1 Tim. 4:1-3).

1. A. According to Romans 11:6, is it possible to combine grace and works for salvation? (No)
   B. Why are we missing it? (We tie God's movement in our lives to our performance)
2. A. Read Romans 1:16-17. What does the word translated "Gospel" mean? (Nearly-too-good-to-be-true news)
   B. What did Paul boldly proclaim? (I'm not ashamed of telling people that God loves them and that their sins are paid for)
3. A. Read James 5:14-15. In addition to forgiveness of sins, what does salvation include? (Healing, deliverance, and prosperity)
   B. According to Colossians 2:16-17 and 1 Timothy 4:1-3, what were these Old Testament dietary laws? (Shadows and types of New Testament realities that are now fulfilled)

4.   Once we understand the Gospel, our natural realm—our body and soul—would improve. Concerning health, the Bible speaks of operating in honor and joy (Prov. 17:22 and Ex. 20:12). If we understood how forgiven and loved we are, we'd start rejoicing and praising God. Our immune system would work better if we weren't beaten down feeling unworthy, defiled, and condemned all the time. Food and exercise are a part of it, but it's much less than people think. If we would keep our minds stayed on the Lord, we would be in perfect peace (Is. 26:3). If we understood the Gospel, it would produce health, joy, peace, and prosperity.

5.   In Romans 1:18-20, Paul basically said, "People already know that they're sinners. It's intuitive knowledge. God has revealed Himself from heaven against all sin and unrighteousness of man." We might know people who say they don't believe in God, but in their hearts they really do. We need to go straight to their hearts and talk to them like they know the truth. We'll find out that people will respond. Everybody knows there's only one God and that they are not Him.

4. A. Read Proverbs 17:22, Exodus 20:12, and Isaiah 26:3. Concerning health, what does the Bible speak of? (Operating in honor and joy)
   B. What does understanding the Gospel produce? (Health, joy, peace, and prosperity)
5. A. What was Paul basically saying in Romans 1:18-20? (People already know that they're sinners. It's intuitive knowledge. God has revealed Himself from heaven against all sin and unrighteousness of man)
   B. What, then, should we do with people who say they don't believe in God? (Go straight to their hearts and talk to them like they know the truth)
   C. What does everybody know? (That there's only one God and that they are not Him)

Understand the Gospel
LESSON 7 – ADDITIONAL INFORMATION

As we look at some highlights from the book of Romans, I'd like to recommend both of my synopsis of Romans for further study: *Grace, the Power of the Gospel* (in audio form as *The Gospel: the Power of God*) and my verse-by-verse commentary (which can be accessed free online at our website), entitled *Life for Today:* the Romans Edition. These go into much more detail than I'm able to here.

Understand the Gospel
LESSON 7 – DISCIPLESHIP QUESTIONS

1. According to Romans 11:6, can we be saved by a combination of grace and works?

2. How did Paul feel about the Gospel of Christ in Romans 1:16-17?

3. What is the power of God unto salvation?

4. What must we do to receive salvation?

5. Where is the righteousness of God revealed?

6. How shall the just live?

7. Who is the one person who can do everything listed in Isaiah 40:12?

8. What does James 5:14-15 instruct a sick person to do?

9. What two things should they do to minister to the sick person?

10. What is it that saves/heals/delivers the sick?

11. Who raises them up?

12. What happens if they have committed sins?

13. According to Colossians 2:16-17, we are to let no one judge us concerning what?
    A. In respect of a holy day.
    B. In drink.
    C. The Sabbath days.
    D. In meat.
    E. All of the above.
    F. None of the above.

14. These were merely shadows of things to come in whom?

15. According to 1 Timothy 4:1-3, when will some depart from the faith?

16. What will they give heed to?

17. Speaking lies in hypocrisy, what will happen to their consciences?

18. In addition to forbidding marrying, what will they command people to abstain from?

19. God has created these things to be received with thanksgiving by whom?

20. According to Proverbs 17:22, what does good like medicine?

21. What does a broken spirit do?

22. Whom should we honor, according to Exodus 20:12?

23. What are we promised if we do?

24. According to Isaiah 26:3, who will be kept in perfect peace?

25. Why?

Understand the Gospel
LESSON 7 – ANSWER KEY

1. No.

2. Not ashamed.

3. The Gospel of Christ.

4. Believe the Gospel.

5. In the Gospel.

6. By faith.

7. God.

8. Call for the elders of the church.

9. Pray over them and anoint them with oil in the name of the Lord.

10. The prayer of faith.

11. The Lord.

12. They are forgiven.

13. A. In respect of a holy day.
    B. In drink.
    C. The Sabbath days.
    D. In meat.
    E. All of the above.

14. Christ.

15. In the latter times.

16. Seducing spirits and doctrines of devils.

17. Be seared with a hot iron.

18. Meats.

19. Those who believe and know the truth.

20. A merry heart.

21. Dries the bones.

22. Our fathers and mothers.

23. Our days will be long upon the land that God gives us.

24. The person whose mind is stayed on the Lord.

25. Because they trust in Him.

Understand the Gospel
LESSON 7 – SCRIPTURES

And if by grace, then is it no more of works: otherwise grace is no more grace. But if it be of works, then is it no more grace: otherwise work is no more work.

ROMANS 11:6

For I am not ashamed of the gospel of Christ: for it is the power of God unto salvation to every one that believeth; to the Jew first, and also to the Greek. For therein is the righteousness of God revealed from faith to faith: as it is written, The just shall live by faith. For the wrath of God is revealed from heaven against all ungodliness and unrighteousness of men, who hold the truth in unrighteousness; because that which may be known of God is manifest in them; for God hath shown it unto them.

ROMANS 1:16-19

Who hath measured the waters in the hollow of his hand, and meted out heaven with the span, and comprehended the dust of the earth in a measure, and weighed the mountains in scales, and the hills in a balance?

ISAIAH 40:12

Is any sick among you? let him call for the elders of the church; and let them pray over him, anointing him with oil in the name of the Lord: and the prayer of faith shall save the sick, and the Lord shall raise him up; and if he have committed sins, they shall be forgiven him.

JAMES 5:14-15

Let no man therefore judge you in meat, or in drink, or in respect of an holyday, or of the new moon, or of the sabbath days: which are a shadow of things to come; but the body is of Christ.

COLOSSIANS 2:16-17

Now the Spirit speaketh expressly, that in the latter times some shall depart from the faith, giving heed to seducing spirits, and doctrines of devils; speaking lies in hypocrisy; having their conscience seared with a hot iron; forbidding to marry, and commanding to abstain from meats, which God hath created to be received with thanksgiving of them which believe and know the truth.

1 TIMOTHY 4:1-3

A merry heart doeth good like a medicine: but a broken spirit drieth the bones.

PROVERBS 17:22

110

Honour thy father and thy mother: that thy days may be long upon the land which the LORD thy God giveth thee.

EXODUS 20:12

Thou wilt keep him in perfect peace, whose mind is stayed on thee: because he trusteth in thee.

ISAIAH 26:3

Justified by Faith
LESSON 8

In Romans 2, Paul showed that religious people are doubly guilty. They not only have the witness of their consciences, but they also have what they know of the Word of God. Therefore, religious people are twice as accountable and doubly guilty before God. So he summed it all up in chapter 3 by saying:

> **All have sinned, and come short of the glory of God.**
>
> ROMANS 3:23

Both religious people and nonreligious people know they have a need in their lives. Whether they are operating only with an intuitive knowledge of God, or also with the Word of God they've been taught, everyone knows they need help.

In Romans 4, Paul went back to speaking primarily to religious people. He took the examples of both Abraham and David, two of the greatest Old Testament patriarchs, and showed how they weren't justified—put in right standing with God—because of their holiness. It was the grace of God.

The Lord was very candid in recording the sins of Bible characters. David ordered to have one of his own soldiers killed, in an effort to cover up his adultery with the soldier's wife. Yet we look at David today and say, "What a great king! What a holy man!" The guy committed adultery and murder, yet he was the man after God's own heart (1 Sam. 13:14). People who say, "God only uses people who are worthy of being used" and "You need to be holy before God will use you" are wrong.

Faith for Righteousness

God hasn't had anyone qualified working for Him yet. I'm not going to be the first, and neither will you! God has never had anybody who deserved to be used. He was very candid about this.

> **For if Abraham were justified by works, he hath whereof to glory; but not before God.**
>
> ROMANS 4:2

In other words, if Abraham would have earned all of these things from God because of his greatness, then he might have been able to boast in front of a person, but not before God.

> **For what saith the scripture? Abraham believed God, and it was counted unto him for righteousness.**
>
> ROMANS 4:3

That's a quotation from Genesis 15:6. God had just told Abraham, "Count the stars in the sky if you can. So shall your seed be" (Gen. 15:5). Abraham just believed God, so his faith **"was counted to him for righteousness."**

Abraham's wife was his half-sister (Gen. 20:11-12). According to Leviticus 18:9, this was a sexual abomination to God. If the Law had been in effect in Abraham's day, he would have been stoned to death. When do you think God decided that marrying a half-sister was wrong? Since He doesn't change, we know it was always wrong (Mal. 3:6 and Heb. 13:8). But until the Law was given, God was dealing with people in mercy and wasn't imputing their sins unto them (Rom. 5:13). Abraham was living in a sexual abomination to God, yet he's the only person in the Old Testament called the friend of God (2 Chr. 20:7 and James 2:23).

He Justifies the Ungodly

God used Abraham because he believed His promise, not because of his goodness or greatness. Abraham wasn't the sharpest knife in the drawer. He paid tithes to Melchizedek. Melchizedek was a much greater man than Abraham. He was the priest of the Most High God. According to Hebrews 7:7, the less is blessed by the greater. Since Melchizedek blessed Abraham (Gen. 14:18-20), he was the greater of the two. Yet God used Abraham instead to start the nation. He wasn't chosen because he was the best person on earth. Abraham just trusted God and believed His promise. God used him because of faith.

> **Now to him that worketh is the reward not reckoned of grace, but of debt. But to him that worketh not, but believeth on <u>him that justifieth the ungodly</u>, his faith is counted for righteousness.**
>
> ROMANS 4:4-5, EMPHASIS MINE

God justifies the ungodly. That's the only type of people He can justify. The reason is that He doesn't have anybody else to justify. We're all ungodly! The word **"ungodly"** means "not like God." Somebody might be better than I am. That person may have lived a better life than I have, but who wants to be the best sinner that ever went to hell? We've all...

> **Sinned, and come short of the glory of God.**
>
> ROMANS 3:23

We're all ungodly! No one has ever consistently acted perfect like God. So God only justifies ungodly people. If you are unwilling to admit that you're ungodly, you can't be justified. This same principle applies to your relationship with God after you've been born again. The only people God can really relate to and fellowship with are those who are willing to admit that it's not their goodness, worth, or value. It's people who come to Him based on His grace and their faith in the Savior.

If you put trust in your own holiness, that's the very thing that is keeping you from receiving from God. It's the fact that you're saying, "God, give it to me. I deserve it. I've done something that makes me worthy." You are the only kind of people whose prayers God can't answer. Why? It's not based on faith in the Savior. You're your own "savior." You're basing God's answer in your life upon your own goodness. That's ungodly!

"The Sacrifices of God"

Even as David also describeth the blessedness of the man, unto whom God imputeth righteousness without works, Saying, Blessed are they whose iniquities are forgiven, and whose sins are covered.

ROMANS 4:6-7

This is a quotation from Psalm 32:1-2. David prophetically saw and spoke of the day of grace when our sins were paid for. David's sins weren't paid for. He had relationship with God by looking forward to the coming payment for his sins, but that payment hadn't yet been made.

The animal sacrifices offered in the Old Testament never really secured forgiveness for anyone's sins. It was impossible for the blood of bulls and goats to take away sins (Heb. 10:4). They were only a picture—a type and shadow—of what was to come. It was a constant reminder to us that without the shedding of blood—without someone giving their life—no one could have a relationship with God.

Even though those sacrifices were enforced under the Old Testament, David never offered them for the sins he committed with Bathsheba and Uriah. Notice what Psalm 51, his prayer of repentance over this, says:

For thou desirest not sacrifice; else would I give it: thou delightest not in burnt offering. The sacrifices of God are a broken spirit: a broken and a contrite heart, O God, thou wilt not despise.

PSALM 51:16-17

A Slap in the Face

David had a revelation that these blood sacrifices of animals were only types and shadows. He knew that what God really wanted was true repentance from the heart. He didn't offer sacrifices. There's no scriptural account of him doing so. David was looking forward to his sins being forgiven, which is the reason he felt separated from God when he sinned. That's what he was expressing when he said:

Create in me a clean heart, O God; and renew a right spirit within me. Cast me not away from thy presence; and take not thy holy spirit from me. Restore unto me the joy of thy salvation; and uphold me with thy free spirit.

PSALM 51:10-12

It was appropriate for David to say these things, because he wasn't a born-again Christian. He didn't have a new heart. But today, every true believer in Christ has been given a totally new heart (2 Cor. 5:17). Jesus promised New Testament believers,

I will never leave thee, nor forsake thee.

HEBREWS 13:5

Since David didn't have this promise, it was okay for him to say these things. But for a New Testament believer to say "Create in me a clean heart and renew a right spirit within me. Cast me not away from Your presence, Lord. And take not Your Holy Spirit from me" is rank unbelief. It's like slapping Jesus in the face! We have the Lord's promise that He will never leave us nor forsake us (Heb. 13:5). Our sins have already been forgiven (1 John 2:2). We received a new heart and a righteous spirit the very moment we were born again (Eph. 4:24). Don't ever ask God to give you a new heart after you've already received one. That's unbelief!

Motivated by Love

There's a difference between the way people approached God in the Old Testament and how we are to approach Him in the New. They were looking forward to the price that would be paid, and we're looking back upon it. The price has already been fully paid, and you are completely forgiven. I'll talk more about forgiveness and confession of sins in a later chapter.

David said:

Blessed are they whose iniquities are forgiven, and whose sins are covered. Blessed is the man to whom the Lord will not [future tense] **impute sin.**
ROMANS 4:7-8, BRACKETS MINE

This wasn't just "did not" or "does not," but future tense **"will not."** David saw that there was coming such a payment for sin that all sin would be wiped out—past, present, and even future sin would be completely dealt with. "But, Andrew, I can't believe you're saying that a person's sins are forgiven before they're even committed!" That's exactly what David saw. That's exactly what this scripture says. All sin—past, present, and even future sin—has been dealt with and forgiven.

You need to get this understanding. Nothing can come between you and God. You can't blow it. You can't send Him away. He will never leave you nor forsake you! God loves you—and there's nothing you can do about it. Some Christians say, "Man, I would never say that! If you give people that kind of assurance, they'll just go live in sin. What will be their motivation for living holy?" For the most part, the church has been using fear of rejection and fear of punishment to keep people on the straight and narrow. As a whole, the church believes that fear is a greater motivation than love. But that's not true. Love is an infinitely stronger motivation. It's the goodness of God that leads people to repentance (Rom. 2:4).

No Fear

There is no fear in love; but perfect love casteth out fear: because fear hath torment. He that feareth is not made perfect in love.
1 JOHN 4:18

Whoever fears hasn't had God's love perfected on the inside of them. Fear has torment, but perfect love casts out fear. Are you serving God because you're afraid that if you don't, He won't answer your prayers, you might lose your salvation, or He will send you to hell? If so, you haven't been made perfect in love. You don't fully understand the Gospel. That's the very reason you don't have power for healing, deliverance, joy, and peace. And that's the reason there is torment in your relationship with the Lord. It's the Gospel, the nearly-too-good-to-be-true news of God's love, that releases everything Jesus provided for you. Very few people know the true Gospel.

David knew it. Remember, Paul told in Romans 4:7-8 what David said about the true Gospel. He continued discussing it in the next verse, saying:

> **Cometh this blessedness then upon the circumcision** [Jews; religious people] **only, or upon the uncircumcision** [Gentiles; nonreligious people] **also? for we say that faith was reckoned to Abraham for righteousness.**
>
> ROMANS 4:9, BRACKETS MINE

Receive His Peace

Then Paul discussed how Abraham was reckoned righteous long before he performed this religious duty of being circumcised. Therefore, it was his faith—not his religious works—that caused God to accept him. Paul used Abraham as an example of faith. Abraham was called the father of many nations before he even had a son. That was faith! After Paul talked about all these things, he said:

> **Therefore being justified by faith, we have peace with God.**
>
> ROMANS 5:1

It's faith that gives us access to the grace of God (Rom. 5:2). This goes right along with…

> **Glory to God in the highest, and on earth peace, good will toward men.**
>
> LUKE 2:14

How do you receive this peace? Through understanding the Gospel. It's through comprehending that God placed your sin upon Jesus. It's not you. You didn't make peace by the fact that you're now going to church, paying your tithes, and that you've promised not to dip or cuss or chew, or go with those who do anymore: "I'll do what's right and then I'll have peace with God." No! Jesus made peace. Christ bore all your sin, and all you can do is receive the gift of salvation. You can't earn it. You can't do anything to make yourself more acceptable to God than what Jesus has made you. The only way you can have peace with God is to be justified by faith.

If you're trying to be justified through your own effort and goodness, that's the reason you have zero peace. It's all on your shoulders, which is why you have no confidence, stability, or security. If I thought that you had to earn the favor of God, then the loving thing to do the moment you're born again is to kill you. I might go to hell for killing you, but that's the only way you would ever make it to heaven. "Oh, I know I blow it. But then I run to Him and get forgiveness." Well, if I thought you had to repent; pray through; get born again, again to get your sins forgiven every time you sin, I'd just kill you. That way, all of the burden of salvation would be placed back on Jesus and not your ability to recognize and confess every sin.

Many of us do a lot of things wrong that we don't even recognize is sin—but others recognize it, and God certainly recognizes it (James 4:17). If it were up to you to repent of every single sin and get it "under the blood," you can't live that way. If that were true, then you'd better hope somebody kills you just as soon as you're born again, because that's the only way you'd ever be able to retain your salvation.

Justified by Faith
LESSON 8 – OUTLINE

I. In Romans 2, Paul showed that religious people are doubly guilty.

    A. They not only have the witness of their consciences, but they also have what they know of the Word of God.

    B. Therefore, religious people are twice as accountable and doubly guilty before God.

    C. So Paul summed it all up in chapter 3 by saying:

> **All have sinned, and come short of the glory of God.**
>
> ROMANS 3:23

    D. Whether they are operating only with an intuitive knowledge of God, or also with the Word of God they've been taught, everyone knows they need help.

II. In Romans 4, Paul went back to speaking primarily to religious people.

    A. He took the examples of both Abraham and David, two of the greatest Old Testament patriarchs, and showed how they weren't justified—put in right standing with God—because of their holiness, but by God's grace.

    B. God hasn't had anyone qualified working for Him yet.

> **For if Abraham were justified by works, he hath whereof to glory; but not before God.**
>
> ROMANS 4:2

    C. In other words, if Abraham would have earned all of these things from God because of his greatness, then he might have been able to boast in front of a person, but not before God.

> **For what saith the scripture? Abraham believed God, and it was counted unto him for righteousness.**
>
> ROMANS 4:3

    D. Abraham just believed God, so his faith **"was counted unto him for righteousness"** (Gen. 15:6).

    E. Abraham was living in a sexual abomination to God, yet he's the only person in the Old Testament called the friend of God (2 Chr. 20:7 and James 2:23).

    F. God used Abraham because he believed His promise, not because of his goodness or greatness.

III. God justifies the ungodly because He doesn't have anybody else to justify.

> **Now to him that worketh is the reward not reckoned of grace, but of debt. But to him that worketh not, but believeth on <u>him that justifieth the ungodly</u>, his faith is counted for righteousness.**
>
> ROMANS 4:4-5, EMPHASIS MINE

A. This same principle applies to our relationship with God after we've been born again.

B. The only people God can really relate to and fellowship with are those who are willing to admit that it's not their goodness, worth, or value. It's people who come to Him based on His grace and their faith in the Savior.

C. If you put trust in your own holiness, that's the very thing that is keeping you from receiving from God.

IV. David prophetically saw and spoke of the day of grace when our sins were paid for (Ps. 32:1-2).

> **Even as David also describeth the blessedness of the man, unto whom God imputeth righteousness without works, Saying, Blessed are they whose iniquities are forgiven, and whose sins are covered.**
>
> ROMANS 4:6-7

A. David had a revelation that the blood sacrifices of animals were only types and shadows. He knew that what God really wanted was true repentance from the heart.

> **For thou desirest not sacrifice; else would I give it: thou delightest not in burnt offering. The sacrifices of God are a broken spirit: a broken and a contrite heart, O God, thou wilt not despise.**
>
> PSALM 51:16-17

B. David was looking forward to his sins being forgiven, which is the reason he felt separated from God when he sinned.

> **Create in me a clean heart, O God; and renew a right spirit within me. Cast me not away from thy presence; and take not thy holy spirit from me. Restore unto me the joy of thy salvation; and uphold me with thy free spirit.**
>
> PSALM 51:10-12

C. Jesus promised New Testament believers:

> **I will never leave thee, nor forsake thee.**
>
> HEBREWS 13:5

V. There's a difference between the way people approached God in the Old Testament and how we are to approach Him in the New.

    A. They were looking forward to the price that would be paid, and we're looking back upon it.

    B. All sin—past, present, and even future sin—has been dealt with and forgiven.

> **Blessed are they whose iniquities are forgiven, and whose sins are covered. Blessed is the man to whom the Lord will not** [future tense] **impute sin.**
>
> ROMANS 4:7-8, BRACKETS MINE

    C. Love is an infinitely stronger motivation than fear.

> **There is no fear in love; but perfect love casteth out fear: because fear hath torment. He that feareth is not made perfect in love.**
>
> 1 JOHN 4:18

VI. Then Paul discussed how Abraham was reckoned righteous long before he performed this religious duty of being circumcised.

> **Cometh this blessedness then upon the circumcision** [Jews; religious people] **only, or upon the uncircumcision** [Gentiles; nonreligious people] **also? for we say that faith was reckoned to Abraham for righteousness.**
>
> ROMANS 4:9, BRACKETS MINE

    A. Therefore, it was his faith—not his religious works—that caused God to accept him.

> **Therefore being justified by faith, we have peace with God.**
>
> ROMANS 5:1

    B. The only way you can have peace with God is to be justified by faith.

> **Glory to God in the highest, and on earth peace, good will toward men.**
>
> LUKE 2:14

Justified by Faith
LESSON 8 – TEACHER'S GUIDE

1.   In Romans 2, Paul showed that religious people are doubly guilty. They not only have the witness of their consciences, but they also have what they know of the Word of God. Therefore, religious people are twice as accountable and doubly guilty before God. So he summed it all up in chapter 3 by saying, **"All have sinned, and come short of the glory of God"** (Rom. 3:23). Whether they are operating only with an intuitive knowledge of God, or also with the Word of God they've been taught, everyone knows that they need help.

2.   In Romans 4, Paul went back to speaking primarily to religious people. He took the examples of both Abraham and David, two of the greatest Old Testament patriarchs, and showed how they weren't justified—put in right standing with God—because of their holiness, but by God's grace. God hasn't had anyone qualified working for Him yet (Rom. 4:2).

In other words, if Abraham would have earned all of these things from God because of his greatness, then he might have been able to boast in front of a person, but not before God (Rom. 4:3). Abraham just believed God, so his faith **"was counted unto him for righteousness"** (Gen. 15:6). Abraham was living in a sexual abomination to God, yet he's the only person in the Old Testament called the friend of God (2 Chr. 20:7 and James 2:23). God used Abraham because he believed His promise, not because of his goodness or greatness.

3.   God justifies the ungodly because He doesn't have anybody else to justify (Rom. 4:4-5). This same principle applies to our relationship with God after we've been born again. The only people God can really relate to and fellowship with are those who are willing to admit that it's not their goodness, worth, or value. It's people who come to Him based on His grace and their faith in the Savior. If we are trusting our own holiness, that's the very thing that is keeping us from receiving from God.

1. A. Why are religious people twice as accountable and doubly guilty before God? (They not only have the witness of their consciences, but they also have what they know of the Word of God)
   B. How did Paul sum all this up in Romans 3:23? (**"All have sinned, and come short of the glory of God"**)
2. A. Read Romans 4:2-3, Genesis 15:6, 2 Chronicles 20:7, and James 2:23. Were Abraham and David justified—put in right standing with God—because of their holiness or God's grace? (God's grace)
   B. What was Abraham's faith counted unto him for? (Righteousness)
3. A. Read Romans 4:4-5. Who does God justify? (The ungodly)
   B. After we're born again, how does this same principle apply to our relationship with God? (The only people God can really relate to and fellowship with are those who are willing to admit that it's not their goodness, worth, or value. It's people who come to Him based on His grace and their faith in the Savior)
   C. What keeps us from receiving from God? (Trusting in our own holiness)

4.   David prophetically saw and spoke of the day of grace when our sins were paid for (Ps. 32:1-2 and Rom. 4:6-7). David had a revelation that the blood sacrifices of animals were only types and shadows. He knew that what God really wanted was true repentance from the heart (Ps. 51:16-17). David was looking forward to his sins being forgiven, which is the reason he felt separated from God when he sinned (Ps. 51:10-12). Jesus promised New Testament believers, **"I will never leave thee, nor forsake thee"** (Heb. 13:5).

5.   There's a difference between the way people approached God in the Old Testament and how we are to approach Him in the New. They were looking forward to the price that would be paid, and we're looking back upon it. All sin—past, present, and even future sin—has been dealt with and forgiven (Rom. 4:7-8). Love is an infinitely stronger motivation than fear (1 John 4:18).

6.   Then Paul discussed how Abraham was reckoned righteous long before he performed this religious duty of being circumcised (Rom. 4:9). Therefore, it was his faith—not his religious works—that caused God to accept him (Rom. 5:1). The only way we can have peace with God is to be justified by faith (Luke 2:14).

4. A. Read Psalm 32:1-2, 51:10-12, 16-17; Romans 4:6-7; and Hebrews 13:5. What did David prophetically see and speak of? (The day of grace when our sins were paid for)
   B. What was it that David knew God really wanted? (True repentance from the heart)
5. A. Read Romans 4:7-8. What is the difference between the way people approached God in the Old Testament and how we are to approach Him in the New? (They were looking forward to the price that would be paid, and we're looking back upon it)
   B. According to 1 John 4:18, what is an infinitely stronger motivation than fear? (Love)
6. A. Read Romans 4:9, 5:1; and Luke 2:14. Was Abraham reckoned righteous before or after he performed this religious duty of being circumcised? (Before)
   B. In light of this, was it his faith or his religious works that caused God to accept him? (It was his faith)
   C. What is the only way we can have peace with God? (To be justified by faith)

Justified by Faith

For an in-depth look at what happens the instant you're born again, please refer to my teachings entitled *The New You* and *Spirit, Soul & Body*.

Justified by Faith
LESSON 8 – DISCIPLESHIP QUESTIONS

1. According to Romans 3:23, who has sinned?

2. What have we come short of?

3. Who had the Lord sought after in 1 Samuel 13:14?

4. According to Romans 4:2-3, was Abraham justified by works?

5. Who did Abraham believe?

6. What did God count Abraham's faith unto him?

7. According to Genesis 15:5-6, God promised Abraham that his seed would be as numerous as what?

8. Genesis 20:11-12 reveals that Abraham's wife was his half-sister through whom?

9. According to Leviticus 18:9, the Law forbade uncovering what?

10. According to Malachi 3:6, does the Lord change?

11. Who does Hebrews 13:8 reveal as being the same yesterday, today, and forever?

12. According to Romans 5:13, was sin in the world before the Law?

13. When was sin not imputed—held against us?

14. According to 2 Chronicles 20:7, who drove out the inhabitants of Israel's land before them?

15. What was Abraham called in this verse and in James 2:23?

16. According to Hebrews 7:7, who blesses whom?
    A. The less is blessed of the better.
    B. The better is blessed of the lesser.

17. Genesis 14:18-20 reveals that Melchizedek, the king of Salem, was also what?

18. Whom did he bless?

19. What was given to Melchizedek after this blessing?

20. According to Romans 4:4-5, what is the reward of work reckoned as?
    A. Grace.
    B. Debt.

21. Those who don't work but instead believe on God, their faith is counted for what?

22. Whom does God justify?

23. According to Romans 4:6-9, how does David describe the person whose iniquities are forgiven and sins are covered?

24. How does God impute righteousness to us?
    A. Without works.
    B. With works.
    C. By faith.
    D. All of the above.
    E. None of the above.

25. Fill in the blank. Blessed is the man to whom the Lord _____ impute sin.
    A. Did not (past tense).
    B. Does not (present tense).
    C. Will not (future tense).

26. According to Psalm 32:1-2, what does David also say concerning this person's spirit?

27. According to Hebrews 10:4, is it possible for the blood of bulls and goats to take away sin?

28. Instead of burnt offerings and sacrifices, what kind of heart does Psalm 51:16-17 reveal that God looks for?

29. What was David asking God to restore unto him in Psalm 51:10-12?

30. Second Corinthians 5:17 reveals that we who are in Christ are what?

31. According to Hebrews 13:5, will Jesus ever leave or forsake one of His children?

32. First John 2:2 reveals that Jesus is the propitiation—atoning sacrifice—for whose sins?

33. According to Ephesians 4:24, our new man was created how?

34. According to Romans 2:4, what leads us to repentance?

35. First John 4:18 reveals that perfect love casts out what?

36. According to Romans 5:1, how are we justified?

37. How does peace with God come?

38. Read Romans 5:2. How do we access this grace wherein we stand?

39. According to Luke 2:14, God now has what toward men?

40. What does James 4:17 call the good we know to do but don't do?

Justified by Faith

1. All.

2. The glory of God.

3. A man after His own heart.

4. No.

5. God.

6. Righteousness.

7. The stars in the sky.

8. Their father.

9. Your sister's nakedness.

10. No.

11. Jesus Christ.

12. Yes.

13. When there is no Law.

14. God.

15. The friend of God.

16. A. The less is blessed of the better.

17. The priest of the Most High God.

18. Abraham.

19. Tithes of all.

20. B. Debt.

21. Righteousness.

22. The ungodly.

23. Blessed.

24. A. Without works.
    C. By faith.

25. C. Will not (future tense).

26. There is no guile.

27. No.

28. A broken and contrite heart.

29. The joy of His salvation.

30. New creatures.

31. No.

32. Ours and the whole world's.

33. After God in righteousness and true holiness.

34. The goodness of God.

35. Fear.

36. By faith.

37. Through our Lord Jesus Christ.

38. By faith.

39. Good will.

40. Sin.

For all have sinned, and come short of the glory of God.

ROMANS 3:23

But now thy kingdom shall not continue: the LORD hath sought him a man after his own heart, and the LORD hath commanded him to be captain over his people, because thou hast not kept that which the LORD commanded thee.

1 SAMUEL 13:14

For if Abraham were justified by works, he hath whereof to glory; but not before God. For what saith the scripture? Abraham believed God, and it was counted unto him for righteousness.

ROMANS 4:2-3

And he brought him forth abroad, and said, Look now toward heaven, and tell the stars, if thou be able to number them: and he said unto him, So shall thy seed be. And he believed in the LORD; and he counted it to him for righteousness.

GENESIS 15:5-6

And Abraham said, Because I thought, Surely the fear of God is not in this place; and they will slay me for my wife's sake. And yet indeed she is my sister; she is the daughter of my father, but not the daughter of my mother; and she became my wife.

GENESIS 20:11-12

The nakedness of thy sister, the daughter of thy father, or daughter of thy mother, whether she be born at home, or born abroad, even their nakedness thou shalt not uncover.

LEVITICUS 18:9

For I am the LORD, I change not; therefore ye sons of Jacob are not consumed.

MALACHI 3:6

Jesus Christ the same yesterday, and to day, and for ever.

HEBREWS 13:8

For until the law sin was in the world: but sin is not imputed when there is no law.

ROMANS 5:13

Art not thou our God, who didst drive out the inhabitants of this land before thy people Israel, and gavest it to the seed of Abraham thy friend for ever?

2 CHRONICLES 20:7

And the scripture was fulfilled which saith, Abraham believed God, and it was imputed unto him for righteousness: and he was called the Friend of God.

JAMES 2:23

And without all contradiction the less is blessed of the better.

HEBREWS 7:7

And Melchizedek king of Salem brought forth bread and wine: and he was the priest of the most high God. And he blessed him, and said, Blessed be Abram of the most high God, possessor of heaven and earth: And blessed be the most high God, which hath delivered thine enemies into thy hand. And he gave him tithes of all.

GENESIS 14:18-20

Now to him that worketh is the reward not reckoned of grace, but of debt. But to him that worketh not, but believeth on him that justifieth the ungodly, his faith is counted for righteousness. Even as David also describeth the blessedness of the man, unto whom God imputeth righteousness without works, Saying, Blessed are they whose iniquities are forgiven, and whose sins are covered. Blessed is the man to whom the Lord will not impute sin. Cometh this blessedness then upon the circumcision only, or upon the uncircumcision also? for we say that faith was reckoned to Abraham for righteousness.

ROMANS 4:4-9

Blessed is he whose transgression is forgiven, whose sin is covered. Blessed is the man unto whom the LORD imputeth not iniquity, and in whose spirit there is no guile.

PSALM 32:1-2

For it is not possible that the blood of bulls and of goats should take away sins.

HEBREWS 10:4

For thou desirest not sacrifice; else would I give it: thou delightest not in burnt offering. The sacrifices of God are a broken spirit: a broken and a contrite heart, O God, thou wilt not despise.

PSALM 51:16-17

Create in me a clean heart, O God; and renew a right spirit within me. Cast me not away from thy presence; and take not thy holy spirit from me. Restore unto me the joy of thy salvation; and uphold me with thy free spirit.

PSALM 51:10-12

Therefore if any man be in Christ, he is a new creature: old things are passed away; behold, all things are become new.

2 CORINTHIANS 5:17

Let your conversation be without covetousness; and be content with such things as ye have: for he hath said, I will never leave thee, nor forsake thee.

HEBREWS 13:5

And he is the propitiation for our sins: and not for ours only, but also for the sins of the whole world.

1 JOHN 2:2

And that ye put on the new man, which after God is created in righteousness and true holiness.

EPHESIANS 4:24

Or despisest thou the riches of his goodness and forbearance and longsuffering; not knowing that the goodness of God leadeth thee to repentance?

ROMANS 2:4

There is no fear in love; but perfect love casteth out fear: because fear hath torment. He that feareth is not made perfect in love.

1 JOHN 4:18

Therefore being justified by faith, we have peace with God through our Lord Jesus Christ: By whom also we have access by faith into this grace wherein we stand, and rejoice in hope of the glory of God.

ROMANS 5:1-2

Glory to God in the highest, and on earth peace, good will toward men.

LUKE 2:14

Therefore to him that knoweth to do good, and doeth it not, to him it is sin.

JAMES 4:17

Shall We Sin?
LESSON 9

By whom also we have access by faith into this grace wherein we stand, and rejoice in hope of the glory of God.

ROMANS 5:2

"Access" here is the same word we get "admission" from. When you go to a movie theater, you pay the admission price and they let you in. This verse is saying you have access—admission—to the grace of God through faith. Faith is what gains you access to God's grace—not your goodness, works, or performance. God loves you because He is love, not because you are lovely. That's good news!

What shall we say then? Shall we continue in sin, that grace may abound?

ROMANS 6:1

Paul had been preaching on grace and emphasizing how God loves us independent of our performance. It has nothing to do with our goodness and worth, whether we've done everything right or not. Immediately, this question was raised: "Are you saying that we should continue in sin so that grace may abound?"

God forbid.

ROMANS 6:2

Paul was adamant, saying, "No, that's not what I'm saying!"

Have You Ever Wondered?

Has the Gospel you've heard preached ever made you wonder, *Can I just live in sin because all my sin has been forgiven?* If you haven't ever had this question come up, then you haven't heard the same Gospel that the Apostle Paul preached. He had to address this question many times. Two of them are right here in Romans 6 (verses 1-2 and 15).

Shall we continue in sin, that grace may abound?

ROMANS 6:1

Is anyone misunderstanding the message you're hearing? Are they asking the question, "Are you saying that we can just live in sin?" If this logical question isn't coming up, then you aren't hearing the same Gospel that the early New Testament church heard. That's the reason we aren't getting the same results that the early New Testament church had. That's why if most Christians were arrested for their faith, there wouldn't be enough evidence to convict them. There isn't any power or victory in their lives. Nobody could even tell they're Christians.

Do the people around you at work know that you're a believer? Is there anything different about you? If not, then it's because you haven't fully understood the Gospel. You haven't fully comprehended how much God loves you.

God Loves You

Is there something in your life that you've done that you're still ashamed of and haven't admitted to anybody? Are you trying to hide it even from God? The truth is, He already knows all about it. He's already dealt with that sin and forgiven you. Jesus bore it on the cross and suffered that shame for you. He loves you in spite of what you've done.

Regardless of how much you've failed in any area, God loves you. And if you could really understand that and receive it, there would be such a reciprocal love on your part toward Him.

We love him, because he first loved us.

1 JOHN 4:19

If you understood how much God loves you, you'd be a stark raving mad fanatic. "Come on, Andrew. That's not my personality." I'm pretty laid back and quiet myself. Many people don't think I'm anointed when I minister, because I don't scream, spit, and yell. But I'm a fanatic. I love God with all my heart. I would follow Him anywhere and do anything He asks, because I have a revelation of His love for me. It doesn't matter what your personality type or situation is, if you understood the Gospel, it would release the power of God in your life more than you could ever dream. Instead of being coerced into doing something out of a sense of debt and being fearful that God will be displeased or angry with you if you don't do it, you'd do it out of love. In fact, you'd do it much better, much stronger, and much more out of love than you'd ever do it out of fear.

You need to let people know how much God loves them. They'll serve Him infinitely more out of love than they ever will out of fear. However, it's easier to motivate people—even lost people—out of fear, rejection, and punishment. So, many preachers say, "If you don't pay your tithe, God's going to judge you. You'll be cursed with a curse!" Unbelievers can relate to that. But those preachers ought to tell them, "You're free. God loves you. Give as you purpose in your own heart, not grudgingly or of necessity, because God loves a cheerful giver" (2 Cor. 9:7). However, even if people are not under a fear of punishment, that still will not cause them to give freely. It's good not to be motivated by fear, but it's only when preachers motivate people by love that people will in turn love God with all their hearts and give more.

Going through the Motions

"But the kingdom of God would suffer!" From our human standpoint, the physical things we monitor and keep statistics on may not look as good, but the Lord isn't impressed with those things anyway. It's only those people who give from their hearts with the right motivation that God is pleased with. Many people are going through the motions—giving, going to church, reading the Bible, and so on—doing all of the right things, but from the wrong motive. They're trying to earn God's favor and make themselves acceptable to Him. The Lord's not pleased with any of that! That's the wood, hay, and stubble that will be torched when we stand before Him (1 Cor. 3:11-15). None of these religious works will endure the fire.

Some of these big churches have thousands and thousands of people attending who aren't really committed to God. There's no peace, joy, or victory in their lives. They're just going through the motions. That's not pleasing to God.

Many people are just as straight as a gun barrel and twice as empty. They don't have any peace or joy in their lives. Why? They haven't been motivated by the Gospel. They're being motivated out of fear and condemnation. That's not the Gospel.

"Live Soberly, Righteously, and Godly"

If no one asks "Can I just live in sin because God has forgiven all of my sins?" then they haven't heard the Gospel that Paul preached. The answer to this question is, "Of course not! God forbid! Living in sin is stupid! God loves you so much that all of your sins are forgiven. His judgment isn't coming on your sin. Satan will take advantage of your sin, so you ought to live as holy as you possibly can. But it's not in order to receive God's blessing, because you have already received it (Eph. 1:3). You're just so thankful, you'll want to live in a way that glorifies God. You don't want to yield yourself to your Enemy, who has come to steal, kill, and destroy" (John 10:10).

I'm glad God raised me up to preach the Gospel, because I've lived a holier life than you have probably ever thought about. Therefore, you can't look at me and say, "Well, he's preaching this because it allows him to go do all of these sins." According to religious standards, I've lived a super holy life. I'm not preaching this so I can indulge my flesh or live in sin. If I were living in sin, people would immediately say, "Well, no wonder he preaches grace. It frees him to live in sin!" But that's not what the Bible says.

> **For the grace of God that bringeth salvation hath appeared to all men, Teaching us that, denying ungodliness and worldly lusts, we should live soberly, righteously, and godly, in this present world.**
>
> TITUS 2:11-12

If you truly understand the grace of God, you'll live holier accidentally than you ever have on purpose. You'll wind up glorifying and serving God, but you'll do it out of a pure heart. God will be pleased, and He'll inhabit the good works that you do because you're not trying to earn anything. They're just done out of love. The Lord will be pleased, and you'll be satisfied. It'll change your whole life.

This is the Gospel, and we need to be proclaiming it. You need to share the Gospel with your friends, coworkers, and family. It'll release people from religious bondage and set them free. Thank You, Jesus!

Shall We Sin?
LESSON 9 – OUTLINE

I. You have access—admission—to the grace of God through faith.

By whom also we have access by faith into this grace wherein we stand, and rejoice in hope of the glory of God.

ROMANS 5:2

   A. Faith is what gains you access to God's grace—not your goodness, works, or performance.

   B. God loves you because He is love, not because you are lovely. That's good news!

II. Since Paul had been preaching on grace and emphasizing how God loves us independent of our performance, immediately this question was raised: "Are you saying that we should continue in sin so that grace may abound?"

What shall we say then? Shall we continue in sin, that grace may abound?

ROMANS 6:1

   A. Paul was adamant, saying, "No, that's not what I'm saying!"

God forbid.

ROMANS 6:2

   B. If this logical question isn't coming up, then you aren't hearing the same Gospel that the early New Testament church heard.

   C. That's the reason we aren't getting the same results that the early New Testament church had.

III. Regardless of how much you've failed in any area, God loves you.

   A. If you could really understand that and receive it, there would be such a reciprocal love on your part toward God.

We love him, because he first loved us.

1 JOHN 4:19

   B. If you understood how much God loves you, you'd be a stark raving mad fanatic.

   C. You need to let people know how much God loves them.

   D. They'll serve Him infinitely more out of love than they ever will out of fear.

IV. Many people are going through the motions—giving, going to church, reading the Bible, and so on—doing all of the right things, but from the wrong motive.

A. They're trying to earn God's favor and make themselves acceptable to Him.

B. That's the wood, hay, and stubble that will be torched when we stand before Him (1 Cor. 3:11-15).

C. None of these religious works will endure the fire.

V. If no one asks, "Can I just live in sin because God has forgiven all of my sins?" then they haven't heard the Gospel that Paul preached.

A. The answer to this question is, "Of course not! God forbid! Living in sin is stupid!"

B. Satan will take advantage of your sin, so you ought to live as holy as you possibly can. But it's not in order to receive God's blessing, because you have already received it (Eph. 1:3).

C. You live holy because you're just so thankful, you'll want to live in a way that glorifies God.

D. You don't want to yield yourself to your Enemy, who has come to steal, kill, and destroy (John 10:10).

VI. If you truly understand the grace of God, you'll live holier accidentally than you ever have on purpose.

For the grace of God that bringeth salvation hath appeared to all men, Teaching us that, denying ungodliness and worldly lusts, we should live soberly, righteously, and godly, in this present world.

Titus 2:11-12

A. You'll wind up glorifying and serving God, but you'll do it out of a pure heart.

B. God will be pleased, and He'll inhabit the good works that you do because you're not trying to earn anything—they're just done out of love.

C. The Lord will be pleased, and you'll be satisfied.

D. This is the Gospel, and we need to be proclaiming it.

E. It'll release people from religious bondage and set them free. Thank You, Jesus!

Shall We Sin?
LESSON 9 – TEACHER'S GUIDE

1.   We have access—admission—to the grace of God through faith (Rom. 5:2). Faith is what gains us access to God's grace—not our goodness, works, or performance. God loves us because He is love, not because we are lovely. That's good news!

2.   Since Paul had been preaching on grace and emphasizing how God loves us independent of our performance, immediately this question was raised: "Are you saying that we should continue in sin so that grace may abound?" (Rom. 6:1). Paul was adamant, saying, "No, that's not what I'm saying!" (Rom. 6:2). If this logical question isn't coming up, then we aren't hearing the same Gospel that the early New Testament church heard. That's the reason we aren't getting the same results that the early New Testament church had.

3.   Regardless of how much we've failed in any area, God loves us. If we could really understand that and receive it, there would be such a reciprocal love on our part toward Him (1 John 4:19). If we understood how much God loves us, we'd be stark raving mad fanatics. We need to let people know how much God loves them. They'll serve Him infinitely more out of love than they ever will out of fear.

1. A. Read Romans 5:2. Does our goodness, works, or performance gain us access to God's grace? (No, it's only through faith)
   B. Why does God love us? (Because He is love)
2. A. Read Romans 6:1-2. What logical question should come up if we're hearing the same Gospel the early New Testament church heard? ("Are you saying that we should continue in sin so that grace may abound?")
   B. How did Paul answer this question? ("No, that's not what I'm saying!")
3. A. According to 1 John 4:19, what would happen if we really understood and received God's love for us? (There would be such a reciprocal love on our part toward Him, and we'd be stark raving mad fanatics)
   B. What do we need to let people know? (How much God loves them)

4.   Many people are going through the motions—giving, going to church, reading the Bible, and so on—doing all of the right things, but from the wrong motive. They're trying to earn God's favor and make themselves acceptable to Him. That's the wood, hay, and stubble that will be torched when they stand before Him (1 Cor. 3:11-15). None of these religious works will endure the fire.

5.   If no one asks "Can I just live in sin because God has forgiven all of my sins?" then they haven't heard the Gospel that Paul preached. The answer to this question is, "Of course not! God forbid! Living in sin is stupid!" Satan will take advantage of our sin, so we ought to live as holy as we possibly can. But it's not in order to receive God's blessing, because we have already received it (Eph. 1:3). We're just so thankful, we'll want to live in a way that glorifies God. We don't want to yield ourselves to our Enemy, who has come to steal, kill, and destroy (John 10:10).

6.   If we truly understand the grace of God, we'll live holier accidentally than we ever have on purpose (Titus 2:11-12). We'll wind up glorifying and serving God, but we'll do it out of pure hearts. God will be pleased, and He'll inhabit the good works that we do because we're not trying to earn anything—they're just done out of love. The Lord will be pleased, and we'll be satisfied. This is the Gospel, and we need to be proclaiming it. It'll release people from religious bondage and set them free. Thank You, Jesus!

4. A. How are many people going through the motions? (They're doing all of the right things—giving, going to church, reading their Bible, and so on—but from the wrong motive)
   B. What are they trying to do? (Earn God's favor and make themselves acceptable to Him)
   C. Read 1 Corinthians 3:11-15. Will any of these religious works endure the fire? (No)
5. A. Who is it that takes advantage of our sin? (Satan)
   B. According to John 10:10, what does he come to do in our lives? (Steal, kill, and destroy)
   C. Read Ephesians 1:3. Out of thankfulness for the blessing of God that we have already received, what do we want to do? (Live in a way that glorifies God)
6. A. Read Titus 2:11-12. What happens when we truly understand the grace of God? (We'll live holier accidentally than we ever have on purpose)
   B. How will we glorify and serve God? (Out of pure hearts)
   C. Why will He inhabit the good works that we do? (Because they aren't trying to earn anything—they're just done out of love)

Shall We Sin?
LESSON 9 – DISCIPLESHIP QUESTIONS

1. According to Romans 5:2, how do we access this grace wherein we stand?

2. As we access this grace, what do we rejoice in hope of?

3. How many questions are included in Romans 6:1-2?

4. Shall we continue in sin that grace may abound?

5. What question does Paul then employ to continue his answer to the previous question?

6. What arc born-again believers dead to?

7. Since we are dead to it, should we live any longer in it?

8. How many questions are asked in Romans 6:15?

9. Shall we sin because we are not under the Law but under grace?

10. Are born-again believers under the Law?

11. What are we under?

12. According to 1 John 4:19, who loved whom first?

13. Why can we love Him now?

14. According to 2 Corinthians 9:7, how should we give?

15. What two ways should we not give?

16. What kind of giver does God love?

17. According to 1 Corinthians 3:11-15, who is the foundation?

18. As we build upon this foundation, how will the nature of our works one day be revealed?

19. What will we receive if our works abide?

20. If all our works are burned, what will we suffer?

21. Will we ourselves be saved?

22. According to Ephesians 1:3, God is the Father of whom?

23. What has He blessed us with?

24. Where are these blessings right now?

25. According to John 10:10, who is it that only comes to steal, kill, and destroy?

26. Who has come that we might have an abundance of life?

27. According to Titus 2:11-12, what does the grace of God bring?

28. What has appeared to all men?

29. What does this grace teach us?
    A. Live righteously.
    B. Deny worldly lusts.
    C. Live godly.
    D. Deny ungodliness.
    E. Live soberly.
    F. All of the above.
    G. None of the above.

30. When and where should we live this way?

Shall We Sin?

Lesson 9 – Answer Key

1. By faith.

2. The glory of God.

3. Three.

4. God forbid.

5. How shall we, who are dead to sin, live any longer therein?

6. Sin.

7. No.

8. Two.

9. God forbid.

10. No.

11. Grace.

12. God loved us.

13. Because He first loved us.

14. As we purpose in our hearts.

15. Grudgingly or of necessity.

16. A cheerful giver.

17. Jesus Christ.

18. By fire.

19. A reward.

20. Loss.

21. Yes.

22. Our Lord Jesus Christ.

23. All spiritual blessings.

24. In heavenly places in Christ—which is in the spirit realm, in our born-again spirits.

25. The thief.

26. Jesus Christ.

27. Salvation.

28. The grace of God that brings salvation.

29. A. Live righteously.
    B. Deny worldly lusts.
    C. Live godly.
    D. Deny ungodliness.
    E. Live soberly.
    F. All of the above.

30. In this present world.

Shall We Sin?
LESSON 9 – SCRIPTURES

By whom also we have access by faith into this grace wherein we stand, and rejoice in hope of the glory of God.

ROMANS 5:2

What shall we say then? Shall we continue in sin, that grace may abound? God forbid. How shall we, that are dead to sin, live any longer therein?

ROMANS 6:1-2

What then? Shall we sin, because we are not under the law, but under grace? God forbid.

ROMANS 6:15

We love him, because he first loved us.

1 JOHN 4:19

Every man according as he purposeth in his heart, so let him give; not grudgingly, or of necessity: for God loveth a cheerful giver.

2 CORINTHIANS 9:7

For other foundation can no man lay than that is laid, which is Jesus Christ. Now if any man build upon this foundation gold, silver, precious stones, wood, hay, stubble; Every man's work shall be made manifest: for the day shall declare it, because it shall be revealed by fire; and the fire shall try every man's work of what sort it is. If any man's work abide which he hath built thereupon, he shall receive a reward. If any man's work shall be burned, he shall suffer loss: but he himself shall be saved; yet so as by fire.

1 CORINTHIANS 3:11-15

Blessed be the God and Father of our Lord Jesus Christ, who hath blessed us with all spiritual blessings in heavenly places in Christ.

EPHESIANS 1:3

The thief cometh not, but for to steal, and to kill, and to destroy: I am come that they might have life, and that they might have it more abundantly.

JOHN 10:10

For the grace of God that bringeth salvation hath appeared to all men, Teaching us that, denying ungodliness and worldly lusts, we should live soberly, righteously, and godly, in this present world.

TITUS 2:11-12

Eternal Redemption
LESSON 10

God has forever settled the sin issue. People aren't really going to hell because of sin. The sins of the entire world have been paid for.

> **He** [Jesus] **is the propitiation** [atoning sacrifice] **for our sins: and not for ours only, but also for the sins of the whole world.**
>
> 1 JOHN 2:2, BRACKETS MINE

The sins of lost people have already been paid for. Jesus bore the sins of everyone—not just those He knew would accept Him. People who reject and hate the Lord have already been forgiven of their sins.

"Then what's the point in getting saved? Are you saying that everyone is saved?" No, that's not what I'm saying. God has made the payment, but you must receive it. Each individual must appropriate by faith what God has already provided by grace, for it to take effect in their life.

By Grace through Faith

> **For by grace are ye saved through faith; and that not of yourselves: it is the gift of God.**
>
> EPHESIANS 2:8

You are saved by grace through faith. You aren't saved by grace alone. You're saved by grace through faith! Grace is what God has done for us independent of us. It's completely separate from anything we deserve. By grace, God has already paid for the sins of the whole world. But for God's grace to affect you, you must put faith in it. Not everybody has responded to God's grace.

> **For the grace of God that bringeth salvation hath appeared to all men.**
>
> TITUS 2:11

God's grace that brings salvation has come to every person. The grace of God had been extended toward someone like Adolph Hitler, who committed horrendous atrocities. All of his sins were forgiven. Jesus paid for every single one of Hitler's sins. But as far as we know, Adolph never put faith in Christ. He consulted astrologers and such. There is no evidence that Hitler was ever truly born again. As far as we know, he went into eternity without God. Since he rejected the payment for his sin, he will answer for those sins. But it's not because the payment wasn't made. In Christ, the payment was made. Hitler just didn't accept it. So he'll have to pay for his sins on his own.

God paid for the sins of the whole world. Every person's sins have already been atoned for. People aren't going to hell for individual sins; they're going to hell because they rejected the payment for their sins. This is not just rebels and God-haters. Multitudes of religious people go to hell because they thought they could pay for their sins by attending church, paying their tithes, reading the Bible, and trying to be good. They falsely believed that God would accept them because of some worth or value of theirs. That's not accepting the payment for their sins. They are still trying to make up for their own sins. There will be many people like that in hell.

Savior or Performance?

A Muslim, a Buddhist, a Hindu, and a Christian all stand before God. He asks them, "What makes you worthy to enter heaven?" The Muslim answers first, saying, "I prayed five times a day and gave alms to the poor. I also fought jihad against the infidels, blowing up myself and many of them for You. Therefore, I'm guaranteed a place and a harem in heaven." The Buddhist answers next, saying, "I shaved my head, wore a robe, and took an oath of poverty. I denied myself every opportunity I had." The Hindu answers next, saying, "I participated in all of the temple rituals. I honored my ancestors by never eating meat. Therefore, I'm entitled to a better reincarnation." If the Christian were to answer "I went to church, paid my tithes, read my Bible, fasted, prayed" and so on, this person wouldn't be any different from the others. Whatever their standards were, all of these people trusted in their own acts of holiness. When asked "What makes you worthy?" they all pointed to their own performance.

However, a true Christian would answer, "It's nothing I did. My faith is in Christ alone, and in His shed blood upon the cross. He's my Savior!" Christianity is the only faith in the world that has a Savior. Every other religious system makes you try to earn God's favor through your own "good works."

It's sad to say, but there are huge amounts of so-called "Christians" trapped in our churches today who are doing the exact same thing as Muslims, Buddhists, Hindus, and others. They are trying to be good enough for God to accept them. They think they have to read the Bible, pray, tithe, and so forth, or God won't answer their prayers. This isn't true Christianity.

Others have truly been born again, but Christ is not profiting them anything in this life (Gal. 5:2-4). Many times, the initial born-again experience is presented as a matter of grace. People humble themselves and ask God to save them, while everyone else in the meeting sings, "Just as I am, without one plea." They respond to His grace with faith, and receive the Lord. But then they fall into a mindset that says, "I've been saved by grace, but now that I'm a Christian, I need to pray, fast, tithe, study, and attend church in order for God to love me, bless me, use me, and answer my prayers." They may be on their way to heaven, but they have fallen back into the same old legalistic mindset and pattern. This is what the book of Galatians was written about. Paul said that if you do that, Christ profits you nothing (Gal. 5:2).

Doubting His Willingness

Friend, I write this to you in love. I'm not trying to scold you. I'm trying to help you see an area that Satan has been deceiving and blinding so many of us in. Have you prayed and received Jesus as your Savior? Are you born again, but right now Christ is profiting you nothing? You can't get healed? You don't have joy or peace? You don't have excitement for the kingdom of God, but you're plagued by fear and unbelief instead? If you were arrested for being a Christian, there wouldn't be enough evidence to convict you? Truthfully speaking, there's very little difference between you and the unsaved people at work? In fact, many of the folks you work with would be shocked to find out you're a Christian? If this describes you, Christ is profiting you nothing.

It's not because Jesus doesn't have power; it's because we've fallen prey to Satan's lie. We know God is powerful, but we think, *How could He ever use His power on my behalf?* That's because you're back under a sin-consciousness, thinking you have to earn God's favor. You know you aren't living as well as you should. Your own heart condemns you. You don't doubt God's ability. What you doubt is His willingness to use His ability on your behalf, because you feel He's still holding sin against you.

God placed your sin upon Jesus. Sin is a non-issue with God. He is aware of it and will tell you to quit doing it, but not because He's going to reject you. He's already paid for your sin. God loves you, and He knows that Satan will destroy you if you choose to live in sin.

The thief cometh not, but for to steal, and to kill, and to destroy.

JOHN 10:10

The Lord will tell you to quit sinning because He knows that the devil will come in, hinder, hurt, and otherwise take advantage of you. God doesn't convict you of sin because He's going to punish or reject you; He's already laid all the punishment and rejection your sin deserved—and then some—upon Jesus. God isn't ignorant of sin in your life, but it doesn't change His attitude toward you. He's paid for your sins—past, present, and even future sins!

If You Miss it, You Miss it

Many people choke on this. They criticize me, saying, "You're a heretic. How dare you say this!" By God's grace, I'm willing to speak the Word in the face of some very dearly held religious traditions.

Some people think that every time you sin, it's a new affront against God and you have to get that sin confessed, under the blood, and forgiven. There are several variations of this. Some people believe you lose your salvation every time there's un-confessed sin in your life. They believe that if you were to die without getting that sin confessed, you'd go directly to hell—it doesn't matter that you've been born again and walking with the Lord for twenty-plus years. They believe you just lose everything if you have un-confessed sin in your life. There are people who teach that if you're driving down the road on your way home from committing adultery (or some other sin) and you have a car wreck and die with that sin un-confessed, you would go straight to hell because you hadn't repented of that sin. That's not what Scripture teaches.

This is the very reason most of us aren't experiencing more of God. It's the reason Christ has become of none effect in our lives. We limit what God can do because we've tied His willingness to use His ability in our lives to our worth and value. The truth is that none of us deserve the blessing of God. Even if we don't commit adultery, murder, or steal, we're not perfect.

For whosoever shall keep the whole law, and yet offend in one point, he is guilty of all.

JAMES 2:10

I've never spoken a word of profanity, taken a drink of liquor, or smoked a cigarette in all my life. But who wants to be the best sinner that ever went to hell? I have sinned and come short of the glory of God (Rom. 3:23). I've broken God's standard. If you miss a little bit, you miss the whole thing. When someone says "Well, I don't do these bad things," I always come back and ask, "So, are you perfect? Are you without sin in your life?" They answer, "Well, no. I have problems. I've sinned." Well, if you miss it, you miss it.

If God said "If you can jump up and touch this thirty-foot ceiling, then you can be saved," you might be able to jump higher than someone else, but nobody can jump that high. If that were the minimum requirement, we'd all die.

That's how the Law works. You can't say to someone else, "I haven't kept them all, but I've done better than you have." There isn't a hell #2 or a hell #3. If you miss it, you miss it!

All Come Short

We've all sinned and come short of the glory of God (Rom. 3:23). For someone to say, "I can't believe a person could commit adultery, have a car wreck, and die on the way home without confessing that sin and still go to heaven. There's no way God could accept someone who has just committed adultery!" Well, the same Bible that tells us not to commit adultery also commands us to obey the laws of the land (Ex. 20:14 and Rom. 13:1-7). What happens if you drive fifty-six miles per hour in a fifty-five zone? You broke the law. You aren't doing what God told you to do. "But, Andrew, that's different. There's a huge difference between committing adultery and going one mile per hour over the speed limit." Well, there is a difference as far as people and the consequences here in this physical life are concerned.

However, the same One who said not to commit adultery also said not to gossip (Lev. 19:16). Gluttony is listed in the same verse as drunkenness (Prov. 23:20-21). The Lord said that if you lust after a person in your heart, it's the same as if you actually committed adultery (Matt. 5:28). If you hate someone in your heart, it's as if you murdered them (1 John 3:15). If you're about to say "I can't believe a person with sin in their life will be accepted by God," then you might as well give it up because all of us have sinned and come short of God's glory (Rom. 3:23).

Entered in Once!

God has dealt with sin.

But Christ being come an high priest of good things to come, by a greater and more perfect tabernacle, not made with hands, that is to say, not of this building; Neither by the blood of goats and calves, but by his own blood he entered in once into the holy place, having obtained eternal redemption for us.

Hebrews 9:11-12

Jesus entered in once—ONCE! This means He doesn't do it over and over again. Every time you sin, the Lord doesn't have to wait until you repent in order to get that sin under the blood. Christ obtained eternal redemption for you (Heb. 9:12). This wasn't a short-term redemption, only good until the next time you sin (and then you have to repent, get the blood reapplied, and be redeemed again). Christ entered in once and obtained for you an eternal redemption. For many people, this pulls the rug out from under them. It shakes them to the foundation of everything they believe.

Backslidden?

Most Christians think that when you come to the Lord, you get your sins forgiven up to that point. Then, every time you sin after you're a Christian, you have to run to the Lord with that sin, repent of it, and confess it. If you don't, then you could die and go to hell with un-confessed sin, or at the very least, you're out of fellowship with God. Religion calls this "backslidden." They say, "You need to repent of that sin and get back into relationship with God."

There's also a milder form of this same erroneous doctrine. People will say, "You won't lose your salvation. If you were to die in a backslidden state or with un-confessed sin, you'd still go to heaven, but you can't enjoy the presence of God. The Lord won't fellowship with a dirty vessel. God can't fill a dirty vessel. He can't answer your prayers if you have any sin in your life." If that were true, then God doesn't have anyone to fellowship with, and He's not going to answer anybody's prayers, because we all have things wrong with us.

Incompatible

Sin isn't only what you're doing; it's also what you're not doing.

Therefore to him that knoweth to do good, and doeth it not, to him it is sin.
JAMES 4:17

Therefore, sin isn't only violating a command; it's also not doing the good we know to do. According to this biblical definition of sin, if we know we're supposed to love somebody, if we know we're supposed to pray, if we have been convicted by God to love our wives as Christ loves the church or to honor our husbands the same way the church is to honor Christ, if we're supposed to do any of these things and we're failing—which, if we're breathing, we're failing—then we've all sinned. If it were true that we can't fellowship with God as long as there's sin in our lives, nobody could ever fellowship with God.

We've adopted this lie that every time we sin, it's a new affront against God that has to be repented of, confessed, and put under the blood. Because of this mentality and the fact that we know in our hearts that we're just blowing it all of the time, we feel unworthy and are void of any real confidence that God truly loves us. We'll say that He loves us, but then we'll turn around and confess, "I know why God hasn't healed me of this cancer. He's letting me suffer. The Lord allowed this car wreck that killed my children. He's the one who sent these terrorist attacks, tsunamis, and hurricanes. God's ticked off!" We say, "God loves us" out of one side of our mouths and "God is judging us because of our sin" out of the other. These are incompatible.

Jesus obtained for us an eternal redemption!

Eternal Redemption
LESSON 10 – OUTLINE

I. Jesus bore the sins of everyone—not just those He knew would accept Him.

> **He** [Jesus] **is the propitiation** [atoning sacrifice] **for our sins: and not for ours only, but also for the sins of the whole world.**
>
> 1 JOHN 2:2, BRACKETS MINE

   A. God has made the payment, but you must receive it.

   B. Each individual must appropriate by faith what God has already provided by grace, for it to take effect in their life.

II. You are saved by grace through faith.

> **For by grace are ye saved through faith; and that not of yourselves: it is the gift of God.**
>
> EPHESIANS 2:8

   A. Grace is what God has done for us independent of us—completely separate from anything we deserve.

   B. For God's grace to affect you, you must put faith in it.

   C. God's grace that brings salvation has come to every person, but not everyone has responded to God's grace.

> **For the grace of God that bringeth salvation hath appeared to all men.**
>
> TITUS 2:11

III. Multitudes of religious people go to hell because they thought that by attending church, paying their tithes, reading the Bible, and trying to be good, they could pay for their sins.

   A. Christianity is the only faith in the world that has a Savior.

   B. Every other religious system makes you try to earn God's favor through your own "good works."

   C. It's sad to say, but there are huge amounts of so-called "Christians" trapped in our churches today who are doing the exact same thing as Muslims, Buddhists, Hindus, and others—trying to be good enough for God to accept them. This isn't true Christianity.

IV. Others have truly been born again, but Christ is not profiting them anything in this life (Gal. 5:2-4).

    A. They may be on their way to heaven, but they have fallen back into the same old legalistic mindset and pattern.

    B. We know God is powerful, but we think, *How could He ever use His power on my behalf?*

    C. What you doubt is His willingness to use His ability on your behalf, because you feel He's still holding sin against you.

    D. The Lord will tell you to quit sinning because He knows that the devil will come in, hinder, hurt, and otherwise take advantage of you.

    E. God doesn't convict you of sin because He's going to punish or reject you.

> **The thief cometh not, but for to steal, and to kill, and to destroy.**
>
> JOHN 10:10

    F. God isn't ignorant of sin in your life, but it doesn't change His attitude toward you.

V. We limit what God can do because we've tied His willingness to use His ability in our lives to our worth and value.

    A. You may not commit adultery, murder, or steal, but you're not perfect.

> **For whosoever shall keep the whole law, and yet offend in one point, he is guilty of all.**
>
> JAMES 2:10

    B. That's how the Law works—if you miss it, you miss it!

    C. We've all sinned and come short of the glory of God (Rom. 3:23).

VI. God has dealt with sin.

> **But Christ being come an high priest of good things to come, by a greater and more perfect tabernacle, not made with hands, that is to say, not of this building; Neither by the blood of goats and calves, but by his own blood he entered in once into the holy place, having obtained eternal redemption for us.**
>
> HEBREWS 9:11-12

    A. This wasn't a short-term redemption—only good until the next time you sin (and then you have to repent, get the blood reapplied, and be redeemed again).

    B. Christ entered in once and obtained for us an eternal redemption.

C. Sin isn't only violating a command not to do something; it's also not doing the good you know to do.

Therefore to him that knoweth to do good, and doeth it not, to him it is sin.
JAMES 4:17

D. If it were true that you can't fellowship with God as long as there's sin in your life, nobody could ever fellowship with God.

E. Jesus obtained for us an eternal redemption!

Eternal Redemption
LESSON 10 – TEACHER'S GUIDE

1.   Jesus bore the sins of everyone—not just those He knew would accept Him (1 John 2:2). God has made the payment, but we must receive it. Each individual must appropriate by faith what God has already provided by grace, for it to take effect in their life.

2.   We are saved by grace through faith (Eph. 2:8). Grace is what God has done for us independent of us—completely separate from anything we deserve. For God's grace to affect us, we must put faith in it. This grace, which brings salvation, has come to every person, but not everyone has responded to it (Titus 2:11).

3.   Multitudes of religious people go to hell because they thought that by attending church, paying their tithes, reading the Bible, and trying to be good, they could pay for their sins.

Christianity is the only faith in the world that has a Savior. Every other religious system makes us try to earn God's favor through our own "good works." It's sad to say, but there are huge amounts of so-called "Christians" trapped in our churches today who are doing the exact same thing as Muslims, Buddhists, Hindus, and others—trying to be good enough for God to accept them. This isn't true Christianity.

1. A. According to 1 John 2:2, who did Jesus bear the sins of? (Everyone—not just those He knew would accept Him)
   B. For grace to take effect in an individual's life, what must they do with what God has already provided by grace? (They must receive and appropriate it by faith)
2. A. Read Ephesians 2:8 and Titus 2:11. How are we saved? (By grace through faith)
   B. What is grace? (It's what God has done for us independent of us—completely separate from anything we deserve)
3. A. Christianity is the only faith in the world with what? (A Savior)
   B. What does every other religious system in the world make us do? (Try to earn God's favor through our own "good works")

4.   Many people have truly been born again, but Christ is profiting them nothing in this life (Gal. 5:2-4). They may be on their way to heaven, but they have fallen back into the same old legalistic mindset and pattern.

We know God is powerful, but we think, *How could He ever use His power on my behalf?* What we doubt is His willingness to use His ability on our behalf, because we feel He's still holding sin against us. The Lord will tell us to quit sinning because He knows that the devil will come in, hinder, hurt, and otherwise take advantage of us—not because He's going to punish or reject us (John 10:10). God isn't ignorant of sin in our lives, but it doesn't change His attitude toward us.

5.   We limit what God can do because we've tied His willingness to use His ability in our lives to our worth and value. We may not commit adultery, murder, or steal, but we're not perfect (James 2:10). That's how the Law works—if we miss it, we miss it! We've all sinned and come short of the glory of God (Rom. 3:23).

6.   God has dealt with sin (Heb. 9:11-12). This wasn't a short-term redemption—only good until the next time we sin (and then we have to repent, get the blood reapplied, and be redeemed again). Christ entered in once and obtained for us an eternal redemption. Sin isn't only violating a command not to do something; it's also not doing the good we know to do (James 4:17). If it were true that we can't fellowship with God as long as there's sin in our lives, nobody could ever fellowship with God. Jesus obtained for us an eternal redemption!

4. A. Read Galatians 5:2-4 and John 10:10. What do many people who have been truly born again fall back into? (The same old legalistic mindset and pattern)
   B. Why do we doubt God's willingness to use His ability on our behalf? (Because we feel He's still holding sin against us)
5. A. How do we limit what God can do? (By tying His willingness to use His ability in our lives to our worth and value)
   B. Read James 2:10 and Romans 3:23. Are any of us perfect? (No)
6. A. According to Hebrews 9:11-12, what did Christ obtain for us? (An eternal redemption)
   B. According to James 4:17, what is sin? (It's not only violating a command not to do something, but it's also not doing the good we know to do)
   C. If it were true that we can't fellowship with God as long as there's sin in our lives, who could ever fellowship with God? (Nobody)

Eternal Redemption
LESSON 10 – DISCIPLESHIP QUESTIONS

1. According to 1 John 2:2, who is the propitiation for our sins?

2. Who is the propitiation for the sins of the whole world?

3. According to Ephesians 2:8, how are we saved?

4. What is not of ourselves, but is the gift of God?
    A. Grace.
    B. Salvation.
    C. Faith.
    D. All of the above.
    E. None of the above.

5. According to Titus 2:11, whose grace has appeared to all men?

6. Who was God speaking through in Galatians 5:2-4?

7. According to Galatians 5:4, if we trust in our own Law keeping and religious works, what will happen?

8. Christ becomes of no effect to those who are trying to be justified (made righteous) how?

9. What have they fallen from?

10. According to John 10:10, why does the thief come?
    A. To kill.
    B. To destroy.
    C. To give life.
    D. To steal.
    E. All of the above.
    F. None of the above.

11. Why did Jesus come?

12. According to James 2:10, is it possible to keep the whole Law and yet offend at one point?

13. What happens when even just one point of the Law is offended?

14. According to Romans 3:23, what happens when we sin?

15. What does Exodus 20:14 command us?

16. The main idea of Romans 13:1-7 is to **"let every soul be subject unto"** whom?
    A. The powers that be.
    B. Rulers.
    C. The higher powers.
    D. All of the above.
    E. None of the above.

17. According to Leviticus 19:16, we should not go up and down as _____ among other people.

18. Proverbs 23:20-21 reveals that drunkards and gluttons come to what?

19. According to Matthew 5:28, at what point does God consider that adultery has taken place in a man's heart?

20. What does 1 John 3:15 call a person who hates his brother?

21. What does this person not have abiding in him?

22. According to Hebrews 9:11-12, who came as high priest of good things to come?

23. Whose blood did Jesus enter into the holy place in heaven with?
    A. The blood of calves.
    B. The blood of goats.
    C. His own blood.
    D. All of the above.
    E. None of the above.

24. How many times did He enter in?

25. What has He obtained for us?

26. What does James 4:17 call sin?

Eternal Redemption
LESSON 10 – ANSWER KEY

1. Jesus.

2. Jesus.

3. By grace through faith.

4. A. Grace.
   B. Salvation.
   C. Faith.
   D. All of the above.

5. God's grace.

6. Paul.

7. Christ shall profit us nothing.

8. By the Law.

9. Grace.

10. A. To kill.
    B. To destroy.
    D. To steal.

11. That we might have life, and have it more abundantly.

12. No.

13. We are guilty of breaking it all.

14. We come short of God's glory.

15. Not to commit adultery.

16. A. The powers that be.
    B. Rulers.
    C. The higher powers.
    D. All of the above.

17. A talebearer (gossip).

18. Poverty.

19. When he looks on a woman to lust after her.

20. A murderer.

21. Eternal life.

22. Jesus Christ.

23. C. His own blood.

24. Once.

25. Eternal redemption.

26. Not doing the good we know to do.

Eternal Redemption

And he is the propitiation for our sins: and not for ours only, but also for the sins of the whole world.

1 JOHN 2:2

For by grace are ye saved through faith; and that not of yourselves: it is the gift of God.

EPHESIANS 2:8

For the grace of God that bringeth salvation hath appeared to all men.

TITUS 2:11

Behold, I Paul say unto you, that if ye be circumcised, Christ shall profit you nothing. For I testify again to every man that is circumcised, that he is a debtor to do the whole law. Christ is become of no effect unto you, whosoever of you are justified by the law; ye are fallen from grace.

GALATIANS 5:2-4

The thief cometh not, but for to steal, and to kill, and to destroy: I am come that they might have life, and that they might have it more abundantly.

JOHN 10:10

For whosoever shall keep the whole law, and yet offend in one point, he is guilty of all.

JAMES 2:10

For all have sinned, and come short of the glory of God.

ROMANS 3:23

Thou shalt not commit adultery.

EXODUS 20:14

Let every soul be subject unto the higher powers. For there is no power but of God: the powers that be are ordained of God. Whosoever therefore resisteth the power, resisteth the ordinance of God: and they that resist shall receive to themselves damnation. For rulers are not a terror to good works, but to the evil. Wilt thou then not be afraid of the power? do that which is good, and thou shalt have praise of the same: For he is the minister of God to thee for good. But if thou do that which is evil, be afraid; for he beareth not the sword in vain: for he is the minister of God, a revenger to execute wrath upon him that doeth evil. Wherefore ye must needs be subject, not only for wrath, but also for conscience sake. For for this cause pay ye tribute also: for they are God's ministers, attending continually upon this very thing. Render therefore to all their dues: tribute to whom tribute is due; custom to whom custom; fear to whom fear; honour to whom honour.

ROMANS 13:1-7

Thou shalt not go up and down as a talebearer among thy people: neither shalt thou stand against the blood of thy neighbour: I am the LORD.

LEVITICUS 19:16

Be not among winebibbers; among riotous eaters of flesh: For the drunkard and the glutton shall come to poverty: and drowsiness shall clothe a man with rags.

PROVERBS 23:20-21

But I say unto you, That whosoever looketh on a woman to lust after her hath committed adultery with her already in his heart.

MATTHEW 5:28

Whosoever hateth his brother is a murderer: and ye know that no murderer hath eternal life abiding in him.

1 JOHN 3:15

But Christ being come an high priest of good things to come, by a greater and more perfect tabernacle, not made with hands, that is to say, not of this building; Neither by the blood of goats and calves, but by his own blood he entered in once into the holy place, having obtained eternal redemption for us.

HEBREWS 9:11-12

Therefore to him that knoweth to do good, and doeth it not, to him it is sin.

JAMES 4:17

The Real Deal
LESSON 11

For if the blood of bulls and of goats, and the ashes of an heifer sprinkling the unclean, sanctifieth to the purifying of the flesh.

HEBREWS 9:13

The author was writing to Jewish Christians. They were aware of all the covenants, laws, and rituals involved in the Old Testament. The author was saying, "If the Old Testament sacrifices had any benefit to them, how much greater, then, is the sacrifice of the Lord Jesus Christ? All those Old Testament sacrifices were pointing toward the sacrifice that Jesus was going to make."

How much more shall the blood of Christ, who through the eternal Spirit offered himself without spot to God, purge your conscience from dead works to serve the living God?

HEBREWS 9:14

The problem is that we have consciences that have been defiled. We haven't purged our consciences with the truth about what Jesus has done with our sins. Satan is digging up things you have done, saying, "Sure, God exists and He has power, but He won't do it for you, you sorry thing!" We're allowing the devil's condemnation to destroy our faith and confidence in God because we know we don't deserve it. There's good news. It's the Gospel!

You don't deserve it, but God isn't giving you what you deserve. You're getting what God deserves. You get to use the name of Jesus, and God isn't angry with you or holding your sins against you. Jesus entered into the holy place one time and obtained for you an eternal redemption. He paid for all of your sins—past, present, and even the ones you haven't committed yet. Your sins have been forgiven.

Eternal Inheritance

"But how can that be?" Keep reading.

And for this cause he is the mediator of the new testament, that by means of death, for the redemption of the transgressions that were under the first testament, they which are called might receive the promise of eternal inheritance.

HEBREWS 9:15

You don't just have inheritance. You aren't just a family member until the next time you sin and then you lose your membership, or at least all of the privileges, and God puts you on a list of children who can't receive anything. He doesn't say, "You don't have any of the benefits because you haven't been living right." No! You get an **"eternal inheritance."**

The very moment you were born again, you became as forgiven as you'll ever be. When you go to be with the Lord in heaven, you aren't going to get more cleansed. In your born-again spirit, you are as perfect and holy as you will ever be. You have a body and a soul that do get defiled by sin. Your conscience gets defiled. Satan comes in and takes advantage of you. Therefore, when you go to be with the Lord, you'll receive a glorified body and soul. But right now—at this very moment—your spirit is as born again as it will ever be! In your born-again spirit, you are as clean, holy, and pure as Jesus Himself (1 John 4:17).

A New Creature

"But, Andrew, how can that be?" You look in the mirror and see zits, bulges, wrinkles, and gray hairs—what's left of them. You look at this and wonder, *How can I be righteous?* The Word isn't talking about your physical body. Then you search your soulish realm and find thoughts, attitudes, and feelings you know aren't the way they're supposed to be. Due to this, you think, *I don't understand—how could I be righteous?* It's your spirit—not your soul—that's born again. Your spirit is the part of you that's created in righteousness and true holiness. However, you can't see your spirit in a mirror or feel it with your senses. Your spirit can only be perceived through the Word of God.

Jesus said:

The words that I speak unto you, they are spirit, and they are life.

JOHN 6:63

If we want to know what we're like in our born-again spirits, we have to look in the Word of God. We have to hold it up like a spiritual mirror (James 1:23-25). When someone asks "How are you?" most of us answer, "Oh, I have this pain over here, and the doctor said this and that." We describe our physical bodies. Or we'll search our souls and say "I'm discouraged" or something similar. But neither our bodies nor our souls are the real us. The real us is the born-again part of us—our spirits. When someone asks us how we are, we ought to hold the Word up, take a look, and say, "I'm blessed with all spiritual blessings (Eph. 1:3). I'm above only, and not beneath. I'm the head, and not the tail (Deut. 28:13). I am blessed, blessed, blessed!" Most of us don't know ourselves in the spirit. We only know ourselves in the outward man.

Therefore if any man be in Christ, he is a new creature: old things are passed away; behold, all things are become new.

2 CORINTHIANS 5:17

"Old things are passed away" and **"all things are become new"** isn't talking about your body or your soul. Those didn't change the instant you became born again, but your spirit did. In your spirit, you became as righteous, holy, and pure as Jesus is (Eph. 4:24 and 1 John 4:17). You're forgiven and cleansed. You have an eternal redemption and an eternal inheritance (Heb. 9:12 and 15). Jesus only purges us one time. He doesn't have to re-purge us.

"But how could God forgive a sin before I even commit it?" I'm not sure exactly how all this happens, but Jesus only died for our sins one time, two thousand years ago. You'd better hope He can forgive a sin before you committed it, because He hasn't died for any of your sins since you committed them. He anticipated. God knows the end from the beginning. He knew the sins of the entire world. Jesus took your sins and paid for them before you ever committed them. That's good news!

Heavenly Patterns

It was therefore necessary that the patterns of things in the heavens should be purified with these; but the heavenly things themselves with better sacrifices than these.

HEBREWS 9:23

The Old Testament tabernacle and temple were full of these symbols of actual things in heaven. There is an actual mercy seat and altar of incense in heaven. God instructed Moses to make sure that everything made was according to the pattern he was given on the mount (Ex. 25:40 and Heb. 8:5). He actually saw into heaven and saw the temple there. All these things were pictures of things that exist in the spiritual realm. Each one symbolized something that Jesus was going to do. The veil of the temple represented the physical body of Jesus that separated the holy of holies and the holy place. When Jesus died…

The veil of the temple was rent in twain from the top to the bottom.

MATTHEW 27:51

This symbolized that Jesus' flesh was broken and that the way to God is now available through Him. All of these Old Testament sacrifices and rituals that they went through over and over were because the people needed to be reminded over and over again. But the real sacrifice that was made for our sins wasn't something that has to be done over and over again. It was only done once.

Jesus died for the sins of the entire world one time. He dealt with all sins of all people for all time. You don't have to go back to the Lord every time you mess up, or feel like you have to work your way back into His favor. That's what this is talking about.

Types, Shadows, and Reality

For Christ is not entered into the holy places made with hands, which are the figures of the true; but into heaven itself, now to appear in the presence of God for us: Nor yet that he should offer himself often, as the high priest entereth into the holy place every year with blood of others; For then must he often have suffered since the foundation of the world.

HEBREWS 9:24-26

The high priest went into the holy of holies every year on the Day of Atonement and made a sacrifice. There were also daily sacrifices, both morning and evening. Then there were all the other sacrifices people brought every time someone sinned. So the constant flowing of blood and offering of sacrifices in the Old Testament were just pictures. They weren't the real thing. The author was contrasting the priest continually entering in with sacrifices with Jesus only entering in once. If Jesus was doing it the way it was done in the Old Testament, He would have had offer Himself many, many times. But He didn't. Jesus only offered Himself for our sins once.

> **For then must he often have suffered since the foundation of the world: but now once in the end of the world hath he appeared to put away sin by the sacrifice of himself. And as it is appointed unto men once to die, but after this the judgment: so Christ was once offered to bear the sins of many; and unto them that look for him shall he appear the second time without sin unto salvation.**
>
> HEBREWS 9:26-28

This whole passage is contrasting the Old Testament sacrifices with the sacrifice of Christ. In the Old Testament, the same sacrifices were offered over and over again, because they couldn't really work. They were only types, shadows, and pictures of the real deal to come. Since Jesus' sacrifice was the real deal, it only had to be offered once. Yet it dealt with all sins for all people at all times. Jesus entered in once and obtained eternal redemption for us.

"No More Conscience of Sins"

> **For the law having a shadow of good things to come, and not the very image of the things, can never with those sacrifices which they offered year by year continually make the comers thereunto perfect. For then would they not have ceased to be offered?**
>
> HEBREWS 10:1-2

Notice the question mark. If the Old Testament sacrifices could have worked, then they would have quit offering them…

> **Because that the worshippers once purged should have had no more conscience of sins.**
>
> HEBREWS 10:2

The Old Testament sacrifices couldn't work, so there was sin-consciousness, and they offered the same sacrifices over and over again. But the New Testament sacrifice of Jesus *did* work, and therefore we should have no more sin-consciousness. That's radical! This is so different from the way most people think.

A Performance-Based World

Most Christians are sin conscious. It's just ground into you. People don't treat you by grace. They don't say, "Whatever you do, I'm going to love you regardless." There isn't a role model for this. Your employer doesn't hire you by grace and say, "I want you to know that whether you ever show up or not, or do your job or not—regardless of how you act—I'm a grace man. It doesn't matter what you do, you have guaranteed cost-of-living raises, promotions, and Christmas bonuses." That's not the way your employer hires you. Like everything else in the world, it's all based on performance. If you don't perform, you get reprimanded, demoted, or fired.

In marriage, we're supposed to love each other unconditionally. However, I've dealt with hundreds of people who have come to me for counseling. They always say, "I'm mad at my spouse for this."

I answer, "Well, you're supposed to forgive them."

"I know, but they did this!"

"Do you know what you're saying? You're giving that person what they deserve instead of loving them unconditionally." Even in marriage we treat people based on performance.

We treat our kids this way too. When they do right, we sing their praises. When they do wrong, we punish them. The entire world around us is based on performance.

However, the Lord made a sacrifice and forgave you. You didn't deserve to be forgiven. God just forgave you because He loves you and because He's a good God. Therefore, we shouldn't have sin-consciousness.

The Real Deal
LESSON 11 – OUTLINE

I. The author of Hebrews was writing to Jewish Christians who were aware of all the covenants, laws, and rituals involved in the Old Testament.

> **For if the blood of bulls and of goats, and the ashes of an heifer sprinkling the unclean, sanctifieth to the purifying of the flesh.**
>
> HEBREWS 9:13

   A. The author was saying, "If the Old Testament sacrifices had any benefit to them, how much greater, then, is the sacrifice of the Lord Jesus Christ? All those Old Testament sacrifices were pointing toward the sacrifice that Jesus was going to make."

> **How much more shall the blood of Christ, who through the eternal Spirit offered himself without spot to God, purge your conscience from dead works to serve the living God?**
>
> HEBREWS 9:14

   B. The problem is that we have consciences that have been defiled—we haven't purged our consciences with the truth about what Jesus has done with our sins.

   C. Jesus entered into the holy place one time and obtained for us an eternal redemption.

   D. He paid for all of your sins—past, present, and even the ones you haven't committed yet.

   E. Your sins have been forgiven.

> **And for this cause he is the mediator of the new testament, that by means of death, for the redemption of the transgressions that were under the first testament, they which are called might receive the promise of eternal inheritance.**
>
> HEBREWS 9:15

II. In your born-again spirit, you are as clean, holy, and pure as Jesus Himself (1 John 4:17).

   A. Your spirit—not your body or soul—is the part of you that's created in righteousness and true holiness.

   B. However, you can't see your spirit in a mirror or feel it with your senses.

   C. If you want to know what you're like in your born-again spirit, you have to look in the Word of God—the spiritual mirror (James 1:23-25).

The words that I speak unto you, they are spirit, and they are life.

JOHN 6:63

D. Your body and soul didn't change the instant you became born again, but your spirit did.

Therefore if any man be in Christ, he is a new creature: old things are passed away; behold, all things are become new.

2 CORINTHIANS 5:17

E. Jesus only purges us one time—He doesn't have to re-purge us (Heb. 9:12 and 15).

III. The Old Testament tabernacle and temple were full of these symbols of actual things in heaven (Ex. 25:40 and Heb. 8:5).

It was therefore necessary that the patterns of things in the heavens should be purified with these; but the heavenly things themselves with better sacrifices than these.

HEBREWS 9:23

A. Each one symbolized something that Jesus was going to do (e.g., the veil).

The veil of the temple was rent in twain from the top to the bottom.

MATTHEW 27:51

B. Jesus died for the sins of the entire world one time.

C. He dealt with all sins of all people for all time.

D. You don't have to go back to the Lord every time you mess up, or feel like you have to work your way back into His favor.

For Christ is not entered into the holy places made with hands, which are the figures of the true; but into heaven itself, now to appear in the presence of God for us: Nor yet that he should offer himself often, as the high priest entereth into the holy place every year with blood of others; For then must he often have suffered since the foundation of the world.

HEBREWS 9:24-26

IV. This whole passage is contrasting the Old Testament sacrifices with the sacrifice of Christ.

For then must he often have suffered since the foundation of the world: but now once in the end of the world hath he appeared to put away sin by the sacrifice of himself. And as it is appointed unto men once to die, but after this the judgment: so Christ was once offered to bear the sins of many; and unto them that look for him shall he appear the second time without sin unto salvation.

HEBREWS 9:26-28

A. In the Old Testament, the same sacrifices were offered over and over again, because they couldn't really work—they were only types, shadows, and pictures of the real deal to come.

B. Since Jesus' sacrifice was the real deal, it only had to be offered once.

> **For the law having a shadow of good things to come, and not the very image of the things, can never with those sacrifices which they offered year by year continually make the comers thereunto perfect. For then would they not have ceased to be offered? Because that the worshippers once purged should have had no more conscience of sins.**
>
> HEBREWS 10:1-2

C. The Old Testament sacrifices couldn't work, so there was sin-consciousness, and they offered the same sacrifices over and over again.

D. But the New Testament sacrifice of Jesus *did* work, and therefore we should have no more sin-consciousness.

V. Most Christians are sin conscious.

A. The entire world around us is based on performance.

B. However, the Lord made a sacrifice and forgave you.

C. Therefore, you shouldn't have sin-consciousness.

The Real Deal

1.   The author of Hebrews was writing to Jewish Christians who were aware of all the covenants, laws, and rituals involved in the Old Testament (Heb. 9:13). The author was saying, "If the Old Testament sacrifices had any benefit to them, how much greater, then, is the sacrifice of the Lord Jesus Christ? All those Old Testament sacrifices were pointing toward the sacrifice that Jesus was going to make" (Heb. 9:14). The problem is that we have consciences that have been defiled—we haven't purged our consciences with the truth about what Jesus has done with our sins. Jesus entered into the holy place one time and obtained for us an eternal redemption. He paid for all of our sins—past, present, and even the ones we haven't committed yet. Our sins have been forgiven (Heb. 9:15).

2.   In our born-again spirits, we are as clean, holy, and pure as Jesus Himself. Our spirits—not our bodies or souls—are the part of us that are created in righteousness and true holiness. However, we can't see our spirits in a mirror or feel them with our senses. If we want to know what we're like in our born-again spirits, we have to look in the Word of God—the spiritual mirror (John 6:63 and James 1:23-25). Our bodies and souls didn't change the instant we became born again, but our spirits did (2 Cor. 5:17). Jesus only purges us one time—He doesn't have to re-purge us (Heb. 9:12 and 15).

3.   The Old Testament tabernacle and temple were full of these symbols of actual things in heaven (Ex. 25:40; Heb. 8:5, and 9:23). Each one symbolized something that Jesus was going to do (e.g., the veil; Matt. 27:51). Jesus died for the sins of the entire world one time. He dealt with all sins of all people for all time. We don't have to go back to the Lord every time we mess up, or feel like we have to work our way back into His favor (Heb. 9:24-26).

1. A. Read Hebrews 9:13-15. What do we need to purge our consciences with? (The truth about what Jesus has done with our sins)
   B. Which of our sins have been paid for and forgiven? (All of our sins—past, present, and even the ones we haven't committed yet)
2. A. In what part of our beings—spirit, soul, or body—are we as clean, holy, and pure as Jesus Himself? (Our born-again spirits)
   B. Read John 6:63, James 1:23-25, and 2 Corinthians 5:17. If we want to know what we're like in our born-again spirits, where must we look? (In the Word of God—the spiritual mirror)
   C. Read Hebrews 9:12 and 15. How many times does Jesus purge us? (Only once)
3. A. Read Exodus 25:40; Hebrews 8:5, 9:23-26; and Matthew 27:51. What were the Old Testament tabernacle and temple full of? (Symbols of actual things in heaven and what Jesus was going to do)
   B. Do we have to go back to the Lord every time we mess up, or feel like we have to work our way back into His favor? (No)

4. Hebrews 9 contrasts the Old Testament sacrifices with the sacrifice of Christ. In the Old Testament, the same sacrifices were offered over and over again, because they couldn't really work—they were only types, shadows, and pictures of the real deal to come. Since Jesus' sacrifice was the real deal, it only had to be offered once (Heb. 9:26-10:2). The Old Testament sacrifices couldn't work, so there was a sin-consciousness, and they offered the same sacrifices over and over again. But the New Testament sacrifice of Jesus *did* work, and therefore we should have no more sin-consciousness.

5. Most Christians are sin conscious. The entire world around us is based on performance. However, the Lord made a sacrifice and forgave us. Therefore, we shouldn't have sin-consciousness.

4. A. Read Hebrews 9:26-10:2. Why couldn't the Old Testament sacrifices, which were offered over and over again, really work? (They were only types, shadows, and pictures of the real deal to come)
    B. Since the New Testament sacrifice of Jesus *did* work, what should we therefore have no more of? (Sin consciousness)
5. A. What is the entire world around us based on? (Performance)
    B. Why shouldn't we have sin-consciousness? (Because the Lord made a sacrifice and forgave us)

The Real Deal

1. What does Hebrews 9:13-15 reveal that the blood of Christ should purge our consciences from to serve the living God?

2. For this cause, Jesus is the mediator of what?

3. Those who are called are to receive what promise?

4. According to 1 John 4:17, how should believers be on the Day of Judgment?

5. We are, right now, as who is?

6. We are as He is where?

7. According to John 6:63, what part of our beings quickens us (gives life)?

8. What part of our beings profits nothing?

9. What are Jesus' words to us?
    A. Flesh.
    B. Life.
    C. Death.
    D. Spirit.

10. According to James 1:23-25, who will be blessed in his deed?
    A. The one who hears the Word, but forgets it and doesn't do it.
    B. The one who hears the Word, continues therein, and does it.

11. According to Ephesians 1:3, who has blessed us?

12. What has He blessed us with?

13. Where are they?

14. According to Deuteronomy 28:13, the Lord has made you what?

15. What shall you be?

16. What are we to hearken (listen) to?

17. According to 2 Corinthians 5:17, what passed away?

18. What have become new?

19. According to Ephesians 4:24, how was our new man created after God?

20. Hebrews 9:12 and 15 reveal that both our redemption and inheritance are what?

21. According to Matthew 27:51, what was ripped in two from top to bottom when Jesus died?

22. According to Hebrews 9:23-28, where did Christ enter into on our behalf?

23. How many times did Jesus appear to put away sin?

24. How did He do it?

25. Once we die, what comes next?

26. How many times was Christ offered to bear the sins of many?

27. According to Exodus 25:40, where was the pattern Moses was shown to follow?

28. What does Hebrews 8:5 reveal as being the example and shadow of heavenly things?

29. According to Hebrews 10:1-2, could the Law and its continual sacrifices make the comers thereunto perfect?

30. What would have happened if it had?

31. Because the worshipers once purged would have had what?

The Real Deal

1. Dead works.

2. The New Testament (New Covenant).

3. The promise of eternal inheritance.

4. Bold.

5. Jesus.

6. In this world.

7. Our spirits.

8. Our flesh.

9. B. Life.
   D. Spirit.

10. B. The one who hears the Word, continues therein, and does it.

11. The God and Father of our Lord Jesus Christ.

12. All spiritual blessings.

13. In heavenly places in Christ (the spirit realm).

14. The head, and not the tail.

15. Above only, and not beneath.

16. The commandments (Word) of the Lord our God.

17. Old things.

18. All things.

19. In righteousness and true holiness.

20. Eternal.

21. The veil of the temple.

22. The holy place in heaven itself.

23. Once.

24. By the sacrifice of Himself.

25. The judgment.

26. Once.

27. On the mount.

28. The tabernacle.

29. No.

30. The sacrifices would have ceased to be offered.

31. No more conscience of sins.

The Real Deal
LESSON 11 – SCRIPTURES

For if the blood of bulls and of goats, and the ashes of an heifer sprinkling the unclean, sanctifieth to the purifying of the flesh: How much more shall the blood of Christ, who through the eternal Spirit offered himself without spot to God, purge your conscience from dead works to serve the living God? And for this cause he is the mediator of the new testament, that by means of death, for the redemption of the transgressions that were under the first testament, they which are called might receive the promise of eternal inheritance.

HEBREWS 9:13-15

Herein is our love made perfect, that we may have boldness in the day of judgment: because as he is, so are we in this world.

1 JOHN 4:17

It is the spirit that quickeneth; the flesh profiteth nothing: the words that I speak unto you, they are spirit, and they are life.

JOHN 6:63

For if any be a hearer of the word, and not a doer, he is like unto a man beholding his natural face in a glass: for he beholdeth himself, and goeth his way, and straightway forgetteth what manner of man he was. But whoso looketh into the perfect law of liberty, and continueth therein, he being not a forgetful hearer, but a doer of the work, this man shall be blessed in his deed.

JAMES 1:23-25

Blessed be the God and Father of our Lord Jesus Christ, who hath blessed us with all spiritual blessings in heavenly places in Christ.

EPHESIANS 1:3

And the LORD shall make thee the head, and not the tail; and thou shalt be above only, and thou shalt not be beneath; if that thou hearken unto the commandments of the LORD thy God, which I command thee this day, to observe and to do them.

DEUTERONOMY 28:13

Therefore if any man be in Christ, he is a new creature: old things are passed away; behold, all things are become new.

2 CORINTHIANS 5:17

And that ye put on the new man, which after God is created in righteousness and true holiness.

EPHESIANS 4:24

Neither by the blood of goats and calves, but by his own blood he entered in once into the holy place, having obtained eternal redemption for us…And for this cause he is the mediator of the new testament, that by means of death, for the redemption of the transgressions that were under the first testament, they which are called might receive the promise of eternal inheritance.

HEBREWS 9:12 AND 15

And, behold, the veil of the temple was rent in twain from the top to the bottom; and the earth did quake, and the rocks rent.

MATTHEW 27:51

It was therefore necessary that the patterns of things in the heavens should be purified with these; but the heavenly things themselves with better sacrifices than these. For Christ is not entered into the holy places made with hands, which are the figures of the true; but into heaven itself, now to appear in the presence of God for us: Nor yet that he should offer himself often, as the high priest entereth into the holy place every year with blood of others; For then must he often have suffered since the foundation of the world: but now once in the end of the world hath he appeared to put away sin by the sacrifice of himself. And as it is appointed unto men once to die, but after this the judgment: So Christ was once offered to bear the sins of many; and unto them that look for him shall he appear the second time without sin unto salvation.

HEBREWS 9:23-28

And look that thou make them after their pattern, which was shewed thee in the mount.

EXODUS 25:40

Who serve unto the example and shadow of heavenly things, as Moses was admonished of God when he was about to make the tabernacle: for, See, saith he, that thou make all things according to the pattern shewed to thee in the mount.

HEBREWS 8:5

For the law having a shadow of good things to come, and not the very image of the things, can never with those sacrifices which they offered year by year continually make the comers thereunto perfect. For then would they not have ceased to be offered? because that the worshippers once purged should have had no more conscience of sins.

HEBREWS 10:1-2

Spirit vs. Flesh
LESSON 12

Most of us are modeling our relationship with God after the way our fathers or someone else has treated us. But God is greater than any person you've ever dealt with. He has forgiven all of your sin, so you should have no more sin-consciousness.

However, the average Christian approaches God, saying, "O Lord. I come before You so humbly today. Please forgive me of my many sins." It's like we feel that if we mention all of our sins—and mention them quickly—then God might not mention them. But if we don't, He'll definitely bring them up. We have a constant sin-consciousness.

When you come before the Lord, are you someone who has to be sad and cry every time? Do you feel so ungodly that you have to plead with Him for mercy? Even if you're acting ungodly in the natural realm, you are righteous in His sight if you've truly been born again. If you approach God, saying "I'm so ungodly and unworthy. How could You love me?" then you're in the flesh. You aren't in the spirit.

Your born-again spirit isn't defiled or ungodly. It's righteous, holy, and pure. "But, Andrew, you don't know what I've been doing." You don't know what God has done!

Preserved and Protected

When you first believed on Jesus, you were sealed with the Holy Spirit.

> **In whom ye also trusted, after that ye heard the word of truth, the gospel of your salvation: in whom also after that ye believed, ye were sealed with that holy Spirit of promise.**
>
> EPHESIANS 1:13

Your born-again spirit, a.k.a. new man, was created in righteousness and true holiness.

> **Put on the new man, which after God is created in righteousness and true holiness.**
>
> EPHESIANS 4:24

As Jesus is, so became your spirit in this world.

> **As he is, so are we in this world.**
>
> 1 JOHN 4:17

Your spirit became one with the Lord.

> **But he that is joined unto the Lord is one spirit.**
>
> 1 CORINTHIANS 6:17

Then, all of this goodness was immediately sealed tight with the Holy Spirit, just as Ephesians 1:13 says.

When people can food, they seal the jar with paraffin. This makes an airtight seal that preserves and protects the food within. Airborne impurities are prevented from getting inside and causing the food to rot and spoil. That's how this word **"sealed"** is used in Ephesians 1:13.

When you were born again, your spirit was immediately encased—vacuum packed—by the Holy Spirit for the purpose of preservation. When you fail in any area of your life after being saved, the rottenness, uncleanness, and defilement that comes to your body and soul doesn't penetrate your spirit. This Holy Spirit seal keeps the good in and the bad out.

God doesn't look at sin the way people do. To Him, sin isn't only doing something wrong by violating a command; it's also not doing something right that you should have done (James 4:17). No husband loves his wife exactly like Christ loved the church. No wife reverences her husband the way the church reverences Christ. No one is as passionate about ministering to others as they should be. None of us meditates on the things of God as much as we could. Therefore, according to God's definition of sin, everyone constantly falls short.

If you don't understand that the Holy Spirit encased your born-again spirit, your conscience will eventually give you the impression that you've lost the righteousness and true holiness your spirit was created in. Your conscience, with its knowledge of right and wrong, constantly bears witness to your mind about your thoughts and actions. If you aren't careful, you'll allow the knowledge of your failures to affect you. You'll think, *Well, when I was born again, God gave me a brand-new start, but I've failed since then.* You may confess, try hard, and get back to where you feel like, *Now I'm back on track and everything's fine!* but it won't be long before your conscience shows you something else. If your life fluctuates like this day after day, year after year (which it does), after a while you'll think, *What's the use?*

Born of God

However, the truth is that your spirit was sealed. Sin and its effects cannot enter your spirit. When you sin, your spirit does not participate. It retains its original holiness and purity—and will for eternity!

> **Whosoever is born of God doth not commit sin; for his seed remaineth in him: and he cannot sin, because he is born of God.**
>
> 1 JOHN 3:9

This means you are as righteous and holy now—in your spirit—as you will ever be. However, many people struggle to understand 1 John 3:9 because its context clearly shows that Christians do sin.

> **If we say that we have no sin, we deceive ourselves, and the truth is not in us.**
>
> 1 JOHN 1:8

If we say that we have not sinned, we make him a liar, and his word is not in us.

1 JOHN 1:10

My little children, these things write I unto you, that ye sin not. And if any man sin, we have an advocate with the Father, Jesus Christ the righteous.

1 JOHN 2:1

These are three instances from the same letter where the writer, the Apostle John, talks about sinning. The first two communicate, "If you say you haven't sinned, you're a liar." He adds, "I'm writing to you so that you will not (future tense) sin. But if you do sin…" Then, in John 3:9, he declares, "If you're born of God, you cannot sin." That sounds very contradictory!

Both Scripture and experience reveal that Christians can sin. The context of 1 John shows that 3:9 isn't saying that it's impossible for a born-again believer to do something that's sin. Yet it also clearly says that if you're born of God, you cannot sin. How can this be?

Big and Little Sins?

Some people take 1 John 3:9 to mean you can't "habitually" sin. Several Bible translations now render it this way. People who think along this line preach, "If you were a drunk before you were saved, you might get drunk once or twice, but if you're truly saved you won't habitually sin. Eventually, you'll see victory in that area, or you weren't truly born again."

In order to embrace this view, you have to categorize sin, which God doesn't. To Him, there are no "big" sins and "little" sins. By His definition, we all habitually sin. We all habitually fail to study God's Word as much as we should. We all habitually fail to love others the way we should. We all habitually fail to be as considerate as we should. We habitually get into self-centeredness, and God has to habitually deal with us about it.

Sometimes, we also pass over things that God calls sin. For instance, the Lord views gluttony the same as drunkenness, adultery, and murder (Deut. 21:20). Gluttony is a sin that can only happen habitually. You can't become overweight by eating just one large meal. Even if you gorged yourself, it would only make a pound or two of difference. In order to gain an extra fifty to a hundred pounds, you'd have to do it again and again and again. Being overweight is a habitual sin. This isn't to condemn anyone but to put things in perspective.

If you interpret 1 John 3:9 to mean that you cannot habitually sin if you're truly born of God, then nobody would qualify, because we all habitually sin. The only way this can be preached is to say, "Well, you can't habitually do the 'big' sins, but the 'little' ones—yes, you can habitually sin." That's not what this verse is saying.

If you understand spirit, soul, and body, the interpretation of 1 John 3:9 is obvious. Your spirit is the only part of you that's been born of God. Your soul and body have been purchased, but not yet redeemed. Therefore, your spirit cannot sin even though your body and soul can. This means your performance doesn't affect the purity and holiness of your spirit.

This truth is pivotal to your relationship with God. If you tie His acceptance to your performance, you'll always come short. You might do better than certain other people, but your own conscience will condemn you. Eventually, it'll keep you from enjoying God's love and blessings, because you know that you've tried and tried but still have faults after all these years. When you understand spirit, soul, and body, you know that it was your spirit that changed. Created in righteousness and true holiness, it's been sealed by the Holy Spirit so no sin can penetrate it. The righteousness you were born again with stays uncontaminated. Since God is a Spirit, He always deals with you Spirit to spirit. No matter how you're performing, you can always approach Him in your born-again spirit. That's awesome!

Approach God with Confidence

When you sin as a Christian, it affects your physical body, mind, and emotions. Satan has an opportunity against your physical and soulish realms, but your born-again spirit remains sealed (Rom. 6:16). Since your spirit was created in righteousness and true holiness—and sin can't penetrate that Holy Spirit seal—you don't lose your right standing with God. Your spirit is as pure right now as it was the instant you were born again. Your spirit is as righteous at this moment as it will ever be throughout all eternity.

You are the righteousness of God in Christ (2 Cor. 5:21). You are righteous in your spirit, and it's sealed. It never fluctuates. God is a Spirit, and He relates to you Spirit to spirit (John 4:24). He sees you as clean, holy, and pure even though you aren't that way in your physical man. Because you are righteous in your born-again spirit, you can approach God with confidence. It doesn't matter that you haven't done everything you should have done in your physical actions. Now, that's good news!

Spirit vs. Flesh
LESSON 12 – OUTLINE

I. Most of us are modeling our relationship with God after the way our fathers or someone else has treated us.

    A. But God is greater than any person you've ever dealt with.

    B. He has forgiven all of your sins, so you should have no more sin-consciousness.

    C. If you approach God, saying "I'm so ungodly and unworthy. How could You love me?" then you're in the flesh.

II. Your born-again spirit isn't defiled or ungodly—it's righteous, holy, and pure.

    A. When you first believed on Jesus, you were sealed with the Holy Spirit.

      In whom ye also trusted, after that ye heard the word of truth, the gospel of your salvation: in whom also after that ye believed, ye were sealed with that holy Spirit of promise.

                                        EPHESIANS 1:13

    B. Your born-again spirit, a.k.a. new man, was created in righteousness and true holiness.

      Put on the new man, which after God is created in righteousness and true holiness.

                                          EPHESIANS 4:24

    C. As Jesus is, so became your spirit in this world.

      As he is, so are we in this world.

                                          1 JOHN 4:17

    D. Your spirit became one with the Lord.

      But he that is joined unto the Lord is one spirit.

                                       1 CORINTHIANS 6:17

    E. Then, all of this goodness was immediately sealed tight with the Holy Spirit (Eph. 1:13).

III. When you were born again, your spirit was immediately encased—vacuum packed—by the Holy Spirit for the purpose of preservation.

    A. When you fail in any area of your life after being saved, the rottenness, uncleanness, and defilement that comes to your body and soul doesn't penetrate your spirit.

B. If you don't understand that the Holy Spirit encased your born-again spirit, your conscience will eventually give you the impression that you've lost the righteousness and true holiness your spirit was created in.

C. However, the truth is that your spirit was sealed.

D. Sin and its effects cannot enter your spirit.

IV. When you sin, your spirit does not participate.

A. It retains its original holiness and purity—and will for eternity!

Whosoever is born of God doth not commit sin; for his seed remaineth in him: and he cannot sin, because he is born of God.
1 JOHN 3:9

B. This means you are as righteous and holy now—in your spirit—as you will ever be.

V. However, many people struggle to understand 1 John 3:9 because its context clearly shows that Christians do sin.

If we say that we have no sin, we deceive ourselves, and the truth is not in us.
1 JOHN 1:8

If we say that we have not sinned, we make him a liar, and his word is not in us.
1 JOHN 1:10

My little children, these things write I unto you, that ye sin not. And if any man sin, we have an advocate with the Father, Jesus Christ the righteous.
1 JOHN 2:1

A. If you interpret 1 John 3:9 to mean that you cannot habitually sin if you're truly born of God, then nobody would qualify, because we all habitually sin.

B. If you understand spirit, soul, and body, the interpretation of 1 John 3:9 is obvious.

C. Your spirit is the only part of you that's been born of God.

D. Your soul and body have been purchased, but not yet redeemed.

E. Therefore, your spirit cannot sin even though your body and soul can, which means your performance doesn't affect the purity and holiness of your spirit.

VI. Since God is a Spirit, He always deals with (and relates to) you Spirit to spirit (John 4:24).

A. When you sin as a Christian, it affects your physical body, mind, and emotions.

B. Satan has an opportunity against your physical and soulish realms, but your born-again spirit remains sealed (Rom. 6:16).

C. Since your spirit was created in righteousness and true holiness—and sin can't penetrate that Holy Spirit seal—you don't lose your right standing with God.

D. Your spirit is as pure right now as it was the instant you were born again, and as righteous this moment as it will ever be throughout all eternity (2 Cor. 5:21).

E. Because you are righteous in your born-again spirit, you can approach God with confidence. It doesn't matter that you haven't done everything you should have done in your physical actions. Now, that's good news!

Spirit vs. Flesh
LESSON 12 – TEACHER'S GUIDE

1.   Most of us are modeling our relationship with God after the way our fathers or someone else has treated us. But God is greater than any person we've ever dealt with. He has forgiven all of our sins, so we should have no more sin-consciousness. If we approach God, saying "I'm so ungodly and unworthy. How could You love me?" then we're in the flesh.

2.   Our born-again spirits aren't defiled or ungodly—they're righteous, holy, and pure. When we first believed on Jesus, we were sealed with the Holy Spirit (Eph. 1:13). Our born-again spirits—a.k.a. new man—were created in righteousness and true holiness (Eph. 4:24). As Jesus is, so became our spirit in this world (1 John 4:17). Our spirits became one with the Lord (1 Cor. 6:17). Then, all of this goodness was immediately sealed tight with the Holy Spirit (Eph. 1:13).

3.   When we were born again, our spirits were immediately encased—vacuum packed—by the Holy Spirit for the purpose of preservation. When we fail in any area of our lives after being saved, the rottenness, uncleanness, and defilement that comes to our bodies and souls don't penetrate our spirits. If we don't understand that the Holy Spirit encased our born-again spirits, our consciences will eventually give us the impression that we've lost the righteousness and true holiness our spirits were created in. However, the truth is our spirits were sealed. Sin and its effects cannot enter our spirits.

1. A. What are most of us modeling our relationship with God after? (The way our fathers or someone else has treated us)
   B. Why should we have no more sin-consciousness? (Because God has forgiven all of our sin)
2. A. Read Ephesians 1:13. What happened when we first believed on Jesus? (We were sealed with the Holy Spirit)
   B. According to Ephesians 4:24, how was our new man created? (In righteousness and true holiness)
   C. Read 1 John 4:17 and 1 Corinthians 6:17. What part of our beings became one with the Lord? (Our spirits)
3. A. What happens if we don't understand that the Holy Spirit encased our born-again spirits? (Our consciences will eventually give us the impression that we've lost the righteousness and true holiness our spirits were created in)
   B. Can sin and its effects enter our spirits? (No)

4.   When we sin, our spirits do not participate. They retains their original holiness and purity—and will for eternity! First John 3:9 means that we are as righteous and holy now—in our spirits—as we will ever be.

5.   However, many people struggle to understand 1 John 3:9 because its context clearly shows that Christians do sin (1 John 1:8, 10; and 2:1). If we interpret 1 John 3:9 to mean that we cannot habitually sin if we're truly born of God, then nobody would qualify, because we all habitually sin. If we understand spirit, soul, and body, the interpretation of 1 John 3:9 is obvious. Our spirits are the only part of us that have been born of God. Our souls and bodies have been purchased, but not yet redeemed. Therefore, our spirits cannot sin even though our bodies and souls can, which means our performance doesn't affect the purity and holiness of our spirits.

6.   Since God is a Spirit, He always deals with (and relates to) us Spirit to spirit (John 4:24). When we sin as a Christian, it affects our physical bodies, minds, and emotions. Satan has an opportunity against our physical and soulish realms, but our born-again spirits remain sealed (Rom. 6:16). Since our spirits were created in righteousness and true holiness—and sin can't penetrate that Holy Spirit seal—we don't lose our right standing with God. Our spirits are as pure right now as they were the instant we were born again, and as righteous this moment as they will ever be throughout all eternity (2 Cor. 5:21). Because we are righteous in our born-again spirits, we can approach God with confidence. It doesn't matter that we haven't done everything we should have done in our physical actions. Now, that's good news!

4. A. Do our spirits participate when we sin? (No)
    B. According to 1 John 3:9, are we as righteous and holy now—in our spirits—as we will ever be? (Yes)
5. A. What is the only part of us that has been born of God—our bodies, souls, or spirits? (Our spirits)
    B. Read 1 John 1:8, 10; and 2:1. What parts of our beings can sin? (Our bodies and souls)
    C. Does our performance affect the purity and holiness of our spirits? (No)
6. A. Read John 4:24. Since God is a Spirit, how does He always deal with and relate to us? (Spirit to spirit)
    B. Read 2 Corinthians 5:21. Can we approach God with confidence even though we haven't done everything we should have done in our physical actions? (Yes)
    C. Why? (Because we are righteous in our born-again spirits)

Spirit vs. Flesh

For further study, I recommend my teaching entitled "Who You Are in the Spirit." You need to renew your mind to these truths!

Spirit vs. Flesh
LESSON 12 – DISCIPLESHIP QUESTIONS

1. Ephesians 1:13 describes the Gospel of our salvation as what?

2. What happened when we first believed?

3. According to Ephesians 4:24, what should we do with our new man, which was created in righteousness and true holiness?

4. According to 1 John 4:17, as who is, so are we in this world?

5. First Corinthians 6:17 reveals that we are what unto the Lord?

6. According to James 4:17, is it enough to know the good we ought to do?

7. According to 1 John 3:9, can someone who is born of God sin?

8. What remains in them?

9. According to 1 John 1:8, what are we if we say we have no sin?

10. What is not in those who say they have no sin?

11. According to 1 John 1:10, what do we make God when we say that we have not sinned?

12. What is not in those who say they haven't sinned?

13. Who was being addressed in 1 John 2:1?

14. What was his purpose in writing them?

15. If anyone sins, who is their advocate with the Father?

16. How is this advocate described?

17. In Deuteronomy 21:20, who were the parents of a stubborn and rebellious child instructed to address?

18. In addition to being a glutton and a drunkard, how was this son's stubbornness and rebellion described?

19. According to Romans 6:16, does it matter who we yield ourselves to?

20. What's the fruit of serving sin?

21. What's the fruit of obedience to God?

22. According to 2 Corinthians 5:21, Jesus became sin for us so that we could become what?

23. Had Jesus known sin before He became sin on the cross?

24. We are made the righteousness of God in whom?

25. Since John 4:24 reveals that God is a Spirit, what must we do in spirit and truth?

Spirit vs. Flesh
LESSON 12 – ANSWER KEY

1. The word of truth.

2. We were sealed with the Holy Spirit.

3. Put him on.

4. He—Jesus.

5. Joined.

6. No.

7. No.

8. His seed.

9. Deceived.

10. The truth.

11. A liar.

12. His Word.

13. His—the Apostle John's—little children.

14. That they sin not.

15. Jesus Christ.

16. The righteous.

17. The elders of their city.

18. That he will not obey the parents' voice.

19. Yes.

20. Death.

21. Righteousness (the righteousness already in our born-again spirits manifested in and through our lives).

22. Righteous.

23. No.

24. Him—Jesus Christ.

25. Worship Him.

Spirit vs. Flesh
LESSON 12 – SCRIPTURES

In whom ye also trusted, after that ye heard the word of truth, the gospel of your salvation: in whom also after that ye believed, ye were sealed with that holy Spirit of promise.

EPHESIANS 1:13

And that ye put on the new man, which after God is created in righteousness and true holiness.

EPHESIANS 4:24

Herein is our love made perfect, that we may have boldness in the day of judgment: because as he is, so are we in this world.

1 JOHN 4:17

But he that is joined unto the Lord is one spirit.

1 CORINTHIANS 6:17

Therefore to him that knoweth to do good, and doeth it not, to him it is sin.

JAMES 4:17

Whosoever is born of God doth not commit sin; for his seed remaineth in him: and he cannot sin, because he is born of God.

1 JOHN 3:9

If we say that we have no sin, we deceive ourselves, and the truth is not in us.

1 JOHN 1:8

If we say that we have not sinned, we make him a liar, and his word is not in us.

1 JOHN 1:10

My little children, these things write I unto you, that ye sin not. And if any man sin, we have an advocate with the Father, Jesus Christ the righteous.

1 JOHN 2:1

And they shall say unto the elders of his city, This our son is stubborn and rebellious, he will not obey our voice; he is a glutton, and a drunkard.

DEUTERONOMY 21:20

Know ye not, that to whom ye yield yourselves servants to obey, his servants ye are to whom ye obey; whether of sin unto death, or of obedience unto righteousness?

ROMANS 6:16

For he hath made him to be sin for us, who knew no sin; that we might be made the righteousness of God in him.

2 CORINTHIANS 5:21

God is a Spirit: and they that worship him must worship him in spirit and in truth.

JOHN 4:24

Born Again Perfect
LESSON 13

Jesus made a covenant with us. He died to put His will into effect and then rose again to enforce—probate—it. Now, that's a good deal!

> **By the which will we are sanctified through the offering of the body of Jesus Christ once for all.**
>
> HEBREWS 10:10

The Word says we are sanctified—made holy—through the offering of the Lord Jesus Christ once and for all. This offering wasn't just "once for all people," but "once for all time."

> **And every priest standeth <u>daily</u> ministering and offering <u>oftentimes</u> the same sacrifices, which can never take away sins: But this man [Jesus], after he had offered <u>one sacrifice for sins for ever</u>, sat down on the right hand of God.**
>
> HEBREWS 10:11-12, EMPHASIS AND BRACKETS MINE

Notice the contrast between the way it was done in the Old Testament (**"daily"** and **"oftentimes"**) and the way it's done in the New (**"one sacrifice for sins for ever"**). Jesus made one sacrifice for your sins forever!

Sanctified

> **From henceforth expecting till his enemies be made his footstool. For by one offering he hath perfected for ever them that are sanctified.**
>
> HEBREWS 10:13-14

According to verse 10, you were sanctified through the offering of the body of Jesus Christ once and for all. Verse 14 says that if you were sanctified, you've also been perfected forever. These verses aren't talking about your body or your soul. You won't find this perfection there. This is speaking of the part of you that totally changed the instant you were born again—your spirit.

Your spirit is identical to the Lord Jesus Christ (1 Cor. 6:17). It's sinless and sealed (Eph. 1:13 and 4:24). When you sin in your physical body, that sin opens a door for Satan to come against you with sickness, poverty, and so forth (Rom. 6:16). When you sin with your soul, he'll come in and defile your thinking. Sin will make you spiritually retarded because of the way it affects your ability to think, but it doesn't penetrate your born-again spirit. Your spirit has been sanctified and perfected forever.

> **But ye are come unto mount Sion, and unto the city of the living God, the heavenly Jerusalem, and to an innumerable company of angels, To the general**

assembly and church of the firstborn, which are written in heaven, and to God the Judge of all, and to <u>the spirits of just men made perfect</u>.

HEBREWS 12:22-23, EMPHASIS MINE

Your spirit is the part of you that has been made perfect. It would've been wonderful if God had given a perfect mind that knew all things, but this has yet to come (1 Cor. 13:9-12). In the meantime, you are in the process of renewing your mind to the truth of God's Word. In your spirit, you are sanctified and perfected forever. God has forgiven you of all sin. He's not mad at you, because He sees you Spirit to born-again spirit (1 Sam. 16:7 and John 4:24). Now, God is aware that you have a physical body and a soul that does things wrong, but He looks at you in the spirit. You are His workmanship (Eph. 2:10). If you've accepted Jesus as your Savior, He looks at you and says, "Perfect, holy, pure, and righteous."

The Spirit of Christ

You have all of the benefits and privileges that Jesus has. This is because your spirit was totally changed, not just dusted off or refurbished.

God hath sent forth the Spirit of his Son into your hearts, crying, Abba, Father.

GALATIANS 4:6

The Spirit of Christ is in you.

Now if any man have not the Spirit of Christ, he is none of his.

ROMANS 8:9

If you say "I don't believe that I have the Spirit of Christ," then you need to be born again. If you don't have the Spirit of Christ, then you don't belong to Him. If you are born again, then you have a born-again spirit that is identical to Jesus, because it's His Spirit on the inside of you. You have His faith, His knowledge, His power, and His victory. Everything that's true of Jesus is true of your born-again spirit, which is sealed by the Holy Spirit so you'll never lose it.

God deals with you based on who you are in the spirit.

God Possessed

For I reckon that the sufferings of this present time are not worthy to be compared with the glory which shall be revealed <u>in</u> us.

ROMANS 8:18, EMPHASIS MINE

Notice how this didn't say, "The glory which shall be revealed <u>to</u> us." Most Christians sing, "When we all get to heaven, what a day that'll be." We think, *Heaven will be so wonderful!* And it will because we'll receive glorified bodies that aren't subject to decay, disease, or death. We'll also receive glorified souls that don't struggle with doubt or unbelief anymore. They will know all things. However, the Word says that the sufferings of this present world are not worthy to be compared with the glory that shall be revealed *in* us—not *to* us!

When we stand before God, all of a sudden we'll know all things (1 Cor. 13:12). In an instant, the Lord will straighten out our theology, and we'll understand everything even as we are known. We'll say, "You mean I was forgiven this whole time I went around feeling ungodly and unworthy? You mean I was righteous and holy the entire time I moped around feeling guilty and condemned? I thought You wouldn't do things for me, because I wasn't good enough and I hadn't done this and that." We're going to find out that we had the glory of God on the inside of us. We'll discover that we were as righteous, pure, and holy as Jesus Himself. The same power that raised Christ from the dead was resident inside us the whole time (Eph. 1:18-19). Yet we spent all of our time praying and asking God to send it down and we believed there were demons stopping our prayers from getting to God. That's stupid.

"But, Andrew, that's what happened to Daniel!" No, it's not. First of all, it was God's answer, not Daniel's prayer, that was hindered (Dan. 10:11-14). Second, Daniel didn't have the Lord living on the inside of him like we do today. I don't care what the devil is doing out there—he's not going to block my prayer from getting to God. That's the reason why I bow my head when I pray—He lives within me. I don't need my prayers to get above the ceiling. In fact, I don't need them to get above my nose. He lives right here on the inside of me. I'm God possessed!

Trust the Spiritual Mirror

That the communication of thy faith may become effectual by the acknowledging of every good thing which is in you in Christ Jesus.

PHILEMON 6

You need to start thinking this way and acknowledging the good things in you in Christ!

The average Christian today believes that God can do anything but that He has done nothing. They are asking, "O God, please heal me. Touch me, and pour out Your love in my life." That's an insult to God! He has already done everything He's going to do to heal you (1 Pet. 2:24). He has already poured out His love (Rom. 5:8). When you were born again, He put His Son on the inside of you. You have the fruit of the Spirit—love, joy, peace, patience, and more (Gal. 5:22-23).

Your spirit is always rejoicing, always healthy, always believing, always full of hope, and always exactly like Jesus. The only reason you don't benefit from it is because your flesh is going more by what it feels in the physical realm than what you see in the Word of God. You trust what you see in a mirror more than you trust what you see in the spiritual mirror. You're basing your life on external things—how you feel and what the situation looks like—rather than on the truth of what God's Word says.

Educate Your Brain

In the spirit, you're changed. You're as clean and pure as you'll ever get. One-third of your salvation is over! When you get to heaven, your spirit isn't going to be dusted off. It won't be given some injection that will bring it up to its full potential. Your spirit doesn't grow and mature. Right now, your born-again spirit is as complete, pure, holy, and mature as it will ever get. Maturity in the Christian life isn't trying to grow your spirit up; it's trying to educate your brain to what you already have in your spirit. You're already perfect!

God loves you not because of what *you* do, but because of what *He* did. That's how He can love you even though you've messed up and aren't yet—in the physical and soulish realms—what you're supposed to be. He gave you an eternal redemption and an eternal inheritance. He has sanctified and perfected you forever. Your spirit is perfect. Right now, you can enter into the presence of God. Right now you have the same rights and privileges that Jesus has because the Spirit of the Lord Jesus Christ lives within you. The only thing hindering you from experiencing all of this is that you don't know what you have.

We've fallen for these thoughts that say, "Every time you sin, God turns His back on you. The Lord is grieved and upset with your sin." No! Jesus paid for all of our sins. He anticipated everything we've ever done—and will do—and He's already paid for all of them. Now, that's not to encourage us to live in sin. If we do, Satan will take advantage of every time we sin. God has already forgiven it, but the devil will walk through that open door into our lives and make us pay for it. Sin will take us further than we want to go, cost more than we want to pay, and keep us longer than we want to stay. We don't want to live in sin. We all fail, but the Lord never turns His back on us.

If you think that God turns away from you, won't answer your prayers, doesn't love you, or isn't pleased because you haven't been studying the Word as much as you once did, Satan will take that kind of thinking and use it to depress and discourage you. He'll use it to keep you from trusting and believing in the presence and power of God. This is where Satan is beating us. It all centers around sin.

The Devil's Only Inroad

Sin is the only inroad the devil has ever had on us. He's not really telling you, "Oh, God can't do that. He can't do miracles"; he's saying, "Sure, God can do it. But you're a sinner. You don't deserve it. He won't do it for you!"

You probably have more faith in my prayers than you do in your own because you see me on television and hear me on the radio. Therefore, you think, *This guy has it all together!* The truth is, if you knew me as well as you know yourself, you wouldn't have any more faith in my prayers than your own. It takes faith for me to believe that God will answer my prayers, because I know me! This is where you're missing it. You're sin conscious and still thinking, *I have to get over these things before the Lord will answer my prayers.*

A woman once asked me to pray with her to get free from smoking. She was ashamed and crying. I said, "You don't go to hell for smoking, even though you smell like you've been there. God isn't mad at you. I don't think it's a good testimony, and it's definitely not good for you. If you don't get free, it makes it hard for you to tell someone else that God can set them free. That's not good." Now, I'm not advocating smoking, and I don't know whether this lady got free or not, but I do know she got free from condemnation.

I received a real education the first time I left the United States and went to Europe. I was raised in a strict denominational home, where we didn't dip, cuss, or chew, or go with those who do. We didn't mow the lawn or do dishes on Sunday. We observed Sunday as the Sabbath, and those things were considered work. We made a real effort to live holy.

My first visit to Austria really played with my denominational mind. There were about two hundred people sitting around tables in this church—and they were serving them beer! Each person received a whole pitcher's worth. They served them all free beer for the entire time I spoke. It was one of the few times nobody minded how long I went. They would have been fine if I had gone on all night long. My little denominational mind was preaching away while all these people were drinking and praising God.

God Isn't Condemning Us

The Christians drank beer in Austria, but they believed that if you drank or even tasted coffee, you went straight to hell. They couldn't believe that a Christian would drink coffee. However, once we crossed the border into Hungary, the Hungarian believers drank both coffee and beer. But they believed that if you smoked a cigarette, you would go directly to hell.

Through this, I began to realize some things. God doesn't treat Americans any different than Austrians or Hungarians. After thinking about it, I realized that some of this is just man's interpretation. However, I'm not saying we should drink or smoke.

> **All things are lawful unto me, but all things are not expedient [helpful]: all things are lawful for me, but I will not be brought under the power of any.**
> 1 CORINTHIANS 6:12, BRACKETS MINE

These things are damaging to our health, and it's not a good witness. But we've condemned ourselves when God isn't condemning us.

Born Again Perfect
LESSON 13 – OUTLINE

I. Jesus died to put His will into effect, and then rose again to enforce—probate—it.

> **By the which will we are sanctified through the offering of the body of Jesus Christ once for all.**
>
> HEBREWS 10:10

A. The Word says we are sanctified—made holy—through the offering of the Lord Jesus Christ once for all.

> **And every priest standeth <u>daily</u> ministering and offering <u>oftentimes</u> the same sacrifices, which can never take away sins: But this man [Jesus], after he had offered <u>one sacrifice for sins for ever</u>, sat down on the right hand of God.**
>
> HEBREWS 10:11-12, EMPHASIS AND BRACKETS MINE

B. Notice the contrast between the way it was done in the Old Testament ("daily" and "oftentimes") and the way it's done in the New ("one sacrifice for sins for ever").

> **From henceforth expecting till his enemies be made his footstool. For by one offering he hath perfected for ever them that are sanctified.**
>
> HEBREWS 10:13-14

C. This is speaking of the part of you that totally changed the instant you were born again—your spirit.

II. Your spirit is identical to the Lord Jesus Christ (1 Cor. 6:17).

A. Your spirit has been sanctified and perfected forever.

> **But ye are come unto mount Sion, and unto the city of the living God, the heavenly Jerusalem, and to an innumerable company of angels, To the general assembly and church of the firstborn, which are written in heaven, and to God the Judge of all, and to <u>the spirits of just men made perfect</u>.**
>
> HEBREWS 12:22-23, EMPHASIS MINE

B. Now, God is aware that you have a physical body and a soul that does things wrong, but He looks at you in the spirit.

C. You are His workmanship (Eph. 2:10).

D. You have all of the benefits and privileges that Jesus has.

> **God hath sent forth the Spirit of his Son into your hearts, crying, Abba, Father.**
>
> GALATIANS 4:6

E. The Spirit of Christ is in you.

Now if any man have not the Spirit of Christ, he is none of his.
ROMANS 8:9

III. God deals with you based on who you are in the spirit.

A. When we stand before God, all of a sudden we'll know all things (1 Cor. 13:9-12).

For I reckon that the sufferings of this present time are not worthy to be compared with the glory which shall be revealed <u>in</u> us.
ROMANS 8:18, EMPHASIS MINE

B. In an instant, the Lord will straighten out our theology, and we'll understand everything even as we are known.

IV. You need to start thinking this way and acknowledging the good things in you in Christ!

That the communication of thy faith may become effectual by the acknowledging of every good thing which is in you in Christ Jesus.
PHILEMON 6

A. When you were born again, God put His Son on the inside of you.

B. You have the fruit of the Spirit—love, joy, peace, patience, and more (Gal. 5:22-23).

C. Your spirit is always rejoicing, always healthy, always believing, always full of hope, and always exactly like Jesus is.

D. The only reason you don't benefit from it is because your flesh is going more by what it feels in the physical realm than what you see in the Word of God.

E. Maturity in the Christian life isn't trying to grow your spirit up; it's trying to educate your brain to what you already have in your spirit.

V. We all fail, but the Lord never turns His back on us.

A. Sin is the only inroad the devil has ever had on us.

B. You're sin conscious and still thinking, *I have to get over these things before the Lord will answer my prayers.*

All things are lawful unto me, but all things are not expedient [helpful]: all things are lawful for me, but I will not be brought under the power of any.
1 CORINTHIANS 6:12, BRACKETS MINE

C. We've condemned ourselves when God isn't condemning us.

Born Again Perfect
LESSON 13 – TEACHER'S GUIDE

1. Jesus died to put His will into effect, and then rose again to enforce—probate—it (Heb. 10:10). The Word says we are sanctified—made holy—through the offering of the Lord Jesus Christ once and for all (Heb. 10:11-14). Notice the contrast between the way it was done in the Old Testament (**"daily"** and **"oftentimes"**) and the way it's done in the New (**"one sacrifice for sins for ever"**). Hebrews 10:14 is speaking of the part of us that totally changed the instant we were born again—our spirits.

2. Our spirits are identical to the Lord Jesus Christ (1 Cor. 6:17). Our spirits have been sanctified and perfected forever (Heb. 12:22-23). Now, God is aware that we have physical bodies and souls that do things wrong, but He looks at us in the spirit. We are His workmanship (Eph. 2:10). We have all of the benefits and privileges that Jesus has (Gal. 4:6). The Spirit of Christ is in us (Rom. 8:9).

3. God deals with us based on who we are in the spirit. When we stand before God, all of a sudden we'll know all things (Rom. 8:18 and 1 Cor. 13:9-12). In an instant, the Lord will straighten out our theology, and we'll understand everything even as we are known.

1. A. Read Hebrews 10:10-14. How does the Word say we are sanctified—made holy? (Through the offering of the Lord Jesus Christ once and for all)
   B. What part of us totally changed the instant we were born again? (Our spirits)
2. A. Read Romans 8:9, 1 Corinthians 6:17, Galatians 4:6, Ephesians 2:10, and Hebrews 12:22-23. How does God look at us? (In the spirit)
   B. What benefits and privileges do we now have? (All that Jesus has)
3. A. How does God deal with us? (Based on who we are in the spirit)
   B. Read Romans 8:18 and 1 Corinthians 13:9-12. What will happen when we stand before God? (All of a sudden we'll know all things)

4.   We need to start thinking this way and acknowledging the good things in us in Christ (Philem. 6). When we were born again, God put His Son on the inside of us. We have the fruit of the Spirit—love, joy, peace, patience, and more (Gal. 5:22-23). Our spirits are always rejoicing, always healthy, always believing, always full of hope, and always exactly like Jesus is. The only reason we don't benefit from it is because our flesh is going more by what it feels in the physical realm than what we see in the Word of God. Maturity in the Christian life isn't trying to grow our spirits up; it's trying to educate our brains to what we already have in our spirits.

5.   We all fail, but the Lord never turns His back on us. Sin is the only inroad the devil has ever had on us. We're sin conscious and still thinking, *I have to get over these things before the Lord will answer my prayers.* We've condemned ourselves when God isn't condemning us (1 Cor. 6:12).

4. A. Read Philemon 6 and Galatians 5:22-23. What do we need to start acknowledging? (The good things in us in Christ)
   B. Is maturity in the Christian life trying to grow our spirits up? (No, it's trying to educate our brains to what we already have in our spirits)
5. A. What is the only inroad the devil has ever had on us? (Sin)
   B. Read 1 Corinthians 6:12. Is it possible to condemn ourselves when God isn't condemning us? (Yes)

Born Again Perfect

My teachings entitled *Spirit, Soul & Body* and *You've Already Got It!* go into much more detail. These are foundational revelations that God has shown me from His Word. I can't imagine how anyone could truly live a victorious Christian life without understanding these basic truths.

Born Again Perfect
LESSON 13 – DISCIPLESHIP QUESTIONS

1. According to Hebrews 10:10-14, how are we sanctified?

2. After Jesus offered one sacrifice for sins forever, what did He do?

3. For by one offering, He has perfected whom forever?

4. According to 1 Corinthians 6:17, who is one spirit with the Lord?

5. Ephesians 4:24 reveals that our new man is created in righteousness and what?

6. According to Ephesians 1:13, what happened immediately after we believed?

7. Romans 6:16 shows us that we are servants to whom?

8. According to Hebrews 12:22-23, what part of just men have been made perfect?

9. In 1 Corinthians 13:9-12, what happens when that which is perfect is come?

10. How do we see now?

11. How will we see then?

12. We know in part now, but then we shall know how?

13. According to 1 Samuel 16:7, does God look at our inner man or our outer man?

14. What does John 4:24 reveal that God is?

15. According to Ephesians 2:10, whose workmanship are we?

16. What were we created in Christ Jesus unto?

17. When was it that God ordained for us to walk in them?

18. What does Galatians 4:6 say that we are?

19. Whom has God sent forth into our hearts?

20. What does He cry to God?

21. If the Spirit of God dwells in us, what does Romans 8:9 reveal that we are?

22. What are we not?

23. People without _____ are none of His.

24. According to Romans 8:18, _____ are not worthy to be compared.

25. Compared with the glory that shall be revealed _____ us.
    A. To.
    B. In.
    C. For.
    D. Above.

26. According to Ephesians 1:18-19, what is being enlightened?

27. What should we know?
    A. The exceeding greatness of His power to us-ward who believe.
    B. The riches of the glory of his inheritance in the saints.
    C. The hope of His calling.
    D. All of the above.
    E. None of the above.

28. In Daniel 10:11-14, what did the angel say when he saw Daniel trembling?

29. When was Daniel's prayer heard and the answer sent by God?

30. How many days had this answer been withstood and delayed?

31. According to Philemon 6, how does the communication of our faith become effective?

32. By whose stripes does 1 Peter 2:24 reveal that we were healed?

33. According to Romans 5:8, who did God commend His love toward?

34. When did He do this?

35. How did He do this?

36. Which of the following does Galatians 5:22-23 include as part of the fruit of the Spirit?
    A. Longsuffering.
    B. Temperance.
    C. Joy.
    D. Love.
    E. Meekness.
    F. Goodness.
    G. Peace.
    H. Faith.
    I. Gentleness.
    J. All of the above.

37. Is there any law against such fruit?

38. According to 1 Corinthians 6:12, what did the Apostle Paul say is lawful unto us?

39. But they are not all what?

40. Was Paul brought under the power of anything?

Born Again Perfect
LESSON 13 – ANSWER KEY

1. Through the offering of the body of Jesus Christ.

2. He sat down on the right hand of God.

3. Them that are sanctified.

4. They who are joined to Him.

5. True holiness.

6. We were sealed with the Holy Spirit.

7. To whom we yield ourselves to obey.

8. Their spirits.

9. Then that which is in part shall be done away.

10. Through a glass, darkly.

11. Face to face.

12. Even as also we are known.

13. Inner man (heart).

14. A Spirit.

15. God's.

16. Good works.

17. Before.

18. Sons.

19. The Spirit of His Son.

20. Abba, Father.

21. In the Spirit.

22. In the flesh.

23. The Spirit of Christ.

24. The sufferings of this present time.

25. B. In.

26. The eyes of our understanding.

27. A. The exceeding greatness of His power to us-ward who believe.
    B. The riches of the glory of his inheritance in the saints.
    C. The hope of His calling.
    D. All of the above.

28. Fear not.

29. The first day.

30. Twenty-one days.

31. By the acknowledging of every good thing which is in us in Christ Jesus.

32. His—Jesus'.

33. Us.

34. While we were yet sinners.

35. Christ died for us.

36. A. Longsuffering.
    B. Temperance.
    C. Joy.
    D. Love.
    E. Meekness.
    F. Goodness.
    G. Peace.
    H. Faith.
    I. Gentleness.
    J. All of the above.

37. No.

38. All things.

39. Expedient (helpful).

40. No.

Born Again Perfect
LESSON 13 – SCRIPTURES

By the which will we are sanctified through the offering of the body of Jesus Christ once for all. And every priest standeth daily ministering and offering oftentimes the same sacrifices, which can never take away sins: But this man, after he had offered one sacrifice for sins for ever, sat down on the right hand of God; From henceforth expecting till his enemies be made his footstool. For by one offering he hath perfected for ever them that are sanctified.

HEBREWS 10:10-14

But he that is joined unto the Lord is one spirit.

1 CORINTHIANS 6:17

And that ye put on the new man, which after God is created in righteousness and true holiness.

EPHESIANS 4:24

In whom ye also trusted, after that ye heard the word of truth, the gospel of your salvation: in whom also after that ye believed, ye were sealed with that holy Spirit of promise.

EPHESIANS 1:13

Know ye not, that to whom ye yield yourselves servants to obey, his servants ye are to whom ye obey; whether of sin unto death, or of obedience unto righteousness?

ROMANS 6:16

But ye are come unto mount Sion, and unto the city of the living God, the heavenly Jerusalem, and to an innumerable company of angels, To the general assembly and church of the firstborn, which are written in heaven, and to God the Judge of all, and to the spirits of just men made perfect.

HEBREWS 12:22-23

For we know in part, and we prophesy in part. But when that which is perfect is come, then that which is in part shall be done away. When I was a child, I spake as a child, I understood as a child, I thought as a child: but when I became a man, I put away childish things. For now we see through a glass, darkly; but then face to face: now I know in part; but then shall I know even as also I am known.

1 CORINTHIANS 13:9-12

But the LORD said unto Samuel, Look not on his countenance, or on the height of his stature; because I have refused him: for the LORD seeth not as man seeth; for man looketh on the outward appearance, but the LORD looketh on the heart.

1 SAMUEL 16:7

God is a Spirit: and they that worship him must worship him in spirit and in truth.

JOHN 4:24

For we are his workmanship, created in Christ Jesus unto good works, which God hath before ordained that we should walk in them.

EPHESIANS 2:10

And because ye are sons, God hath sent forth the Spirit of his Son into your hearts, crying, Abba, Father.

GALATIANS 4:6

But ye are not in the flesh, but in the Spirit, if so be that the Spirit of God dwell in you. Now if any man have not the Spirit of Christ, he is none of his.

ROMANS 8:9

For I reckon that the sufferings of this present time are not worthy to be compared with the glory which shall be revealed in us.

ROMANS 8:18

The eyes of your understanding being enlightened; that ye may know what is the hope of his calling, and what the riches of the glory of his inheritance in the saints, And what is the exceeding greatness of his power to us-ward who believe, according to the working of his mighty power.

EPHESIANS 1:18-19

And he said unto me, O Daniel, a man greatly beloved, understand the words that I speak unto thee, and stand upright: for unto thee am I now sent. And when he had spoken this word unto me, I stood trembling. Then said he unto me, Fear not, Daniel: for from the first day that thou didst set thine heart to understand, and to chasten thyself before thy God, thy words were heard, and I am come for thy words. But the prince of the kingdom of Persia withstood me one and twenty days: but, lo, Michael, one of the chief princes, came to help me; and I remained there with the kings of Persia. Now I am come to make thee understand what shall befall thy people in the latter days: for yet the vision is for many days.

DANIEL 10:11-14

That the communication of thy faith may become effectual by the acknowledging of every good thing which is in you in Christ Jesus.

PHILEMON 6

Who his own self bare our sins in his own body on the tree, that we, being dead to sins, should live unto righteousness: by whose stripes ye were healed.

1 PETER 2:24

But God commendeth his love toward us, in that, while we were yet sinners, Christ died for us.

ROMANS 5:8

But the fruit of the Spirit is love, joy, peace, longsuffering, gentleness, goodness, faith, Meekness, temperance: against such there is no law.

GALATIANS 5:22-23

All things are lawful unto me, but all things are not expedient: all things are lawful for me, but I will not be brought under the power of any.

1 CORINTHIANS 6:12

Steady and Secure
LESSON 14

For if our heart condemn us, God is greater than our heart, and knoweth all things.

1 John 3:20

You can feel condemned when God isn't the one condemning you. Many of us say, "God's been on my case beating me up over this sin." No, that's just your religion. The first time I ever skipped a Wednesday night church service was because of my girlfriend. She invited me over to her house. I felt bad about it but went anyway. Once I arrived, there were two other couples already there—dancing! It was bad enough to skip out on church for the first time in my life, but they were *dancing*. I felt so condemned that I thought the Lord was going to kill me. As a ninth grader, I wasn't driving yet, so I called my older brother and asked him to come and get me. I was at church that night before it was over, on my knees at the altar, and begging forgiveness so God wouldn't strike me dead. I felt defiled for weeks! But God wasn't the one condemning me; it was my own religious thinking.

Many Christians can't even blame the devil for all the condemnation they suffer. All he did was teach them something, and they've been doing such a good job ever since, he's been on vacation.

The devil doesn't have to condemn you; you're doing a bang-up job on your own! But God really isn't mad at you. He isn't even in a bad mood. He loves you. He looks at you in the spirit and says, "You're awesome." God sees your potential. He sees His own glory that He's placed on the inside of you.

Stupid Prayers

If it's possible for God to be confused, I believe He would be confused listening to so many of our stupid prayers. "O Lord, take not Your Holy Spirit from me." God's thinking, *Somewhere in the Book, I promised never to leave them nor forsake them*. "O Father, please be with us tonight as we meet." What a stupid prayer! In light of that promise—and the one in Matthew 18:20—how could He answer that? "O God, come visit us!" Is the Lord a visitor, or a permanent resident? Visitors come only for a brief while, and then they're expected to leave. If you're a visitor, you leave after a day or a week, but you don't move in. What a terrible concept! God is with us all the time (Matt. 28:20). He never leaves us nor forsakes us (Heb.13:5).

We pray stupid prayers because we don't understand that what we're asking for is already done. In our spirits, we have all of God we can get. We don't need Him to "stretch forth His hand and touch us." He's already put Himself on the inside of us. The same power that raised Christ from the dead already indwells us (Rom. 8:11 and Eph. 1:19-20). We don't need more of God; we just need to find out what we have. Then we need to acknowledge the good things that are in us in Christ Jesus, and our faith will start working (Philem. 6).

213

God has already done everything in the death, burial, and resurrection of the Lord Jesus Christ. You already have everything you're looking and praying for. It's already happened. You're begging God "Oh, please forgive me of this sin" when the truth is that He's already forgiven you before you even ask.

"Are you saying that you don't have to repent?" The word *repent* means "to turn and go the other way." Yes, you need to repent—turn and go the other way—because if you persist in sin, Satan will eat your lunch and pop the bag. You don't need to give the Enemy that kind of inroad into your life. It's stupid to live in sin. So yes, repent and turn from it, but for what purpose? Is it so God will accept you? Is it so you won't go to hell because you lose your salvation every time you sin? No. If you believe that, how in the world are you ever going to grow and progress? You don't go a day without sinning, meaning you're failing to be everything you should be. What would it be like if a little child never grew but every day had to be born all over again? That child would never progress in life.

You don't have to get born again, again. There is no such thing as being born again, again. You don't lose your salvation every time you sin. God doesn't fall off His throne because you messed up. He knew you were going sin and has already dealt with it.

"I Still Love You"

My sister is a Christian. She's seen people raised from the dead, and she loves God with all her heart. Her daughter was very rebellious as a teenager. She really knew how to push people's "hot buttons." One night, my sister was fixing supper in preparation for the dinner guest her husband, a college professor, was bringing home. My niece was in the kitchen smarting off and agitating my sister. She just kept herself busy getting ready. Finally, my niece said something that pushed her over the edge, and she hauled off and hit her—knocked her flat on her back! As soon as she did that, my born-again, Spirit-filled sister dropped what she was doing, ran upstairs, and threw herself across her bed, saying, "God, You have to help me. If I start crying, I'm not going to come out of here until the morning. I need to get supper ready and pull things together. Lord, I need a word. Help!"

God answered her and said, "When you were eight years old and asked Me to save you, I knew you were going to do this. I've already forgiven it. It's okay. I still love you." That allowed my sister to deal with it and not let sin have dominion over her. She was able to get up and go back downstairs. It didn't make her say "Hey, I'm forgiven" and then go beat her daughter up. She went down, asked her daughter's forgiveness, and then got on with the evening. My sister was able to go on because she didn't feel like it was something brand new that had just offended the Lord and that He had to be appeased. He already knew about it and had forgiven her.

It's totally unnecessary for you to agonize over the things you've done. You don't have to feel like you just can't repent of it until you suffer for a while and do penance. "God can't love me. I really blew it this time!" God doesn't look at it that way. He's already paid for your sins. He was satisfied when He saw Jesus suffer for your sins. Every sin you've ever committed, Jesus paid for it. For your sin, God the Father punished, forsook, and actually released anger and rejection toward His Son. He's not going to make you pay for what His Son has already paid for. There's nothing left to pay! You can't add anything to what Jesus has done. There's nothing more you can do. Your wallowing on the ground isn't going to make God love you any more.

God loves you not because of your goodness but because of Christ's goodness and what He did for you. You need to change the basis of your relationship with God from being on your own goodness and performance to relating to God based on faith in what Jesus did for you. When you do that, you'll find that Jesus is the same yesterday, today, and forever (Heb. 13:8). He never changes. Therefore, your relationship will become steady and secure. You won't have highs and lows. You won't go through the pit-and-valley feeling like God has forsaken you.

Raised from the Dead

Since the Lord showed me this over thirty-five years ago, I haven't been depressed a single time. Now, I've had depressing things happen, and I've been tempted to be depressed, but I know God loves me. In my spirit, there is love, joy, peace, patience, and all the fruit of the Spirit (Gal. 5:22-23). I've been able to refuse and reject those depressing things and live a happy life. I'm steady and secure.

Even when I was told that my son had died, I was tempted to get into pity, fear, hurt, pain, and grief the same as anybody else would. But I don't like feeling that way! I just decided, "I'm not going to grieve over this. I am not going to be upset. Instead of giving in to sorrow, I'm just going to start praising and worshiping God." As soon as I did, faith rose up on the inside. I told Jamie, "Watch this. This is going to be some awesome miracle!" After our son had been dead for almost five hours, God raised him up. He had turned black, was toe tagged, and lying in the hospital cooler, but now he's alive and well. Praise the Lord!

I discovered that I'm a new person in Christ, and I'm not going to let what I feel in my flesh dominate me. People who are depressed and discouraged are people living in the flesh, looking at the physical realm, and people who don't know who they are in Christ. If you know who you are in Christ and that your sins have been forgiven, the worst thing that could happen is you die and go directly into the presence of God. You'll walk on streets of pure gold and inherit the mansion you'll live in for the rest of eternity. You'll get to personally meet the one who has loved you and died for you. What a great deal! You have nothing to be discouraged over. If the doctor tells you you're going to die, just kiss him and say, "Awesome! 'For to me to live is Christ, and to die is gain'!" (Phil. 1:21.)

"Aw, that's just some preacher stuff. You can't live that way!" I do, and you can too. God is awesome. He's been good to us, and it's only our own religious bondage that's keeping us from appreciating and receiving it.

Don't Be Destroyed

My people are destroyed for lack of knowledge.

HOSEA 4:6

Take these truths I'm sharing and meditate on them. God wants to use them in your life in a mighty way.

You don't have to fluctuate between a strong and weak relationship with God. If you would get into Jesus and start basing your life on what He has done and not letting Satan put you back under the sin you've been redeemed from, nothing—absolutely nothing—could destroy you. Your faith would go through the roof!

Steady and Secure
LESSON 14 – OUTLINE

I. You can feel condemned when God isn't the one condemning you.

> **For if our heart condemn us, God is greater than our heart, and knoweth all things.**
>
> 1 JOHN 3:20

    A. It was my own religious thinking.

    B. Many Christians can't even blame the devil for all the condemnation they suffer.

    C. All he did was teach them something, and they've been doing such a good job ever since, he's been on vacation.

II. We pray stupid prayers because we don't understand that what we're asking for is already done.

    A. In your spirit, you have all of God you can get (Matt. 28:20 and Heb. 13:5).

    B. The same power that raised Christ from the dead already indwells you (Rom. 8:11 and Eph. 1:19-20).

    C. You just need to find out what you have.

    D. Then acknowledge the good things that are in you in Christ Jesus, and your faith will start working (Philem. 6).

    E. God has already done everything in the death, burial, and resurrection of the Lord Jesus Christ.

III. *Repent* means "to turn and go the other way."

    A. Yes, you need to repent—turn and go the other way—because if you persist in sin, Satan will eat your lunch and pop the bag.

    B. You don't need to give the Enemy that kind of inroad into your life.

    C. You don't lose your salvation every time you sin.

    D. God knew you were going to sin and has already dealt with it.

    E. He's not going to make you pay for what His Son has already paid for.

    F. You can't add anything to what Jesus has done.

IV. God loves you not because of your goodness but because of Christ's goodness and what He did for you.

    A. You need to change the basis of your relationship with God from being on your own goodness and performance to relating to God based on faith in what Jesus did for you.

    B. When you do that, you'll find that Jesus is the same yesterday, today, and forever (Heb. 13:8).

    C. Therefore, your relationship will become steady and secure.

V. God has been good to us, and it's only our own religious bondage that is keeping us from appreciating and receiving it.

> **My people are destroyed for lack of knowledge.**
>
> Hosea 4:6

    A. You don't have to fluctuate between a strong and weak relationship with God.

    B. If you would get into Jesus and start basing your life on what He has done and not letting Satan put you back under the sin you've been redeemed from, nothing—absolutely nothing—could destroy you.

Steady and Secure
LESSON 14 – TEACHER'S GUIDE

1. We can feel condemned when God isn't the one condemning us (1 John 3:20). It was our own religious thinking. Many Christians can't even blame the devil for all the condemnation they suffer. All he did was teach them something, and they've been doing such a good job ever since, he's been on vacation.

2. We pray stupid prayers because we don't understand that what we're asking for is already done. In our spirits, we have all of God we can get (Matt. 28:20 and Heb. 13:5). The same power that raised Christ from the dead already indwells us (Rom. 8:11 and Eph. 1:19-20). We just need to find out what we have. Then we need to acknowledge the good things that are in us in Christ Jesus, and our faith will start working (Philem. 6). God has already done everything in the death, burial, and resurrection of the Lord Jesus Christ.

3. *Repent* means "to turn and go the other way." Yes, we need to repent—turn and go the other way—because if we persist in sin, Satan will eat our lunches and pop the bags. We don't need to give the Enemy that kind of inroad into our lives. We don't lose our salvation every time we sin. God knew you were going to sin and has already dealt with it. He's not going to make us pay for what His Son has already paid for. We can't add anything to what Jesus has done.

1. A. According to 1 John 3:20, can we feel condemned when God isn't the one condemning us? (Yes)
   B. What's condemning us? (Our own religious thinking)
2. A. Read Matthew 28:20, Hebrews 13:5, Romans 8:11, Ephesians 1:19-20, and Philemon 6. Why do we pray stupid prayers? (Because we don't understand that God has already done everything in the death, burial, and resurrection of the Lord Jesus Christ)
   B. What happens when we acknowledge the good things that are in us in Christ Jesus? (Our faith starts working)
3. A. What does *repent* mean? ("To turn and go the other way")
   B. Why don't we lose our salvation every time we sin? (Because God knew we were going to sin and has already dealt with it)

4.   God loves us not because of our goodness but because of Christ's goodness and what He did for us. We need to change the basis of our relationship with God from being our on own goodness and performance to relating to God based on faith in what Jesus did for us. When we do that, we'll find that Jesus is the same yesterday, today, and forever (Heb. 13:8). Therefore, our relationship will become steady and secure.

5.   God has been good to us, and it's only our own religious bondage that is keeping us from appreciating and receiving it (Hos. 4:6). We don't have to fluctuate between a strong and weak relationship with God. If we would get into Jesus and start basing our lives on what He has done and not letting Satan put us back under the sin we've been redeemed from, nothing—absolutely nothing—could destroy us.

4. A. From what to what do we need to change the basis of our relationship with God? (From our own goodness and performance to relating to God based on faith in what Jesus did for us)
   B. Read Hebrews 13:8. What happens when we base our relationship with God on faith in what Jesus did for us? (Our relationship with Him will become steady and secure)
5. A. Read Hosea 4:6. What is it that has been keeping us from appreciating and receiving God's goodness? (Our own religious bondage)
   B. What must we do to get to the place where nothing—absolutely nothing—could destroy us? (We must get into Jesus and start basing our life on what He has done and not letting Satan put us back under the sin we've been redeemed from)

Steady and Secure
LESSON 14 – DISCIPLESHIP QUESTIONS

1. According to 1 John 3:20, what is it that condemns us?

2. Who is greater than that?

3. What does He know?

4. According to Matthew 18:20, how should we gather?

5. What minimum number must gather before He's there in the midst of us?

6. According to Matthew 28:20, what should be taught for disciples to observe?

7. Who is with us?

8. For how long?

9. According to Hebrews 13:5, what can we be since Jesus will never leave us nor forsake us?

10. Romans 8:11 reveals that what Spirit lives in us?

11. What shall He also do to our mortal bodies?

12. How?

13. According to Ephesians 1:19-20, the exceeding greatness of His power is toward us who what?

14. This same power raised whom from the dead?

15. This same power set Him where?

16. According to Philemon 6, what happens when we acknowledge the good things in us in Christ?

17. According to Hebrews 13:8, who is the same yesterday, today, and forever?

18. The love, joy, peace, longsuffering, gentleness, goodness, faith, meekness, and temperance listed in Galatians 5:22-23 are all part of what?

19. Fill in the blanks from Philippians 1:21. For to me to live is _____, and to die is _____.
    A. Christ, gain.
    B. Gain, loss.
    C. Gain, Christ.
    D. Christ, loss.

20. According to Hosea 4:6, why are God's people destroyed?

221

Steady and Secure
LESSON 14 – ANSWER KEY

1. Our hearts.

2. God.

3. All things.

4. In Jesus' name.

5. Two or three.

6. All things whatsoever Jesus has commanded us.

7. Jesus.

8. Always, even unto the end of the world.

9. Without covetousness and content.

10. The Spirit of Him that raised Jesus from the dead.

11. Quicken them (give life to them).

12. By His Spirit that dwells in us.

13. Believe.

14. Christ.

15. At God's own right hand in the heavenly places.

16. Our faith becomes effective.

17. Jesus Christ.

18. The fruit of the Spirit.

19. A. Christ, gain.

20. For lack of knowledge.

Steady and Secure
LESSON 14 – SCRIPTURES

For if our heart condemn us, God is greater than our heart, and knoweth all things.

1 John 3:20

For where two or three are gathered together in my name, there am I in the midst of them.

Matthew 18:20

Teaching them to observe all things whatsoever I have commanded you: and, lo, I am with you alway, even unto the end of the world. Amen.

Matthew 28:20

Let your conversation be without covetousness; and be content with such things as ye have: for he hath said, I will never leave thee, nor forsake thee.

Hebrews 13:5

But if the Spirit of him that raised up Jesus from the dead dwell in you, he that raised up Christ from the dead shall also quicken your mortal bodies by his Spirit that dwelleth in you.

Romans 8:11

And what is the exceeding greatness of his power to us-ward who believe, according to the working of his mighty power, Which he wrought in Christ, when he raised him from the dead, and set him at his own right hand in the heavenly places.

Ephesians 1:19-20

That the communication of thy faith may become effectual by the acknowledging of every good thing which is in you in Christ Jesus.

Philemon 6

Jesus Christ the same yesterday, and to day, and for ever.

Hebrews 13:8

But the fruit of the Spirit is love, joy, peace, longsuffering, gentleness, goodness, faith, Meekness, temperance: against such there is no law.

Galatians 5:22-23

For to me to live is Christ, and to die is gain.

Philippians 1:21

My people are destroyed for lack of knowledge: because thou hast rejected knowledge, I will also reject thee, that thou shalt be no priest to me: seeing thou hast forgotten the law of thy God, I will also forget thy children.

Hosea 4:6

What about 1 John 1:9?
LESSON 15

You may be wondering, *If our born-again spirits are sanctified and perfected forever (Heb. 10:10, 14; and 12:23), then why confess our sins? If God is a Spirit and deals with us based on who we are in the spirit (John 4:24), what about 1 John 1:9?*

> **If we confess our sins, he is faithful and just to forgive us our sins, and to cleanse us from all unrighteousness.**
>
> 1 JOHN 1:9

Before I answer those questions, let me make some statements.

First John 1:9 is the only scripture in the New Testament I'm aware of where we are told that if we confess our sins, God will forgive us. There are lots of New Testament scriptures that speak of our sins already being forgiven. We've looked at many of those verses in this book. But this is the only New Testament scripture I know of that makes God's forgiveness of our sins conditional on us confessing them. That is a major point.

In Matthew 18:16, Jesus referred to Deuteronomy 17:6 and 19:15, which speak of every truth being established in the mouth of two or three witnesses. This should be the minimum number of scriptures to establish any point of doctrine. Yet the belief that we won't be forgiven if we don't confess our sins is a major doctrine of the church, and it only has one supporting verse in New Testament scriptures.

Jesus' Blood

Having to repent and ask forgiveness before the Lord forgives our sins is an Old Testament concept. Scriptures such as Leviticus 26:40-42; 1 Kings 8:47; 2 Chronicles 6:37-38, 7:14; Nehemiah 1:6, 9:2; and many others make this a condition of receiving forgiveness. When John the Baptist came preaching in the wilderness, he was still a preacher under the Old Covenant (Luke 16:16). He was announcing the coming of the kingdom of God, but the new birth and all the "in Christ" realities didn't come into being until after the resurrection of Jesus. Therefore, John preached the baptism of repentance *for* the remission of sins (Mark 1:4 and Luke 3:3). But Jesus said,

> **For this is my blood of the new testament, which is shed for many for the remission of sins.**
>
> MATTHEW 26:28

Under the New Covenant, remission of our sins comes through faith in the atoning sacrifice of Jesus' blood (Rom. 3:25, Eph. 1:7, Col. 1:14, and Heb. 9:22). It is no longer the turning from our sins that saves us, but the turning to Christ in faith in what He did for us. In Acts 16:30, the

Philippian jailer asked Paul what he needed to do to be saved. Paul didn't ask him what he had done to see what measures he needed to take. It didn't matter what he had done. It was all paid for (John 16:8-9 and 1 John 2:2). All of his sins—past, present, and even future ones—were already forgiven. It was simply a matter of whether he would accept what Jesus had already done for him. So Paul answered:

> **Believe on the Lord Jesus Christ, and thou shalt be saved.**
>
> Acts 16:31

Faith in Christ

In the New Covenant, we confess our faith in Christ—not our sins—in order to receive the salvation Jesus has already provided. Romans 10:9-10 clearly expresses this truth, saying:

> **That if thou shalt confess with thy mouth the Lord Jesus, and shalt believe in thine heart that God hath raised him from the dead, thou shalt be saved. For with the heart man believeth unto righteousness; and with the mouth confession is made unto salvation.**

I am not saying repentance isn't a New Testament doctrine. There are many New Testament scriptures that promote repentance (Acts 20:21, 26:20; Rom. 2:4; and 2 Cor. 7:10). There's even one that links repentance and remission of sins together.

> **And that repentance and remission of sins should be preached in his name among all nations, beginning at Jerusalem.**
>
> Luke 24:47

But there is a difference between preaching repentance and faith toward God (Acts 20:21 and Heb. 6:1) and preaching repentance for the remission of sins, which John the Baptist and the Old Testament prophets preached.

Constantly Cleansed

Let me ask you this question: If you interpret 1 John 1:9 the way it is traditionally interpreted so that we have to confess our sins in order to get them forgiven, what happens if we don't confess them? Are they not forgiven? And what happens to the Christian who has made Jesus their Lord but has not confessed every sin? Can you see the problem this presents? For one thing, no one knows all of the sins they commit. Sin is not only the things we do wrong, but it's also our failure to do what we know we should be doing (James 4:17). Anything not done in faith is sin (Rom. 14:23).

We are constantly falling short of what God wants us to be. That's what fallen humans do, even saved and forgiven humans. But the very context of 1 John 1:9 deals with this problem. First John 1:7 says:

But if we walk in the light, as he is in the light, we have fellowship one with another, and the blood of Jesus Christ his Son cleanseth us from all sin.

Commenting on *katarizo*—the Greek word translated **"cleanseth"** in this verse—Fritz Rienecker's *Linguistic Key to the Greek New Testament* says, "The verbs suggest that God does more than forgive; He erases the stain of sin and the present tense shows that it is a continuous process (Scott)." When we walk in the light of God that we have, the blood of Jesus constantly cleanses us from sins of ignorance and omission. What a wonderful truth!

"But what about the things we do that are wrong, and we know they are wrong? Don't we have to ask forgiveness for them?" Yes we do, but that needs to be clarified too. Our spirits are the part of us that was born again (2 Cor. 5:17). In our born-again spirits, there is no sin (Eph. 4:24). We are as righteous, holy, and pure as Jesus (1 John 4:17 and 1 Cor. 6:17). And once we received our pure, born-again spirits, we were sealed with the Holy Spirit so that no impurity reaches our spirits even when we sin (Eph. 1:13). In our spirits, we've been sanctified and perfected forever (Heb. 10:10, 14; and 12:23). Since God is a Spirit and we must worship Him through our born-again spirits (John 4:24), our relationship and fellowship with Him isn't conditional on our outward actions but rather on the inward condition of our hearts.

Yielding to Satan

However, every known act of sin puts us in a place of submission to Satan.

Know ye not, that to whom ye yield yourselves servants to obey, his servants ye are to whom ye obey; whether of sin unto death, or of obedience unto righteousness?

ROMANS 6:16

Every time we knowingly yield to sin, we are yielding to Satan—the author of that sin. We place ourselves under his dominion. That doesn't mean we lose our salvation. It just means we have opened a door into our lives for the devil to come in and do what he wants. Jesus said:

The thief cometh not, but for to steal, and to kill, and to destroy.

JOHN 10:10

Satan is the ultimate thief and father of all thievery. So when we give him place in our lives through knowingly violating God's direction, we can be sure destruction from the devil is on the way. How do we deal with this? That's what 1 John 1:9 addresses.

Shut the Door

First John 1:9 isn't for the purpose of getting our spirits cleansed. We have eternal redemption and eternal inheritance in our born-again spirits (Heb. 9:12 and 15). However, our souls and bodies aren't sealed, and sin opens them to the power of the devil. How do we reverse that? How do we cancel Satan's legal claim to inflict pain in our lives when we have given him that right?

We confess those known sins, and the forgiveness that is already a reality in our born-again spirits comes out into our flesh and drives the Enemy out. The law of the Spirit of life, which is in Christ Jesus, makes us free from the law of sin and death (Rom. 8:2).

When I realize I've sinned, I repent immediately and ask the Lord's forgiveness. I don't ask in the sense that I think that sin has come between the Lord and me. God is a Spirit. He sees me and deals with me based on who I am in Christ. His love for me doesn't fluctuate based on my performance. I am eternally redeemed (Heb. 9:12). But my flesh—body and soul—was yielded to Satan through that sin, so therefore I confess it.

The Greek word translated **"confess"** in 1 John 1:9 is *homologeo*, which literally means "to say the same thing." When Christians confess their sins, they are simply saying the same thing as God—that their sins were wrong. They are coming back into agreement with the Lord and turning away from Satan. This shuts the door on him and stops his work in their life.

Therefore, I believe it is necessary for Christians to repent and ask forgiveness for their sins. But it *must* be understood that this only affects their relationship with the devil—not with God.

Perfect in Christ

If you make your relationship, or fellowship, with the Lord dependent on your confession of every known sin, there will be some sins that don't get confessed or turned from. That would lead to the broken relationship and fellowship syndrome that religion constantly preaches. This could very well be what has placed you in your current position. You know God exists. You don't doubt that. You know He has the power to move in your life. You don't doubt that either. You just doubt that God is willing to move on your behalf, because you don't feel worthy. You believe your sins have separated you from God (Is. 59:1-2). That's not true for the New Testament believer (Rom. 8:35-39).

All sin does to the believer is open a door to the devil. That's bad enough. In fact, that's terrible. So as much as possible, don't sin. But when you do sin, recognize that it didn't separate you from the love of God. He still sees you perfect in Christ, and all your rights and privileges are still intact. However, you have made your life miserable by inviting Satan into your affairs. Therefore, be quick to repent, confess that sin, and get the forgiveness—which is already resident in your spirit—out into your flesh so the devil can't have his way with you.

Praise God for 1 John 1:9, and the truths it reveals to us!

What about 1 John 1:9?
LESSON 15 – OUTLINE

I. First John 1:9 is the only New Testament scripture I know of that makes God's forgiveness of our sins conditional on us confessing them.

> **If we confess our sins, he is faithful and just to forgive us our sins, and to cleanse us from all unrighteousness.**
>
> 1 JOHN 1:9

A. The belief that we won't be forgiven if we don't confess our sins is a major doctrine of the church, and it only has one supporting verse in New Testament scriptures (Matt. 18:16; Deut. 17:6, and 19:15).

B. Having to repent and ask forgiveness before the Lord forgives our sins is an Old Testament concept (Lev. 26:40-42; 1 Kin. 8:47; 2 Chr. 6:37-38, 7:14; Neh. 1:6, and 9:2).

C. When John the Baptist came preaching in the wilderness, he was still a preacher under the Old Covenant (Mark 1:4; Luke 3:3, and 16:16).

D. He was announcing the coming of the kingdom of God, but the new birth and all the "in Christ" realities didn't come into being until after the resurrection of Jesus.

II. Under the New Covenant, remission of our sins comes through faith in the atoning sacrifice of Jesus' blood (Rom. 3:25; Eph. 1:7; Col. 1:14; and Heb. 9:22).

> **For this is my blood of the new testament, which is shed for many for the remission of sins.**
>
> MATTHEW 26:28

A. It is no longer the turning from our sins that saves us, but the turning to Christ in faith in what He did for us (John 16:8-9 and 1 John 2:2).

> **Believe on the Lord Jesus Christ, and thou shalt be saved.**
>
> ACTS 16:31

B. In the New Covenant, we confess our faith in Christ—not our sins—in order to receive the salvation that Jesus has already provided.

> **That if thou shalt confess with thy mouth the Lord Jesus, and shalt believe in thine heart that God hath raised him from the dead, thou shalt be saved. For with the heart man believeth unto righteousness; and with the mouth confession is made unto salvation.**
>
> ROMANS 10:9-10

C. Many New Testament scriptures promote repentance (Acts 26:20, Rom. 2:4, and 2 Cor. 7:10).

> **And that repentance and remission of sins should be preached in his name among all nations, beginning at Jerusalem.**
>
> LUKE 24:47

D. But there is a difference between preaching repentance and faith toward God (Acts 20:21 and Heb. 6:1) and preaching repentance *for* the remission of sins, which is what John the Baptist and the Old Testament prophets preached.

III. We are constantly falling short of what God wants us to be.

A. That's what fallen humans do, even saved and forgiven humans.

B. But the very context of 1 John 1:9 deals with this problem.

> **But if we walk in the light, as he is in the light, we have fellowship one with another, and the blood of Jesus Christ his Son cleanseth us** [a continuous process] **from all sin.**
>
> 1 JOHN 1:7, BRACKETS MINE

C. When we walk in the light of God that we have, the blood of Jesus constantly cleanses us from sins of ignorance and omission.

IV. Every time we knowingly yield to sin, we are yielding to Satan—the author of that sin.

> **Know ye not, that to whom ye yield yourselves servants to obey, his servants ye are to whom ye obey; whether of sin unto death, or of obedience unto righteousness?**
>
> ROMANS 6:16

A. That doesn't mean we lose our salvation—it just means we have opened a door into our lives for the devil to come in and do what he wants.

> **The thief cometh not, but for to steal, and to kill, and to destroy.**
>
> JOHN 10:10

B. How do we cancel Satan's legal claim to inflict pain in our lives when we have given him that right?

C. We confess those known sins, and the forgiveness that is already a reality in our born-again spirits comes out into our flesh (souls and bodies) and drives the Enemy out (1 John 1:9).

D. When Christians confess their sins, they are simply saying the same thing as God—that their sins were wrong.

    1. They are coming back into agreement with the Lord and turning away from Satan.

    2. This shuts the door on him and stops his work in their life.

V. It is necessary for Christians to repent and ask forgiveness for their sins, but it *must* be understood that this only affects their relationship with the devil—not with God.

    A. All sin does to the believer is open a door to the devil.

        1. When you sin, recognize that it didn't separate you from the love of God—He still sees you perfect in Christ, and all your rights and privileges are still intact.

        2. However, you have made your life miserable by inviting Satan into your affairs.

        3. Therefore, be quick to repent, confess that sin, and get the forgiveness—which is already resident in your spirit—out into your flesh so the devil can't have his way with you.

    B. Praise God for 1 John 1:9, and the truths it reveals to us!

What about 1 John 1:9?
LESSON 15 – TEACHER'S GUIDE

1.   First John 1:9 is the only New Testament scripture I know of that makes God's forgiveness of our sins conditional on us confessing them. The belief that we won't be forgiven if we don't confess our sins is a major doctrine of the church, and it only has one supporting verse in New Testament scriptures (Matt. 18:16; Deut. 17:6, and 19:15). Having to repent and ask forgiveness before the Lord forgives our sins is an Old Testament concept (Lev. 26:40-42; 1 Kin. 8:47; 2 Chr. 6:37-38, 7:14; Neh. 1:6, and 9:2). When John the Baptist came preaching in the wilderness, he was still a preacher under the Old Covenant (Mark 1:4; Luke 3:3, and 16:16). He was announcing the coming of the kingdom of God, but the new birth and all the "in Christ" realities didn't come into being until after the resurrection of Jesus.

2.   Under the New Covenant, remission of our sins comes through faith in the atoning sacrifice of Jesus' blood (Matt. 26:28, Rom. 3:25, Eph. 1:7, Col. 1:14, and Heb. 9:22). It is no longer the turning from our sins that saves us, but the turning to Christ in faith in what He did for us (John 16:8-9 and 1 John 2:2). In the New Covenant, we confess our faith in Christ—not our sins—in order to receive the salvation that Jesus has already provided (Acts 16:31 and Rom. 10:9-10). Many New Testament scriptures promote repentance (Acts 26:20, Rom. 2:4, and 2 Cor. 7:10). But there is a difference between preaching repentance and faith toward God (Luke 24:47, Acts 20:21, and Heb. 6:1) and preaching repentance *for* the remission of sins, which is what John the Baptist and the Old Testament prophets preached.

3.   We are constantly falling short of what God wants us to be. That's what fallen humans do, even saved and forgiven humans. But the very context of 1 John 1:9 deals with this problem. When we walk in the light of God that we have, the blood of Jesus constantly cleanses us from sins of ignorance and omission (1 John 1:7).

1. A. Read 1 John 1:9. What belief is a major doctrine of the church without other supporting New Testament scriptures? (If we don't confess our sins, they won't be forgiven)
   B. Where did this concept of God forgiving us after we have repented and asked forgiveness come from? (The Old Testament)
   C. What didn't come into being until after the resurrection of Jesus? (The new birth and all the "in Christ" realities)
2. A. According to Matthew 26:28, Romans 3:25, Ephesians 1:7, Colossians 1:14, and Hebrews 9:22, how does remission of our sins come under the New Covenant? (Through faith in the atoning sacrifice of Jesus' blood)
   B. According to Acts 16:31 and Romans 10:9-10, what do we confess in order to receive the salvation that Jesus has already provided? (Our faith in Christ)
   C. What did John the Baptist and the other Old Testament prophets preach? (Repentance *for* the remission of sins)
3. A. Do even saved and forgiven humans constantly fall short of what God wants them to be? (Yes)
   B. Read 1 John 1:7. What happens when we walk in the light of God that we have? (The blood of Jesus constantly cleanses us from all these sins of ignorance and omission)

4.   Every time we knowingly yield to sin, we are yielding to Satan—the author of that sin (Rom. 6:16). That doesn't mean we lose our salvation. It just means we have opened a door into our lives for the devil to come in and do what he wants (John 10:10). How do we cancel Satan's legal claim to inflict pain in our lives when we have given him that right? We confess those known sins, and the forgiveness that is already a reality in our born-again spirits comes out into our flesh (souls and bodies) and drives the Enemy out (1 John 1:9).

When Christians confess their sins, they are simply saying the same thing as God—that their sins were wrong. They are coming back into agreement with the Lord and turning away from Satan. This shuts the door on him and stops his work in their life.

5.   It is necessary for us to repent and ask forgiveness for our sins, but it *must* be understood that this only affects our relationship with the devil—not with God. All sin does to us is open a door to the devil. When we do sin, we must recognize that it didn't separate us from the love of God—He still sees us perfect in Christ, and all our rights and privileges are still intact. However, we have made our lives miserable by inviting Satan into our affairs. Therefore, let's be quick to repent, confess that sin, and get the forgiveness—which is already resident in our spirits—out into our flesh so the devil can't have his way with us. Praise God for 1 John 1:9, and the truths it reveals to us!

4. A. Read John 10:10 and Romans 6:16. Who are we yielding to every time we knowingly yield to sin? (Satan—the author of that sin)
   B. According to 1 John 1:9, what happens when we confess those known sins? (The forgiveness that is already a reality in our born-again spirits comes out into our flesh—souls and bodies—and drives the Enemy out)
5. A. When we repent and ask forgiveness for our sins, this only affects our relationship with whom? (The devil)
   B. When we do sin, does it separate us from the love of God? (No)
   C. How does He see us? (Still perfect in Christ, with all our rights and privileges still intact)
   D. Why, then, should we be quick to repent, confess our sin, and get the forgiveness that is already resident in our spirits out into our flesh? (So the devil can't have his way with us)

What about 1 John 1:9?
LESSON 15 – DISCIPLESHIP QUESTIONS

1. According to Hebrews 10:10 and 14, who is sanctified through the offering of the body of Jesus Christ?

2. By this one offering, He has perfected those who are sanctified for how long?

3. According to Hebrews 12:23, what part of just—righteous—people has been made perfect?

4. According to John 4:24, how must we worship God?

5. Who does 1 John 1:9 reveal as faithful and just to forgive us our sins?

6. What does He do with all our unrighteousness?

7. According to Deuteronomy 17:6, 19:15; and Matthew 18:16, in the mouth of how many witnesses should every word/matter be established?

8. Old Testament scriptures like Leviticus 26:40-42; 1 Kings 8:47; 2 Chronicles 6:37-38, 7:14; Nehemiah 1:6, and 9:2 all make _____ a condition of receiving forgiveness.

9. According to Luke 16:16, the Law and the Prophets were until whom?

10. Since that time, what is preached?

11. According to Mark 1:4 and Luke 3:3, what did John the Baptist preach?

12. According to Matthew 26:28, what was Jesus' blood of the New Covenant shed for?

13. Romans 3:25 reveals that we are to place our faith in what?

14. What does Ephesians 1:7 and Colossians 1:14 say we have through Jesus' blood?

15. According to Hebrews 9:22, there is no _____ without the shedding of blood.

16. What does Acts 16:30-31 say we must do to be saved?

17. According to John 16:8-9, what will the Holy Spirit reprove the world of?
    A. Sin.
    B. Righteousness.
    C. Judgment.
    D. All of the above.
    E. None of the above.

18. First John 2:2 reveals that Jesus is the propitiation—atoning sacrifice—for the whole world's what?

19. According to Romans 10:9-10, what must we confess with?

20. What must we believe with?

21. Who must we confess?

22. What must we believe?

23. This results in what?

24. Acts 20:21, 26:20; Romans 2:4; 2 Corinthians 7:10; and Luke 24:47 all refer to what?

25. What does Hebrews 6:1 say we should repent from?

26. According to James 4:17, what should we do?

27. Romans 14:23 reveals that whatsoever is not of faith is what?

28. According to 1 John 1:7, what happens when we walk in the light as Jesus is in the light?

29. The good things mentioned in 2 Corinthians 5:17 are true of any man in whom?

30. What part of our beings is Ephesians 4:24, 1 John 4:17, and 1 Corinthians 6:17 speaking of?

31. Ephesians 1:13 reveals that the Holy Spirit did what the instant we believed the Word and received salvation?

32. According to Romans 6:16 and John 10:10, who brings death into our lives?

33. Who brings righteousness and abundant life?

34. According to Hebrews 9:12 and 15, who is the mediator of the New Covenant (Testament)?

35. According to Romans 8:2, what has the law of the Spirit of life in Christ Jesus made us free from?

36. Isaiah 59:1-2 reveals that under the Old Covenant, people's iniquities did what between them and God?

37. What else did their sins do?

38. According to Romans 8:35-39, what are we through Him who loved us?

39. Is there anything or anyone that can separate us from the love of God?

40. Where is this love?

What about 1 John 1:9?

1. We are.

2. Forever.

3. Their spirits.

4. In spirit and in truth.

5. God.

6. Constantly cleanses us from it.

7. Two or three.

8. Confession of sins.

9. John (the Baptist).

10. The kingdom of God.

11. The baptism of repentance for the remission of sins.

12. The remission of sins.

13. Jesus' blood.

14. Redemption—the forgiveness of sins.

15. Remission.

16. Believe on the Lord Jesus Christ.

17. A. Sin.
    B. Righteousness.
    C. Judgment.
    D. All of the above.

18. Sins.

19. Our mouths.

20. Our hearts.

21. The Lord Jesus.

22. That God has raised Him from the dead.

23. Righteousness and salvation.

24. Repentance.

25. Dead works.

26. The good we know to do.

27. Sin.

28. We have fellowship with one another, and the blood of Jesus cleanses us from all sin.

29. In Christ.

30. Our born-again spirits.

31. He sealed us.

32. The devil.

33. Jesus.

34. Jesus.

35. The law of sin and death.

36. Their iniquities separated them.

37. They hid His face from us.

38. More than conquerors.

39. No.

40. In Christ Jesus our Lord.

What About 1 John 1:9?
LESSON 15 – SCRIPTURES

By the which will we are sanctified through the offering of the body of Jesus Christ once for all…For by one offering he hath perfected for ever them that are sanctified.

HEBREWS 10:10 AND 14

To the general assembly and church of the firstborn, which are written in heaven, and to God the Judge of all, and to the spirits of just men made perfect.

HEBREWS 12:23

God is a Spirit: and they that worship him must worship him in spirit and in truth.

JOHN 4:24

If we confess our sins, he is faithful and just to forgive us our sins, and to cleanse us from all unrighteousness.

1 JOHN 1:9

But if he will not hear thee, then take with thee one or two more, that in the mouth of two or three witnesses every word may be established.

MATTHEW 18:16

At the mouth of two witnesses, or three witnesses, shall he that is worthy of death be put to death; but at the mouth of one witness he shall not be put to death.

DEUTERONOMY 17:6

One witness shall not rise up against a man for any iniquity, or for any sin, in any sin that he sinneth: at the mouth of two witnesses, or at the mouth of three witnesses, shall the matter be established.

DEUTERONOMY 19:15

If they shall confess their iniquity, and the iniquity of their fathers, with their trespass which they trespassed against me, and that also they have walked contrary unto me; And that I also have walked contrary unto them, and have brought them into the land of their enemies; if then their uncircumcised hearts be humbled, and they then accept of the punishment of their iniquity: Then will I remember my covenant with Jacob, and also my covenant with Isaac, and also my covenant with Abraham will I remember; and I will remember the land.

LEVITICUS 26:40-42

Yet if they shall bethink themselves in the land whither they were carried captives, and repent, and make supplication unto thee in the land of them that carried them captives, saying, We have sinned, and have done perversely, we have committed wickedness.

1 Kings 8:47

Yet if they bethink themselves in the land whither they are carried captive, and turn and pray unto thee in the land of their captivity, saying, We have sinned, we have done amiss, and have dealt wickedly; If they return to thee with all their heart and with all their soul in the land of their captivity, whither they have carried them captives, and pray toward their land, which thou gavest unto their fathers, and toward the city which thou hast chosen, and toward the house which I have built for thy name.

2 Chronicles 6:37-38

If my people, which are called by my name, shall humble themselves, and pray, and seek my face, and turn from their wicked ways; then will I hear from heaven, and will forgive their sin, and will heal their land.

2 Chronicles 7:14

Let thine ear now be attentive, and thine eyes open, that thou mayest hear the prayer of thy servant, which I pray before thee now, day and night, for the children of Israel thy servants, and confess the sins of the children of Israel, which we have sinned against thee: both I and my father's house have sinned.

Nehemiah 1:6

And the seed of Israel separated themselves from all strangers, and stood and confessed their sins, and the iniquities of their fathers.

Nehemiah 9:2

The law and the prophets were until John: since that time the kingdom of God is preached, and every man presseth into it.

Luke 16:16

John did baptize in the wilderness, and preach the baptism of repentance for the remission of sins.

Mark 1:4

And he came into all the country about Jordan, preaching the baptism of repentance for the remission of sins.

Luke 3:3

For this is my blood of the new testament, which is shed for many for the remission of sins.

Matthew 26:28

Whom God hath set forth to be a propitiation through faith in his blood, to declare his righteousness for the remission of sins that are past, through the forbearance of God.

ROMANS 3:25

In whom we have redemption through his blood, the forgiveness of sins, according to the riches of his grace.

EPHESIANS 1:7

In whom we have redemption through his blood, even the forgiveness of sins.

COLOSSIANS 1:14

And almost all things are by the law purged with blood; and without shedding of blood is no remission.

HEBREWS 9:22

And brought them out, and said, Sirs, what must I do to be saved? And they said, Believe on the Lord Jesus Christ, and thou shalt be saved, and thy house.

ACTS 16:30-31

And when he is come, he will reprove the world of sin, and of righteousness, and of judgment: Of sin, because they believe not on me.

JOHN 16:8-9

And he is the propitiation for our sins: and not for ours only, but also for the sins of the whole world.

1 JOHN 2:2

That if thou shalt confess with thy mouth the Lord Jesus, and shalt believe in thine heart that God hath raised him from the dead, thou shalt be saved. For with the heart man believeth unto righteousness; and with the mouth confession is made unto salvation.

ROMANS 10:9-10

Testifying both to the Jews, and also to the Greeks, repentance toward God, and faith toward our Lord Jesus Christ.

ACTS 20:21

But shewed first unto them of Damascus, and at Jerusalem, and throughout all the coasts of Judaea, and then to the Gentiles, that they should repent and turn to God, and do works meet for repentance.

ACTS 26:20

Or despisest thou the riches of his goodness and forbearance and longsuffering; not knowing that the goodness of God leadeth thee to repentance?

ROMANS 2:4

For godly sorrow worketh repentance to salvation not to be repented of: but the sorrow of the world worketh death.

2 Corinthians 7:10

And that repentance and remission of sins should be preached in his name among all nations, beginning at Jerusalem.

Luke 24:47

Therefore leaving the principles of the doctrine of Christ, let us go on unto perfection; not laying again the foundation of repentance from dead works, and of faith toward God.

Hebrews 6:1

Therefore to him that knoweth to do good, and doeth it not, to him it is sin.

James 4:17

And he that doubteth is damned if he eat, because he eateth not of faith: for whatsoever is not of faith is sin.

Romans 14:23

But if we walk in the light, as he is in the light, we have fellowship one with another, and the blood of Jesus Christ his Son cleanseth us from all sin.

1 John 1:7

Therefore if any man be in Christ, he is a new creature: old things are passed away; behold, all things are become new.

2 Corinthians 5:17

And that ye put on the new man, which after God is created in righteousness and true holiness.

Ephesians 4:24

Herein is our love made perfect, that we may have boldness in the day of judgment: because as he is, so are we in this world.

1 John 4:17

But he that is joined unto the Lord is one spirit.

1 Corinthians 6:17

In whom ye also trusted, after that ye heard the word of truth, the gospel of your salvation: in whom also after that ye believed, ye were sealed with that holy Spirit of promise.

Ephesians 1:13

Know ye not, that to whom ye yield yourselves servants to obey, his servants ye are to whom ye obey; whether of sin unto death, or of obedience unto righteousness?

Romans 6:16

The thief cometh not, but for to steal, and to kill, and to destroy: I am come that they might have life, and that they might have it more abundantly.

John 10:10

Neither by the blood of goats and calves, but by his own blood he entered in once into the holy place, having obtained eternal redemption for us…And for this cause he is the mediator of the new testament, that by means of death, for the redemption of the transgressions that were under the first testament, that which are called might receive the promise of eternal inheritance.

Hebrews 9:12 and 15

For the law of the Spirit of life in Christ Jesus hath made me free from the law of sin and death.

Romans 8:2

Behold, the LORD'S hand is not shortened, that it cannot save; neither his ear heavy, that it cannot hear: But your iniquities have separated between you and your God, and your sins have hid his face from you, that he will not hear.

Isaiah 59:1-2

Who shall separate us from the love of Christ? shall tribulation, or distress, or persecution, or famine, or nakedness, or peril, or sword? As it is written, For thy sake we are killed all the day long; we are accounted as sheep for the slaughter. Nay, in all these things we are more than conquerors through him that loved us. For I am persuaded, that neither death, nor life, nor angels, nor principalities, nor powers, nor things present, nor things to come, Nor height, nor depth, nor any other creature, shall be able to separate us from the love of God, which is in Christ Jesus our Lord.

Romans 8:35-39

God's True Nature
LESSON 16

When I first started understanding the grace of God, I had many questions. I saw that Jesus had paid for all of my sins and that God wasn't angry with me anymore. I received a revelation of the truth that God wasn't imputing man's sins unto him, and I experienced His unconditional love. I knew by experience that God loved me totally independent of my performance. It had nothing to do with who I was and everything to do with who God was. God is a merciful God. I knew that, but as I studied the Word, I ran across a number of things that seemed contrary to this.

Take, for instance, when Ahaziah hurt himself and sent messengers to inquire of Beelzebub whether he would live or die. Elijah intercepted them and said, "Tell the king that he'll surely die because he inquired of Beelzebub instead of God." So the king became mad at Elijah and sent a captain and fifty soldiers out to get him.

> **Behold, he** [Elijah] **sat on top of an hill. And he** [the captain] **spake unto him, Thou man of God, the king hath said, Come down. And Elijah answered and said to the captain of fifty, If I be a man of God, then let fire come down from heaven, and consume thee and thy fifty. And there came down fire from heaven, and consumed him and his fifty.**
>
> 2 KINGS 1:9-10, BRACKETS MINE

So the king sent another captain with his fifty. This captain addressed Elijah and said:

> **O man of God, thus hath the king said, Come down quickly.**
>
> 2 KINGS 1:11

Elijah answered the same as the first time, and the fire of God fell and consumed all 51 men again (2 Kin. 1:12). That's 102 men killed!

"Have Mercy on Me!"

Finally, the third captain the king sent had sense enough to fall on his knees and say, "Have mercy on me and my men! We're just doing what the king commanded us!"

Then the Lord told Elijah, "Go with them and I'll protect you." He spoke to the king, reiterated his previous message, and everything was fine.

Do you know what? Elijah didn't have to kill those 102 men. He didn't have to handle the situation this way. Yet people want to imitate these kinds of things today. They say, "I'm called to be a prophet—a hellfire and damnation prophet. I'm going to point my finger like Moses did when the earth opened up, swallowed 250 people, and then closed again" (Num. 16:28-33). That's the way people want to be today.

There are just some things in the Bible that look contrary to this truth that the war is over. However, a closer examination confirms that the Lord is now truly at peace with us.

As Jesus walked along with His disciples, the people of Samaria wouldn't receive Him, because His face was set to go to Jerusalem (Luke 9:51-53). The Jews in Jerusalem hated the Samaritans because they were a mixed race and had polluted the true worship of God. The Samaritans had already accepted Jesus before. The whole city of Sychar had believed on Him (John 4). Yet when the Samaritans saw the Lord heading for Jerusalem to worship with those hypocritical Jews this time around, they wouldn't even let Him enter into their village. Due to the two most powerful prejudices known to man—racial and religious prejudice—they totally snubbed and rejected Christ.

The Difference

When James and John, a.k.a. "the sons of thunder," saw this, they wanted to call fire down out of heaven (Luke 9:54). They said, "Lord, do You want us to call fire down out of heaven the way Elijah did?" They desired to emulate the renowned Old Testament prophet. What could be wrong with that? But Jesus turned around and rebuked them, saying:

Ye know not what manner of spirit ye are of. For the Son of man is not come to destroy men's lives, but to save them.

LUKE 9:55-56

Jesus rebuked His disciples for wanting to do the same thing Elijah had done. If Christ had been on the earth in His physical ministry back in the days of Elijah, He would have rebuked him for calling fire down from heaven. That was never God's best! It's not a true representation of Him. Yet it was appropriate under the Old Covenant.

There is a difference between the way God dealt with mankind under the Old Covenant and the way He deals with us now under the New. If you try to act like an Old Covenant person and relate to God the way Old Covenant people did, it's no wonder you feel the wrath of God. You're afraid He's going to judge you and separate Himself from you because of the sin in your life. Those kinds of things happened under the Old Testament.

How do we harmonize this? Is God schizophrenic? Is there a God of the Old Testament who changed His mind, got converted in the New Testament, and now He's different? No, God is the same all the time (Mal. 3:6 and Heb. 13:8). So how do we harmonize the judgment we see under the Old Covenant with the mercy we see under the New? We need to understand the true nature of God.

"Until the Law"

For until the law sin was in the world: but sin is not imputed when there is no law.

ROMANS 5:13

Romans 5:13 is a pivotal scripture that's helped me understand the entire Bible. It says, **"Until the law."** That's during the time of Moses. The Law was given nearly 2,500 years after the Fall of Adam. Until then, God wasn't imputing man's sins unto him. Until the time that the Law was given, man sinned, but God wasn't holding his sins against him. This is a major piece of information!

Basically, our religious system has taught us that God is this holy, stern, austere God who's angry and cannot tolerate sin. It's like He's just leaning over a rail in heaven with a lightning bolt just waiting for someone to get out of line and—BOOM! For many people, this is their impression of God.

Religion has taught us that when Adam and Eve sinned, God instantly cast them out of His presence because He couldn't stand to put up with sinful man. We're told that the wrath of God was instantly vented upon the earth. That's not what Romans 5:13 is saying.

Until the time of Moses, God wasn't holding man's sins against him. God is a merciful God. He didn't instantly start judging man and bringing punishment upon his sin. God was actually operating in mercy toward man for nearly the first 2,500 years of existence. Then the Law came and was in effect for the following 1,500 years, until the time when Christ came.

Grace and Truth

> **The law and the prophets were until John** [the Baptist]**: since that time the kingdom of God is preached, and every man presseth into it.**
>
> LUKE 16:16, BRACKETS MINE

The Law was only temporary until Jesus came to end it.

> **But before faith came, we were kept under the law, shut up unto the faith which should afterwards be revealed. Wherefore the law was our schoolmaster to bring us unto Christ, that we might be justified by faith. But after that faith is come, we are no longer under a schoolmaster. For ye are all the children of God by faith in Christ Jesus.**
>
> GALATIANS 3:23-26

Jesus established grace and truth.

> **For the law was given by Moses, but grace and truth came by Jesus Christ.**
>
> JOHN 1:17

In the nearly 6,000 years since creation—2,500 from the Fall to Moses; 1,500 from Moses to Jesus; and 2,000 from Christ until now—it was less than 2,000 that people were actually under the Law with sin being imputed unto them. The first 2,500 years, God was dealing in mercy with people before the Law. Since the time of Christ, the Law has ceased being the way God deals with people. He's not imputing people's sins unto them anymore.

However, the church has come along and proclaimed, "God is holding your sins against you!" So even though we've not been under the Law for 2,000 years, most people don't know it. Most Christians are still living under the Law.

"Kicked" Out?

Before the Law came, sin was not counted against man. (Rom. 5:13.) Here's how God dealt with Adam and Eve when they sinned against Him:

> **The LORD God said, Behold, the man is become as one of us, to know good and evil: and now, lest he put forth his hand, and take also of the tree of life, and eat, and live for ever: <u>Therefore</u> the LORD God sent him forth from the garden of Eden, to till the ground from whence he was taken.**
>
> GENESIS 3:22-23, EMPHASIS MINE

Notice the placement of the word **"Therefore."** This means that verse 23 is dependent upon what was said in verse 22. The reason God sent Adam and Eve out of the Garden was so they wouldn't eat of the Tree of Life and so live forever.

These verses don't say that God "kicked" Adam and Eve out of the Garden because "He was holy, and a holy God could have no communion or fellowship with unholy man." That's been preached and proclaimed for a long time. "As long as there is any sin, any impurity in our lives, a holy God can't have anything to do with us." That's not what these verses say. The Lord made Adam and Eve leave the Garden specifically so they wouldn't eat of the Tree of Life and so live forever.

Still Fellowshipping

Then in the next chapter, after they left the Garden of Eden, we find God still walking and talking with man. He was still talking with them in an audible voice and fellowshipping with them.

> **And Cain went out from the presence of the LORD, and dwelt in the land of Nod, east of Eden.**
>
> GENESIS 4:16

Cain left the presence of God. God didn't take His presence away from man. Man left the presence of God. We walked away from Him. God didn't cast us away from His presence. He didn't quit fellowshipping with man. God was still dealing with man in mercy, not imputing his sins unto him until the time of the Law.

Why did God send them out of the Garden of Eden? So they wouldn't take of the Tree of Life, eat, and live forever in that fallen state (Gen. 3:22-23). It would have been terrible to live forever in a sinful state.

The Benefit of Death

I don't see very many movies, but I do remember one that had a similar theme. This family drank this certain water that made them "live forever." They had already lived over two hundred years and couldn't die. Even when they got shot, they popped right back up again! An evil man had stumbled onto them and their secret. He was tracking them in order to find this water so he could drink it and live forever too. If he had, it would have been impossible to get rid of him. Through this story, the Lord showed me some things.

Because we live in a sinful world, death is actually a blessing. If people couldn't die, then all of the Hitlers, Stalins, Pol Pots, and Idi Amins of the whole human race would still be alive and spewing out their poison. Death ends a lot of things.

What would it be like to live in a fallen world but not be able to die? You would live forever in a place where lying, cheating, stealing, and every kind of conceivable evil practice is going on everywhere all the time. In light of this, death really is a benefit.

God knew that living forever in sin isn't what He intended for His people. So if you know the Lord, death is a positive thing. We get ushered into a different kingdom where everything will be perfect. No more sorrow, crying, or anything like this. The Lord saw this and didn't want people living forever in a corrupted state. Therefore, death is actually a blessing. God didn't want Adam and Eve to eat of the Tree of Life and have the ability to live forever in corruption and sin. Love—not rejection—motivated God to send Adam and Eve out of the Garden.

God's True Nature
LESSON 16 – OUTLINE

I. When I first started understanding the grace of God, I had many questions.

    A. I saw that Jesus had paid for all of my sins and that God wasn't angry with me anymore.

    B. I received a revelation of the truth that God wasn't imputing man's sins unto him, and I experienced His unconditional love.

    C. God is a merciful God.

    D. I knew that, but as I studied the Word, I ran across a number of things that seemed contrary to this.

II. Take, for instance, when Ahaziah hurt himself and sent messengers to inquire of Beelzebub whether he would live or die.

    A. The king became mad at Elijah and sent a captain and fifty soldiers out to get him.

> **Behold, he [Elijah] sat on top of an hill. And he [the captain] spake unto him, Thou man of God, the king hath said, Come down. And Elijah answered and said to the captain of fifty, If I be a man of God, then let fire come down from heaven, and consume thee and thy fifty. And there came down fire from heaven, and consumed him and his fifty.**
>
> 2 KINGS 1:9-10, BRACKETS MINE

    B. Elijah didn't have to kill those 102 men (2 Kin. 1:11-12).

    C. He didn't have to handle the situation this way.

    D. Although there are some things in the Bible that look contrary to this truth that the war is over, a closer examination confirms that the Lord is now truly at peace with us.

    E. Jesus rebuked His disciples for wanting to do the same thing Elijah had done (Luke 9:51-56).

> **Ye know not what manner of spirit ye are of. For the Son of man is not come to destroy men's lives, but to save them.**
>
> LUKE 9:55-56

    F. If Christ had been on the earth in His physical ministry back in the days of Elijah, He would have rebuked him for calling fire down from heaven too.

III. There is a difference between the way God dealt with mankind under the Old Covenant and the way He deals with us now under the New.

    A. How do we harmonize the judgment we see under the Old Covenant with the mercy we see under the New?

    B. We need to understand the true nature of God (Mal. 3:6 and Heb. 13:8).

IV. God is a merciful God.

    A. Romans 5:13 is a pivotal scripture that's helped me understand the entire Bible.

> **For until the law sin was in the world: but sin is not imputed when there is no law.**
>
> ROMANS 5:13

    B. Until the time of Moses, God wasn't holding men's sins against them.

    C. Then the Law came and was in effect for the following 1,500 years, until the time when Christ came.

> **The law and the prophets were until John** [the Baptist]**: since that time the kingdom of God is preached, and every man presseth into it.**
>
> LUKE 16:16, BRACKETS MINE

    D. The Law was only temporary until Jesus came to end it.

> **But before faith came, we were kept under the law, shut up unto the faith which should afterwards be revealed. Wherefore the law was our schoolmaster to bring us unto Christ, that we might be justified by faith. But after that faith is come, we are no longer under a schoolmaster. For ye are all the children of God by faith in Christ Jesus.**
>
> GALATIANS 3:23-26

    E. Jesus established grace and truth.

> **For the law was given by Moses, but grace and truth came by Jesus Christ.**
>
> JOHN 1:17

    F. In the nearly 6,000 years since creation—2,500 from the Fall to Moses; 1,500 from Moses to Jesus; and 2,000 from Christ until now—it was less than 2,000 that people were actually under the Law with sin being imputed unto them.

    G. Since the time of Christ, the Law has ceased being the way God deals with people—He's not imputing men's sins unto them anymore.

V. The reason God sent Adam and Eve out of the Garden was so they wouldn't eat of the Tree of Life and so live forever.

> **The LORD God said, Behold, the man is become as one of us, to know good and evil: and now, lest he put forth his hand, and take also of the tree of life, and eat, and live for ever: <u>Therefore</u> the LORD God sent him forth from the garden of Eden, to till the ground from whence he was taken.**
>
> GENESIS 3:22-23, EMPHASIS MINE

A. These verses don't say that God "kicked" Adam and Eve out of the Garden because "He was holy, and a holy God could have no communion or fellowship with unholy man."

B. In the next chapter, after they left the Garden of Eden, we find God still walking and talking with man—He's still talking with them in an audible voice and fellowshipping with them.

> **And Cain went out from the presence of the LORD, and dwelt in the land of Nod, east of Eden.**
>
> GENESIS 4:16

C. God didn't take His presence away from man—man left the presence of God.

D. God was still dealing with man in mercy, not imputing his sins unto him until the time of the Law.

E. God didn't want Adam and Eve to eat of the Tree of Life and have the ability to live forever in corruption and sin.

F. Love—not rejection—motivated God to send Adam and Eve out of the Garden.

God's True Nature
LESSON 16 – TEACHER'S GUIDE

1.   When Andrew first started understanding the grace of God, he had many questions. He saw that Jesus had paid for all of his sins and that God wasn't angry with him anymore. He received a revelation of the truth that God wasn't imputing man's sins unto him, and he experienced His unconditional love. Andrew knew that God is a merciful God, but as he studied the Word, he ran across a number of things that seemed contrary to this.

2.   Take, for instance, when Ahaziah hurt himself and sent messengers to inquire of Beelzebub whether he would live or die. The king became mad at Elijah and sent a captain and 50 soldiers out to get him (2 Kin. 1:9-10). Elijah didn't have to kill those 102 men (2 Kin. 1:11-12). He didn't have to handle the situation this way.

   Although there are some things in the Bible that look contrary to this truth that the war is over, a closer examination confirms that the Lord is now truly at peace with us. Jesus rebuked His disciples for wanting to do the same thing Elijah had done (Luke 9:51-56). If Christ had been on the earth in His physical ministry back in the days of Elijah, He would have rebuked him for calling fire down from heaven.

3.   There is a difference between the way God dealt with mankind under the Old Covenant and the way He deals with us now under the New. How do we harmonize the judgment we see under the Old Covenant with the mercy we see under the New? We need to understand the true nature of God (Mal. 3:6 and Heb. 13:8).

1. A. What happened when Andrew first started understanding the grace of God? (He had many questions)
   B. He knew that God is a merciful God, but as he studied the Word, what did he run across? (A number of things that seemed contrary to this)
2. A. Although there are some things in the Bible that look contrary to this truth that the war is over, what does a closer examination confirm? (That the Lord is now truly at peace with us)
   B. Read 2 Kings 1:9-12 and Luke 9:51-56. If Christ had been on the earth in His physical ministry back in the days of Elijah, what would He have done? (He would have rebuked Elijah for calling fire down from heaven)
3. A. Is there a difference between the way God dealt with mankind under the Old Covenant and the way He deals with us now under the New? (Yes)
   B. Read Malachi 3:6 and Hebrews 13:8. How do we harmonize the judgment we see under the Old Covenant with the mercy we see under the New? (We need to understand the true nature of God)

4. God is a merciful God. Romans 5:13 is a pivotal scripture that helped Andrew understand the entire Bible. Until the time of Moses, God wasn't holding men's sins against them. Then the Law came and was in effect for the following 2,000 years, until the time when Christ came (Luke 16:16). The Law was only temporary until Jesus came to end it (Gal. 3:23-26). Jesus established grace and truth (John 1:17). In the nearly 6,000 years since creation—2,500 from the Fall to Moses; 1,500 from Moses to Jesus; and 2,000 from Christ until now—it was less than 2,000 that people were actually under the Law with sin being imputed unto them. Since the time of Christ, the Law has ceased being the way God deals with people—He's not imputing man's sins unto him anymore.

5. The reason God sent Adam and Eve out of the Garden was so they wouldn't eat of the Tree of Life and so live forever (Gen. 3:22-23). These verses don't say that God "kicked" them out of the Garden because "He was holy, and a holy God could have no communion or fellowship with unholy man." In the next chapter, after they left the Garden of Eden, we find God still walking and talking with man—He was still talking with them in an audible voice and fellowshipping with them. God didn't take His presence away from man—man left the presence of God (Gen. 4:16). God was still dealing with mankind in mercy, not imputing their sins unto them until the time of the Law. God didn't want Adam and Eve to eat of the Tree of Life and have the ability to live forever in corruption and sin. Love—not rejection—motivated God to send Adam and Eve out of the Garden.

4. A. Read Romans 5:13, Luke 16:16, Galatians 3:23-26, and John 1:17. For how many years was mankind actually under the Law, with sin being imputed unto them? (1,500 years—from Moses to Jesus)
   B. Since when has the Law ceased being the way God deals with people? (Since the time of Christ)
   C. Is the Lord currently imputing man's sins unto him? (No)
5. A. Read Genesis 3:22-23. Why did God send Adam and Eve out of the Garden? (So they wouldn't eat of the Tree of Life and so live forever in corruption and sin)
   B. According to Genesis 4:16, did God take His presence away from man, or did man leave God's presence? (Man left God's presence)
   C. Was it love or rejection that motivated God to send Adam and Eve out of the Garden? (Love)

God's True Nature
LESSON 16 – DISCIPLESHIP QUESTIONS

1. Which Old Testament prophet was 2 Kings 1:9-12 talking about?

2. How many captains of fifty addressed him in these verses?

3. What did he do to both them and their men?

4. How many people were killed through this?

5. In Numbers 16:28-33, who was the prophet God had sent to do all these works?

6. Who had provoked the Lord?

7. In Luke 9:51-56, where was Jesus traveling to?

8. Where was He traveling through?

9. When they would not receive Him, which two disciples spoke up?

10. What did they ask Jesus?

11. How did Jesus respond?

12. Did the Son of Man come to destroy men's lives, or to save them?

13. According to Malachi 3:6, who never changes?

14. According to Hebrews 13:8, when is Jesus Christ the same?

15. Romans 5:13 reveals that sin was in the world before what?

16. When there is no Law, sin is not what?

17. According to Luke 16:16, the Law and the Prophets were until whom?

18. Since that time, what is preached?

19. Read Galatians 3:23-26. When were we kept under the Law?

20. The Law shut us up (kept us) until what came?

21. The Law was our schoolmaster to bring us unto whom?

22. How are we justified—made righteous?

23. When are we no longer under the schoolmaster?

24. How did we become the children of God?

25. According to John 1:17, who gave us the Law?

26. Grace and truth came by whom?

27. According to Genesis 2:22-23, what did God say man had become?

28. What did they know?

29. What would have happened if man had put forth his hand and eaten of the Tree of Life?

30. To prevent that from happening, what did God do?

31. What was Adam to do out there?

32. According to Genesis 4:16, what did Cain go out from?

God's True Nature

1. Elijah.

2. Two.

3. He called fire down from heaven to consume them.

4. One hundred and two.

5. Moses.

6. Korah and those with him.

7. Jerusalem.

8. A village of the Samaritans.

9. James and John.

10. Do you want us to command fire to come down from heaven and consume them like Elijah did?

11. He rebuked them.

12. Save them.

13. The Lord.

14. Yesterday, today, and forever.

15. The Law.

16. Imputed.

17. John the Baptist.

18. The kingdom of God.

19. Before faith came.

20. The faith.

21. Christ.

22. By faith.

23. After faith has come.

24. By faith in Christ Jesus.

25. Moses.

26. Jesus Christ.

27. As one like Him.

28. Good and evil.

29. Man would have lived forever (in his fallen state).

30. He sent them out of the Garden of Eden.

31. Till the ground.

32. The presence of the Lord.

God's True Nature
LESSON 16 – SCRIPTURES

Then the king sent unto him a captain of fifty with his fifty. And he went up to him: and, behold, he sat on top of an hill. And he spake unto him, Thou man of God, the king hath said, Come down. And Elijah answered and said to the captain of fifty, If I be a man of God, then let fire come down from heaven, and consume thee and thy fifty. And there came down fire from heaven, and consumed him and his fifty. Again also he sent unto him another captain of fifty with his fifty. And he answered and said unto him, O man of God, thus hath the king said, Come down quickly. And Elijah answered and said unto them, If I be a man of God, let fire come down from heaven, and consume thee and thy fifty. And the fire of God came down from heaven, and consumed him and his fifty.

2 KINGS 1:9-12

And Moses said, Hereby ye shall know that the LORD hath sent me to do all these works; for I have not done them of mine own mind. If these men die the common death of all men, or if they be visited after the visitation of all men; then the LORD hath not sent me. But if the LORD make a new thing, and the earth open her mouth, and swallow them up, with all that appertain unto them, and they go down quick into the pit; then ye shall understand that these men have provoked the LORD. And it came to pass, as he had made an end of speaking all these words, that the ground clave asunder that was under them: And the earth opened her mouth, and swallowed them up, and their houses, and all the men that appertained unto Korah, and all their goods. They, and all that appertained to them, went down alive into the pit, and the earth closed upon them: and they perished from among the congregation.

NUMBERS 16:28-33

And it came to pass, when the time was come that he should be received up, he stedfastly set his face to go to Jerusalem, And sent messengers before his face: and they went, and entered into a village of the Samaritans, to make ready for him. And they did not receive him, because his face was as though he would go to Jerusalem. And when his disciples James and John saw this, they said, Lord, wilt thou that we command fire to come down from heaven, and consume them, even as Elias did? But he turned, and rebuked them, and said, Ye know not what manner of spirit ye are of. For the Son of man is not come to destroy men's lives, but to save them. And they went to another village.

LUKE 9:51-56

For I am the LORD, I change not; therefore ye sons of Jacob are not consumed.

MALACHI 3:6

Jesus Christ the same yesterday, and to day, and for ever.

HEBREWS 13:8

For until the law sin was in the world: but sin is not imputed when there is no law.

ROMANS 5:13

The law and the prophets were until John: since that time the kingdom of God is preached, and every man presseth into it.

LUKE 16:16

But before faith came, we were kept under the law, shut up unto the faith which should afterwards be revealed. Wherefore the law was our schoolmaster to bring us unto Christ, that we might be justified by faith. But after that faith is come, we are no longer under a schoolmaster. For ye are all the children of God by faith in Christ Jesus.

GALATIANS 3:23-26

For the law was given by Moses, but grace and truth came by Jesus Christ.

JOHN 1:17

And the LORD God said, Behold, the man is become as one of us, to know good and evil: and now, lest he put forth his hand, and take also of the tree of life, and eat, and live for ever: Therefore the LORD God sent him forth from the garden of Eden, to till the ground from whence he was taken.

GENESIS 3:22-23

And Cain went out from the presence of the LORD, and dwelt in the land of Nod, on the east of Eden.

GENESIS 4:16

Acting in Mercy
LESSON 17

God didn't quit fellowshipping with Adam and Eve, or their descendants, after He sent them out of the Garden. This is evident in Genesis 4.

> **And in process of time it came to pass, that Cain brought of the fruit of the ground an offering unto the LORD. And Abel, he also brought of the firstlings of his flock and of the fat thereof. And the LORD had respect unto Abel and to his offering.**
>
> GENESIS 4:3-4

Most people just read through this and miss the subtle truths embedded within. How did Cain and Abel know that they were supposed to offer sacrifices? Where did they get this knowledge? Was it just intuitive? Did they automatically know these things? Were they born with this knowledge of sacrifice? Although the Scripture doesn't explain, a couple of verses later God spoke to them in an audible voice.

> **And the LORD said unto Cain, Why art thou wroth?**
>
> GENESIS 4:6

There is no reason to believe this was anything other than the same thing that was going on previously in the Garden of Eden. God was walking and talking with them. There was an audible voice. This would be the obvious interpretation due to the context before and after He sent them out of the Garden. God was still talking with these people. They were hearing from Him. What was the difference between being in the Garden and being out of the Garden? God was still walking and talking with them.

How did they know that God approved of Abel's offering and disapproved of Cain's? Scripture doesn't say, but it had to be either some visible or audible manifestation of God, something that showed acceptance and rejection.

Still Walking and Talking

Some people say the reason Cain's offering was rejected was because it didn't have blood in it. A blood sacrifice is definitely typical of Jesus, but there were other kinds of sacrifices commanded too. What Cain did—offering the first fruits of his crops to the Lord—was commanded nearly 2,500 years later in the Law (Ex. 22:29). However, the Word makes a strong case that the real issue wasn't the substance being sacrificed, but the heart of the person making it.

> **By faith Abel offered unto God a more excellent sacrifice than Cain.**
>
> HEBREWS 11:4

The difference was the faith—or lack thereof—in the heart of the one making the offering. I can understand the logic and symbolism of the blood sacrifice argument, but the Word doesn't say that here. Besides, first fruits offerings are later commanded by God as well (Ex. 22:29). These things aside, where did they get this knowledge about bringing these sacrifices? It's obvious to me that God was still walking and talking with man. God was still fellowshipping with man, not imputing his sins unto him (Rom. 5:13). God had respect unto Abel's offering but not Cain's. There was something visible or audible that showed this.

But unto Cain and to his offering he had not respect. And Cain was very wroth, and his countenance fell. And the LORD said unto Cain.

GENESIS 4:5-6

Again, there's no indication that they had a spirit that was in communion with God or that this was just intuition. From the context, this appears as if God spoke in an audible voice.

Familiarity Breeds Contempt

Why art thou wroth? and why is thy countenance fallen? If thou doest well, shalt thou not be accepted? and if thou doest not well, sin lieth at the door. And unto thee shall be his desire, and thou shalt rule over him.

GENESIS 4:6-7

God was talking to Cain in an audible voice, the same way He talked to Adam and Eve in the chapter before.

And Cain talked with Abel his brother: and it came to pass, when they were in the field, that Cain rose up against Abel his brother, and slew him. And the LORD said unto Cain, Where is Abel thy brother?

GENESIS 4:8-9

By the time the average teenager graduates from high school, they will have seen in excess of 250,000 brutal murders on television and in movies. It was totally different back in Cain and Abel's day. They didn't have television. There had never been a single person on the face of the earth killed. This was the very first person to ever murder another person. And while he still had the blood on his hands, God spoke in an audible voice from heaven, asking, "Where is your brother, Abel?"

If you were the first murderer on the face of the earth, having killed your own brother, and you heard an *audible* voice from heaven asking "What have you done?" what do you think would happen to you? You'd probably drop dead right there, after hearing that voice. You'd be thinking, *It's over for me!*

For Cain to respond the way he did, putting his hands behind his back and lying after hearing the audible voice of God, speaks volumes. Basically, Cain said, "I don't know where he is. Am I responsible for my brother?" (Gen. 4:9.) It's obvious that Cain was used to hearing the voice of God. He was accustomed to God talking to him. Familiarity breeds contempt.

All of this proves that God was still walking and talking with man. This whole concept that when Adam and Eve sinned, there was immediate rejection by God simply isn't true. God was extending mercy toward man. He was still dealing with him in love and compassion. God was still walking and talking with him.

A Covenant with God

And Cain went out from the presence of the LORD, and dwelt in the land of Nod, on the east of Eden.

GENESIS 4:16

Cain was the one who left God's presence, not vice versa. He couldn't stand to be in the presence of a holy God, because his own conscience was condemning him. So he left the presence of God. You can't leave something you don't have. The presence of God had to be with him. God was walking with man, still being merciful to him and not imputing his sins unto him during those first 2,500 years.

Abraham married his half-sister. This was an abomination in the sight of the Lord (Lev. 18:9 and 11). Under the Law, the Israelites were commanded to kill people who did this (Lev. 18:29). Abraham was living in a sexual abomination to God. When do you think He decided it was wrong to marry a half-sister? Although this wasn't communicated until the Law came, God is the same yesterday, today, and forever (Heb. 13:8). He never intended for these kinds of things to happen. Abraham married his half-sister, but instead of God punishing him, He dealt with him in mercy and made him His friend (2 Chr. 20:7, Is. 41:8, and James 2:23).

Then Abraham lied twice (Gen. 12:10-20 and 20:1-18). On two separate occasions, Abraham was going to let someone else commit adultery with his wife in order to save his own neck. Any way you slice it, that's wrong. It's not integrity. If a wealthy, powerful man in another country took a liking to my wife, and I thought *He's going to kill me to get to her* so I told him "I've never seen this woman in my life; help yourself," there'd be a scandal! I'd be criticized—and rightly so. It was wrong on Abraham's part, yet God blessed him and rebuked the king as if he were the one who was wrong. Why? It was because Abraham had a covenant with God, and the king didn't.

God deals with people based on covenant, not who's right and who's wrong. He protected Abraham.

"Show No Mercy"

Then Abraham's grandchildren came along. Jacob married two sisters—Leah and Rachel—while they were both alive. That's an abomination in God's sight (Lev. 18:18). Under the Law, people were supposed to be put to death for that (Lev. 18:29). Yet Jacob wrestled with God and prevailed. So the Lord changed his name from Jacob to Israel (Gen. 32:24-28). The children of Israel were named after him. On and on you could go.

The Lord was dealing with people in mercy. If the Law would have been in effect, they would have been under the wrath and punishment of God. But prior to the Law, God dealt with people in mercy, not imputing their sins unto them (Rom. 5:13).

When Cain killed his brother, he lied to God about it and tried to cover it up. There wasn't any repentance on his part. Cain was sorry he'd been caught, but he wasn't sorry he had killed his brother. Cain told God, "I'm afraid people will hear about this and try to kill me." So God put a mark on his forehead and said, "If anyone touches Cain, I'll avenge him sevenfold" (Gen. 4:15). God protected the first murderer on the face of the earth. Instead of judging and killing him, God extended mercy.

Compare this to the first man who broke the Law (Num. 15:32-36). He went out on the Sabbath day to pick up sticks. The first person who ever broke the commandment of Moses was a man who was just gathering sticks so he could fix a fire and cook some food. They shut him up until they could hear what God wanted to do. The Lord appeared in a visible form of a cloud, and an audible voice spoke, saying, "Kill him. Show no mercy."

Under the Law, the first person to violate the Law was killed for picking up sticks to make a fire. The first person who transgressed after the Fall of Adam and Eve killed his brother, and the Lord extended mercy toward him. Can you see the difference between God's dealings with people during the Law, and before and after? The Law wasn't truly God's heart.

Cutting Out Cancer

If God really was as ticked off as people have presented Him to be, and as the Law sometimes makes Him look, then God would have just started judging people. He would have killed them. But instead, we see mercy extended toward people.

"But what about the Flood and the destruction of Sodom and Gomorrah? Those happened before the Law." In these two cases, God acted in judgment toward a certain segment of mankind in order to show mercy toward the human race as a whole. It's like a person who has an infection in their arm or leg. This infection is starting to spread, and it can't be stopped. Therefore, the only thing to do is lop off the arm or cut off the leg. It's a terrible judgment on that individual member, but it preserves the life of the body as a whole. Sometimes drastic measures are necessary for the overall good.

During the days of Noah, God destroyed the earth—except for eight people and a bunch of animals—with a flood. During the time of Lot, He destroyed the cities of Sodom and Gomorrah. It was like there was a cancer in the earth. These people couldn't be purged and cleansed of their sin, because they couldn't be born again (Jesus hadn't come, died, and been resurrected yet). They were very demonic. I could go into a lot of detail on this, but the Bible says that we are just now beginning to approach a time that is as bad as those days.

> **And as it was in the days of Noe [Noah], so shall it be also in the days of the Son of man…Likewise also as it was in the days of Lot…Even thus shall it be in the day when the Son of man is revealed.**
> LUKE 17:26, 28, AND 30, BRACKETS MINE

262

Therefore, when you look at all the corruption and sin of today, it isn't as bad now as it was back in the days of Sodom and Gomorrah. The sin cancer was so bad in the earth that if God had not destroyed those people, there wouldn't have been a virgin left for Him to fulfill His promise through. That's how corrupt the earth was becoming. Acting in mercy toward mankind as a whole, God cut out the cancer so the corruption couldn't escalate and spread to a point of defiling the entire human race.

"I'm Going to Spank You"

As a whole, God wasn't holding man's sins against him (Rom. 5:13). He was being merciful to people. So we find mercy and grace extended toward people and God using people who were doing things that later proved to be totally against His will. Yet He used and blessed them.

Then the Law came and began holding people's sins against them. It served as a…

Schoolmaster to bring us unto Christ.

GALATIANS 3:24

The Law shut us up…

Unto the faith which should afterwards be revealed

GALATIANS 3:23

But now that Christ has come, we're no longer under this schoolmaster (Gal. 3:25). The Law was only temporary. When a child is only one year old, you have to tell them right from wrong and help them start establishing patterns of choosing good things and rejecting bad. Yet a one-year-old doesn't have the ability to comprehend everything. You can't just reason with a one-year-old and explain things to them. Yet you still must get them to obey. You must get a child to where they obey you, not because they understand what's going on, but basically because they fear you. "If you do that again, I'm going to spank you." You can't just sit down with them and say, "Now, look, if you go over there and take that toy from your sibling, then you're responding to the devil. Satan is a taker, not a giver. The Lord says, 'It's more blessed to give than to receive.' So you're yielding yourself to the devil and establishing a bad life pattern. You'll never have friends, because you'll be a selfish person. People don't like selfish people. You'll never be able to hold a job, because if you get one, it'll only be all about you. Your marriage will fail if you continue in this selfishness." If you try to explain that to a one-year-old, they'll just look at you. They can't comprehend all that!

But you can say, "Take that toy again, and I'm going to spank you." They may not even know there is a God or devil, heaven or hell, but when they feel this desire to take the toy, they'll say no because they know they'll be punished for it. So until they get old enough to understand, you can actually, through fear, get someone to do the right thing. There is a certain benefit to that.

Right and Wrong

When our oldest son was just about two years old, we were walking out in the country on a dirt road. The weeds were around four or five feet high. He was just a tiny little kid, running up about thirty yards ahead of us. We were walking and talking. Nobody ever came down this dirt road. But there was an intersection up ahead. And although it was unusual, there was a car coming down that dirt road at fifty or sixty miles per hour. The car was coming so fast that I couldn't have run quick enough to physically stop my son. Joshua reached this intersection at the exact moment the car was whizzing by. The weeds were high, and the driver couldn't see him. They were on a collision course.

But we had been training him to obey us. If he didn't, he got a spanking. So I shouted, "Joshua, stop!" Boy, he froze mid-stride while that car zoomed on by just a few feet away.

Many people don't discipline their kids. They just think they ought to reason with them. They're just making their children susceptible to temptation. Children need to learn to do what's right before they're able to reason.

> **The natural man receiveth not the things of the Spirit of God: for they are foolishness unto him: neither can he know them, because they are spiritually discerned.**
>
> 1 CORINTHIANS 2:14

Before someone is born again, they just don't have the capacity to understand spiritual things. So, then, how could God restrict the amount of sin being committed? How could He get us pointed in the right direction and doing the right thing, even though we didn't have the capacity for spiritual understanding before being born again? Simple. God said, "Do that again and I'll kill you. Pick up sticks on the Sabbath day and you're dead. Do this and you're hit with the botch, mildew, and emerods." The Law taught people right from wrong, but their motivation for obedience was fear.

Acting in Mercy
LESSON 17 – OUTLINE

I. God didn't quit fellowshipping with Adam and Eve, or their descendants, after He sent them out of the Garden.

> **And in process of time it came to pass, that Cain brought of the fruit of the ground an offering unto the LORD. And Abel, he also brought of the firstlings of his flock and of the fat thereof. And the LORD had respect unto Abel and to his offering.**
>
> GENESIS 4:3-4

A. Most people just read through this and miss the subtle truths embedded within.

B. A couple of verses later, God spoke to them in an audible voice.

> **And the LORD said unto Cain, Why art thou wroth?**
>
> GENESIS 4:6

C. God was still walking and talking with them.

> **But unto Cain and to his offering he had not respect. And Cain was very wroth, and his countenance fell. And the LORD said unto Cain.**
>
> GENESIS 4:5-6

D. God was talking to Cain in an audible voice, the same way He talked to Adam and Eve in the chapter before.

> **Why art thou wroth? and why is thy countenance fallen? If thou doest well, shalt thou not be accepted? and if thou doest not well, sin lieth at the door. And unto thee shall be his desire, and thou shalt rule over him.**
>
> GENESIS 4:6-7

II. Cain was the very first person to ever murder another person.

> **And Cain talked with Abel his brother: and it came to pass, when they were in the field, that Cain rose up against Abel his brother, and slew him. And the LORD said unto Cain, Where is Abel thy brother?**
>
> GENESIS 4:8-9

A. For Cain to respond the way he did, putting his hands behind his back and lying after hearing the audible voice of God, speaks volumes.

B. It's obvious that Cain was used to hearing the voice of God—familiarity breeds contempt.

C. Cain was the one who left God's presence, not vice versa.

> **And Cain went out from the presence of the LORD, and dwelt in the land of Nod, on the east of Eden.**
>
> GENESIS 4:16

III. God was walking with man, still being merciful to him and not imputing his sins unto him during those first 2,500 years.

A. Abraham married his half-sister, but instead of God punishing him, He dealt with him in mercy and made him His friend (Lev. 18:9, 2 Chr. 20:7, Is. 41:8, and James 2:23).

B. On two separate occasions, Abraham was going to let someone else commit adultery with his wife in order to save his own neck.

C. It was wrong on Abraham's part, yet God blessed him and rebuked the king as if he were the one who was wrong.

D. Jacob married two sisters—Leah and Rachel—while they were both alive, which is an abomination in God's sight (Lev. 18:18).

E. Yet Jacob wrestled with God and prevailed, so the Lord changed his name from Jacob to Israel (Gen. 32:24-28).

F. God deals with people based on covenant, not who's right and who's wrong.

IV. Prior to the Law, God dealt with people in mercy, not imputing their sins unto them (Rom. 5:13).

A. Under the Law, the first person to violate the Law was killed for picking up sticks to make a fire (Num. 15:32-36).

B. The first person who transgressed after the Fall of Adam and Eve killed his brother, and the Lord extended mercy toward him and protected him (Gen. 4:15).

C. Can you see the difference between God's dealings with people during the Law, and before and after?

D. The Law wasn't truly God's heart.

V. "But what about the Flood and the destruction of Sodom and Gomorrah? Those happened before the Law."

A. In these two cases, God acted in judgment toward a certain segment of mankind in order to show mercy toward the human race as a whole.

B. These people couldn't be purged and cleansed of their sin, because they couldn't be born again (Jesus hadn't come, died, and been resurrected yet).

C. We are just now beginning to approach a time that is as bad as those days.

> **And as it was in the days of Noe** [Noah]**, so shall it be also in the days of the Son of man…Likewise also as it was in the days of Lot…Even thus shall it be in the day when the Son of man is revealed.**
>
> Luke 17:26, 28, and 30, brackets mine

D. The sin cancer was so bad in the earth that if God had not destroyed those people, there wouldn't have been a virgin left for Him to fulfill His promise through.

E. Acting in mercy toward mankind as a whole, God cut out the cancer so the corruption couldn't escalate and spread to a point of defiling the whole human race.

VI. The Law was only temporary.

A. It served as a **"schoolmaster to bring us unto Christ"** (Gal. 3:24).

B. The Law shut us up **"unto the faith which should afterwards be revealed"** (Gal. 3:23).

C. But now that Christ has come, we're no longer under this schoolmaster (Gal. 3:25).

D. Before someone is born again, they don't have the capacity to understand spiritual things.

> **The natural man receiveth not the things of the Spirit of God: for they are foolishness unto him: neither can he know them, because they are spiritually discerned.**
>
> 1 Corinthians 2:14

E. The Law taught people right from wrong, but their motivation for obedience was fear.

Acting in Mercy
LESSON 17 – TEACHER'S GUIDE

1.   God didn't quit fellowshipping with Adam and Eve, or their descendants, after He sent them out of the Garden (Gen. 4:3-4). Most people just read through this and miss the subtle truths embedded within. A couple of verses later, God spoke to them in an audible voice (Gen. 4:5-7). God was still walking and talking with them. God was talking to Cain in an audible voice, the same way He talked to Adam and Eve in the chapter before.

2.   Cain was the very first person to ever murder another person (Gen. 4:8-9). For Cain to respond the way he did, putting his hands behind his back and lying after hearing the audible voice of God, speaks volumes. It's obvious that Cain was used to hearing the voice of God—familiarity breeds contempt. Cain was the one who left God's presence, not vice versa (Gen. 4:16).

3.   God was walking with man, still being merciful to him and not imputing his sins unto him during those first 2,500 years. Abraham married his half-sister, but instead of God punishing him, He dealt with him in mercy and made him His friend (Lev. 18:9, 2 Chr. 20:7, Is. 41:8, and James 2:23). On two separate occasions, Abraham was going to let someone else commit adultery with his wife in order to save his own neck. It was wrong on Abraham's part, yet God blessed him and rebuked the king as if he were the one who was wrong. Jacob married two sisters—Leah and Rachel—while they were both alive, which is an abomination in God's sight (Lev. 18:18). Yet Jacob wrestled with God and prevailed. So the Lord changed his name from Jacob to Israel (Gen. 32:24-28). God deals with people based on covenant, not who's right and who's wrong.

1. A. Read Genesis 4:3-7. Did God quit fellowshipping with Adam and Eve, or their descendants, after He sent them out of the Garden? (No)
   B. What did God do that reveals this? (He spoke to them in an audible voice)
2. A. Read Genesis 4:8-9 and 16. After murdering his brother, how did Cain respond after hearing the audible voice of God? (He put his hands behind his back and lied)
   B. Based on Cain's response, what is obvious? (Cain was used to the voice of God)
3. A. Read Leviticus 18:9, 18:18; 2 Chronicles 20:7; Isaiah 41:8; James 2:23; and Genesis 32:24-28. During those first 2,500 years, what was God doing? (He was walking with man, still being merciful to him and not imputing his sins unto him)
   B. Does God deal with people based on who's right and who's wrong? (No, He deals with people based on covenant)

4.   Prior to the Law, God dealt with people in mercy, not imputing their sins unto them (Rom. 5:13). Under the Law, the first person to violate the Law was killed for picking up sticks to make a fire (Num. 15:32-36). The first person who transgressed after the Fall of Adam and Eve killed his brother, and the Lord extended mercy toward him and protected him (Gen. 4:15). Can you see the difference between God's dealings with people during the Law, and before and after? The Law wasn't truly God's heart.

5.   "But what about the Flood and the destruction of Sodom and Gomorrah? Those happened before the Law." In these two cases, God acted in judgment toward a certain segment of mankind in order to show mercy toward the human race as a whole. These people couldn't be purged and cleansed of their sin, because they couldn't be born again (Jesus hadn't come, died, and been resurrected yet). We are just now beginning to approach a time that is as bad as those days (Luke 17:26-30). The sin cancer was so bad in the earth that if God had not destroyed those people, there wouldn't have been a virgin left for Him to fulfill His promise through. Acting in mercy toward mankind as a whole, God cut out the cancer so the corruption couldn't escalate and spread to a point of defiling the whole human race.

6.   The Law was only temporary; it served as a **"schoolmaster to bring us unto Christ"** (Gal. 3:24). The Law shut us up **"unto the faith which should afterwards be revealed"** (Gal. 3:23). But now that Christ has come, we're no longer under this schoolmaster (Gal. 3:25). Before someone is born again, they just don't have the capacity to understand spiritual things (1 Cor. 2:14). The Law taught people right from wrong, but their motivation for obedience was fear.

4. A. Read Numbers 15:32-36. Under the Law, what happened to the first person who violated the Law? (He was killed)
   B. Read Romans 5:13 and Genesis 4:15. Prior to the Law, what happened to the first person who transgressed after the Fall of Adam and Eve? (The Lord extended mercy toward him and protected him)
   C. What does the difference between God's dealings with people during the Law, and before and after, reveal to us? (The Law wasn't truly God's heart)
5. A. Read Luke 17:26-30. What did God do in the Flood and the destruction of Sodom and Gomorrah? (He acted in judgment toward a certain segment of mankind in order to show mercy toward the human race as a whole)
   B. Why couldn't these people be purged and cleansed of their sin? (Because Jesus hadn't come, died, and been resurrected yet)
   C. What would have happened if God had not destroyed those people? (The sin cancer would have escalated and spread to a point of defiling the whole human race, and there wouldn't have been a virgin left for God to fulfill His promise through)
6. A. Read Galatians 3:23-25 and 1 Corinthians 2:14. Before someone is born again, do they have the capacity to understand spiritual things? (No)
   B. Although the Law taught people right from wrong, what was their motivation for obedience? (Fear)

Acting in Mercy
LESSON 17 – DISCIPLESHIP QUESTIONS

1. According to Genesis 4:3-5, what did Cain and Abel bring to the Lord?

2. What kind did Cain bring?

3. What kind did Abel bring?

4. The Lord had respect unto whom and what?

5. The Lord did not have respect unto whom and what?

6. Who was very wroth and whose countenance fell?

7. According to Genesis 4:6-7, what did the Lord do?

8. What does Exodus 22:29 say concerning the first of our ripe fruits?

9. According to Hebrews 11:4, how did Cain offer unto God a more excellent sacrifice than Abel?

10. After speaking to him, what did Cain do to his brother, Abel, in Genesis 4:8-9?

11. What did the Lord do?

12. How did Cain answer?

13. After leaving the presence of God, where does Genesis 4:16 say Cain dwelt?

14. What does Leviticus 18:9 forbid the uncovering of?

15. What does Leviticus 18:29 say will happen to anyone who commits any of these abominations?

16. Who does Hebrews 13:8 reveal as always the same?

17. What does the Word call Abraham in 2 Chronicles 20:7, Isaiah 41:8, and James 2:23?

18. In Genesis 12:10-20, what king did God protect Sarai from?

19. In Genesis 20:1-18, what king did God protect Sarah from?

20. Who does Leviticus 18:18 forbid a man from marrying—uncovering her nakedness—while his wife is still alive?

21. Even though he had married sisters at the same time, what did Jacob do in Genesis 32:24-28?

22. God changed Jacob's name to what?

23. According to Genesis 4:15, how did the Lord treat the first murderer?
    A. With vengeance.
    B. With mercy.
    C. By killing him.
    D. By protecting him.

24. According to Numbers 15:32-36, how did the Lord instruct Moses to treat the first person who had broken the Law?
    A. With mercy.
    B. To protect him.
    C. To put him to death.
    D. To stone him.

25. According to Luke 17:26-30, whose days will it be like in the day when the Son of man is revealed?
    A. Moses and Joshua.
    B. Peter and Paul.
    C. Elijah and Elisha.
    D. Noah and Lot.

26. According to Romans 5:13, what was in the world before the Law?

27. When there is no Law, what is not imputed?

28. According to Galatians 3:23-25, what were we kept under before faith came?

29. Who did the Law bring us to?

30. How are we justified?

31. What happens after that faith is come?

32. According to 1 Corinthians 2:14, does the natural man receive the things of the Spirit of God?

33. What are they to him?

34. Can he know the things of the Spirit of God?

35. Why?

Acting in Mercy

1. An offering.

2. Of the fruit of the ground.

3. Of the firstlings of his flock, and the fat thereof.

4. Abel and his offering.

5. Cain and his offering.

6. Cain.

7. He spoke to Cain.

8. Do not delay to offer them to the Lord.

9. By faith.

10. He rose up against him and slew him.

11. He asked Cain, "Where is your brother, Abel?"

12. "I don't know. Am I responsible for my brother?"

13. In the land of Nod, on the east of Eden.

14. The nakedness of one's own sister.

15. They shall be cut off from among their people.

16. Jesus Christ.

17. The friend of God.

18. Pharaoh, king of Egypt.

19. Abimelech, king of Gerar.

20. Her sister.

21. He wrestled with God and prevailed.

22. Israel.

23. B. With mercy.
    D. By protecting him.

24. C. To put him to death.
    D. To stone him.

25. D. Noah and Lot.

26. Sin.

27. Sin.

28. The Law.

29. Christ.

30. By faith.

31. We are no longer under a schoolmaster.

32. No.

33. Foolishness.

34. No.

35. Because they are spiritually discerned.

Acting in Mercy
LESSON 17 – SCRIPTURES

And in process of time it came to pass, that Cain brought of the fruit of the ground an offering unto the LORD. And Abel, he also brought of the firstlings of his flock and of the fat thereof. And the LORD had respect unto Abel and to his offering: But unto Cain and to his offering he had not respect. And Cain was very wroth, and his countenance fell. And the LORD said unto Cain, Why art thou wroth? and why is thy countenance fallen? If thou doest well, shalt thou not be accepted? and if thou doest not well, sin lieth at the door. And unto thee shall be his desire, and thou shalt rule over him. And Cain talked with Abel his brother: and it came to pass, when they were in the field, that Cain rose up against Abel his brother, and slew him. And the LORD said unto Cain, Where is Abel thy brother? And he said, I know not: Am I my brother's keeper?

GENESIS 4:3-9

Thou shalt not delay to offer the first of thy ripe fruits, and of thy liquors: the firstborn of thy sons shalt thou give unto me.

EXODUS 22:29

By faith Abel offered unto God a more excellent sacrifice than Cain, by which he obtained witness that he was righteous, God testifying of his gifts: and by it he being dead yet speaketh.

HEBREWS 11:4

For until the law sin was in the world: but sin is not imputed when there is no law.

ROMANS 5:13

And Cain went out from the presence of the LORD, and dwelt in the land of Nod, on the east of Eden.

GENESIS 4:16

The nakedness of thy sister, the daughter of thy father, or daughter of thy mother, whether she be born at home, or born abroad, even their nakedness thou shalt not uncover.

LEVITICUS 18:9

For whosoever shall commit any of these abominations, even the souls that commit them shall be cut off from among their people.

LEVITICUS 18:29

Jesus Christ the same yesterday, and to day, and for ever.

HEBREWS 13:8

Art not thou our God, who didst drive out the inhabitants of this land before thy people Israel, and gavest it to the seed of Abraham thy friend for ever?

2 Chronicles 20:7

But thou, Israel, art my servant, Jacob whom I have chosen, the seed of Abraham my friend.

Isaiah 41:8

And the scripture was fulfilled which saith, Abraham believed God, and it was imputed unto him for righteousness: and he was called the Friend of God.

James 2:23

And there was a famine in the land: and Abram went down into Egypt to sojourn there; for the famine was grievous in the land. And it came to pass, when he was come near to enter into Egypt, that he said unto Sarai his wife, Behold now, I know that thou art a fair woman to look upon: Therefore it shall come to pass, when the Egyptians shall see thee, that they shall say, This is his wife: and they will kill me, but they will save thee alive. Say, I pray thee, thou art my sister: that it may be well with me for thy sake; and my soul shall live because of thee.

Genesis 12:10-13

And it came to pass, that, when Abram was come into Egypt, the Egyptians beheld the woman that she was very fair. The princes also of Pharaoh saw her, and commended her before Pharaoh: and the woman was taken into Pharaoh's house. And he entreated Abram well for her sake: and he had sheep, and oxen, and he asses, and menservants, and maidservants, and she asses, and camels. And the LORD plagued Pharaoh and his house with great plagues because of Sarai Abram's wife.

Genesis 12:14-17

And Pharaoh called Abram, and said, What is this that thou hast done unto me? why didst thou not tell me that she was thy wife? Why saidst thou, She is my sister? so I might have taken her to me to wife: now therefore behold thy wife, take her, and go thy way. And Pharaoh commanded his men concerning him: and they sent him away, and his wife, and all that he had.

Genesis 12:18-20

And Abraham journeyed from thence toward the south country, and dwelled between Kadesh and Shur, and sojourned in Gerar. And Abraham said of Sarah his wife, She is my sister: and Abimelech king of Gerar sent, and took Sarah. But God came to Abimelech in a dream by night, and said to him, Behold, thou art but a dead man, for the woman which thou hast taken; for she is a man's wife. But Abimelech had not come near her: and he said, Lord, wilt thou slay also a righteous nation? Said he not unto me, She is my sister? and she, even she herself said, He is my brother: in the integrity of my heart and innocency of my hands have I done this. And God said unto him in a dream, Yea, I know that thou didst this in the integrity of thy heart; for I also withheld thee from sinning against me: therefore suffered I thee not to touch her. Now therefore restore the man his wife; for he is a prophet, and he shall pray for thee, and thou shalt live: and if thou restore her not, know thou that thou shalt surely die, thou, and all that are thine.

GENESIS 20:1-7

Therefore Abimelech rose early in the morning, and called all his servants, and told all these things in their ears: and the men were sore afraid. Then Abimelech called Abraham, and said unto him, What hast thou done unto us? and what have I offended thee, that thou hast brought on me and on my kingdom a great sin? thou hast done deeds unto me that ought not to be done. And Abimelech said unto Abraham, What sawest thou, that thou hast done this thing?

GENESIS 20:8-10

And Abraham said, Because I thought, Surely the fear of God is not in this place; and they will slay me for my wife's sake. And yet indeed she is my sister; she is the daughter of my father, but not the daughter of my mother; and she became my wife. And it came to pass, when God caused me to wander from my father's house, that I said unto her, This is thy kindness which thou shalt shew unto me; at every place whither we shall come, say of me, He is my brother.

GENESIS 20:11-13

And Abimelech took sheep, and oxen, and menservants, and womenservants, and gave them unto Abraham, and restored him Sarah his wife. And Abimelech said, Behold, my land is before thee: dwell where it pleaseth thee. And unto Sarah he said, Behold, I have given thy brother a thousand pieces of silver: behold, he is to thee a covering of the eyes, unto all that are with thee, and with all other: thus she was reproved. So Abraham prayed unto God: and God healed Abimelech, and his wife, and his maidservants; and they bare children. For the LORD had fast closed up all the wombs of the house of Abimelech, because of Sarah Abraham's wife.

GENESIS 20:14-18

Neither shalt thou take a wife to her sister, to vex her, to uncover her nakedness, beside the other in her life time.

LEVITICUS 18:18

And Jacob was left alone; and there wrestled a man with him until the breaking of the day. And when he saw that he prevailed not against him, he touched the hollow of his thigh; and the hollow of Jacob's thigh was out of joint, as he wrestled with him. And he said, Let me go, for the day breaketh. And he said, I will not let thee go, except thou bless me. And he said unto him, What is thy name? And he said, Jacob. And he said, Thy name shall be called no more Jacob, but Israel: for as a prince hast thou power with God and with men, and hast prevailed.

GENESIS 32:24-28

And the LORD said unto him, Therefore whosoever slayeth Cain, vengeance shall be taken on him sevenfold. And the LORD set a mark upon Cain, lest any finding him should kill him.

GENESIS 4:15

And while the children of Israel were in the wilderness, they found a man that gathered sticks upon the sabbath day. And they that found him gathering sticks brought him unto Moses and Aaron, and unto all the congregation. And they put him in ward, because it was not declared what should be done to him. And the LORD said unto Moses, The man shall be surely put to death: all the congregation shall stone him with stones without the camp. And all the congregation brought him without the camp, and stoned him with stones, and he died; as the LORD commanded Moses.

NUMBERS 15:32-36

And as it was in the days of Noe, so shall it be also in the days of the Son of man. They did eat, they drank, they married wives, they were given in marriage, until the day that Noe entered into the ark, and the flood came, and destroyed them all. Likewise also as it was in the days of Lot; they did eat, they drank, they bought, they sold, they planted, they builded; But the same day that Lot went out of Sodom it rained fire and brimstone from heaven, and destroyed them all. Even thus shall it be in the day when the Son of man is revealed.

LUKE 17:26-30

But before faith came, we were kept under the law, shut up unto the faith which should afterwards be revealed. Wherefore the law was our schoolmaster to bring us unto Christ, that we might be justified by faith. But after that faith is come, we are no longer under a schoolmaster.

GALATIANS 3:23-25

But the natural man receiveth not the things of the Spirit of God: for they are foolishness unto him: neither can he know them, because they are spiritually discerned.

1 CORINTHIANS 2:14

Old vs. New
LESSON 18

There is no fear in love; but perfect love casteth out fear: because fear hath torment. He that feareth is not made perfect in love.

1 John 4:18

In the New Covenant, we aren't supposed to serve God out of fear of punishment. However, most people haven't understood this. They're still operating under Old Covenant fear. They're afraid that God is angry with them and that He's imputing sin unto them. This needs to change! That was only a temporary way God dealt with us, until we could be born again. Now that we're new creatures in Christ, we have an intuitive knowledge. God is inside us, informing us of right and wrong, and leading us in the way we should go. As Christians, we don't have to fear the wrath and judgment of God.

I grew up near a busy city street. My dad died when I was a young boy, so my mother raised me. She'd beat me within an inch of my life if I ever crossed that street without looking both ways. I received many whippings over that. So here I am, almost sixty, and I still look both ways two or three times whenever I cross a street. "Look both ways before you cross the street!" was just drilled into me. Now I understand that it's not the fact my mother will give me a spanking that causes me to do this. I've gone way beyond that. I do what's right not because I'll get in trouble but because I don't want to be hit by a car.

What would you think if we were talking, I forgot what I was doing, we crossed a street, then I realized that I didn't look both ways and said, "Oh, no, I didn't look both ways. Please don't tell my mom! She'll give me a whipping"? You'd probably look at me and say, "What's wrong with you?" Mom is ninety-five now. If I had to, I could take her. I don't have to be afraid of her beating me. Now I do what's right, but with a totally different motivation.

The Law Was Never God's Best

I'm not saying we no longer do what's right, but the Old Testament Law was a brief period of time—until people could be born again—that God used fear, wrath, and punishment to motivate people. The negative side effect of fear is torment (1 John 4:18). Most people are tormented. They aren't able to enter into the closeness and relationship God desires, which is the reason He didn't start imputing man's sins unto him from the very beginning.

If God wanted to just impute man's sins unto him, He could have told Adam and Eve, "All right, let Me show you what your transgression has just done. Let Me show you what's going to happen in the human race." Just in the past century alone, God could have showed them the world wars, Hitler, Stalin, Pol Pot, and all the people these people killed.

If God would have just told Adam the heartache, hurt, pain, sickness, disease, anger, bitterness, and all of these things that just your extended family has experienced, I don't think

Adam could have lived with himself. He wouldn't have been able to handle it. God could have shown him His wrath. He could have shown him how bad he was. But the Lord didn't say to him "Thou shalt not kill, thou shalt not commit adultery" and so on. Why didn't He give the Ten Commandments to Adam and Eve? He was talking to them in an audible voice. It seems like it would have been a great opportunity to do it. Why did He wait another 2,500 years? It was because the Law was never God's best.

God didn't want us to know the depths of our sin. He didn't want Adam to feel so bad that he would run from Him. God extended mercy to people for 2,500 years, but they were taking His lack of judgment as approval. After Cain got by with murder, his great, great, great-grandson, Lamech, killed a man in self-defense. He said:

If Cain shall be avenged sevenfold, truly Lamech seventy and sevenfold.
GENESIS 4:24

In other words, "I am more justified in my murder than Cain was. So if God protected Cain, then He has to protect me that much more." They began comparing themselves among themselves and got to where it wasn't wrong to murder people (2 Cor. 10:12). It wasn't wrong to commit adultery, sexual immorality, or sodomy. People were losing their standard of right and wrong. God had to do something to impose a standard on people because they didn't know what was right or wrong anymore.

"God Will Accept Me"

The same exact thing has been happening in our society. Fifty years ago, homosexuality was considered wrong. It wasn't accepted, so it wasn't flaunted openly as it is now. Homosexuals didn't have parades and promote themselves as "gay." Then a few rock stars, a politician, and a movie star—with all of their fame and fortune—"came out" as homosexuals, and all of a sudden people felt differently about it. They see people living in sin who are famous, rich, on the covers of magazines, and respected, so they don't feel as bad about it as they once did. However, homosexuality is still as wrong as it ever was. Most people today don't have an absolute standard established in their hearts—it's just relative.

Christians try to be a little bit better than the average in society, but as a whole, they don't go by what the Word says. That's wrong! Christians ought to go by what God's Word says. But they're comparing themselves among themselves. How did God break that? He established a standard that showed man the wrath of God. Those who had a desire for Him all of a sudden realized, *If this is what He's demanding, I'm in big trouble!*

One of the main purposes of the Law isn't to get you to obey everything in it. If you really study the Law, it's very detailed. If you're wearing a garment today that has part wool and part cotton in it, you've broken the Law (Lev. 19:19). It covers some very specific details. Did you know that there were things in the Law that told you how to go to the bathroom? It's true. There's a right and wrong way to go to the bathroom (Deut. 23:12-14). The Law had requirements for everything.

Some folks say, "I believe you have to keep the Law." They've criticized me, saying, "I still think we have to keep the Ten Commandments." No one who's told me that, though, has been able to give me all ten of the commandments. And there are many more than just ten commandments. There are hundreds of commandments about everything!

Some people who have seen the scriptures about being delivered from the Old Testament Law say that it was only the "ceremonial" Law that passed away. By "ceremonial" they mean the feast days, sacrifices, and such. However, 2 Corinthians 3:7 speaks of the Law that was written and engraved in stone as passing away. That's referring to the Ten Commandments. The Ten Commandments are still right and holy, but God doesn't relate to us based on our adherence to them anymore. Therefore, the scriptures that speak of us being delivered from the Law are talking about the whole Law—Ten Commandments and ceremonial.

One of the reasons God gave the Law was for people who had been comparing themselves among themselves, thinking, *I'm a pretty good person. I know I'm not everything I should be, but I'm a relatively good person.* People who believe God grades on a curve know that He has to accept somebody. They believe that since nobody's perfect, it doesn't really matter whether they are or not. It's just depends on how a person is in relation to everyone else. *God will accept me if I'm in the top ten percentile.* That's the way many people think.

The Standard

Do you know what God did? For those who were thinking, *Well, I'm pretty good. I don't dip, cuss, or chew, or go with those who do. At least I'm not like this publican over here. I fast twice a week* (Luke 18:11-12), God said, "You think you're good enough? Let Me show you what real holiness is." Then He gave a standard that nobody could keep.

The Law wasn't really given for you to keep. Now, there is benefit in keeping it to the degree that you can. This keeps Satan off your back. But nobody could ever keep the Law perfectly— except Jesus. The Law was given to give you such a standard that it would condemn you.

> **The strength of sin is the law.**
>
> 1 CORINTHIANS 15:56

> **The letter** [of the Law] **killeth.**
>
> 2 CORINTHIANS 3:6, BRACKETS MINE

The Law stops your excuses, makes you guilty, and focuses your attention on sin (Rom. 3:19-20). It also releases wrath and gives sin dominion over you (Rom. 4:15 and 6:14).

> **I had not known sin, but by the law...For without the law sin was dead. For I was alive without the law once: but when the commandment came, sin revived, and I died.**
>
> ROMANS 7:7-9

The Law wasn't something given to help you; it was given to beat you down and hurt you. It was given to take away your self-righteousness, condemn you, and make you feel unworthy.

Basically, it was to knock you flat on your face before God, saying, "If this is what You demand, I have no chance. Have mercy on me, a sinner!" The purpose of the Law was to drive you to the mercy and grace of God.

"What Makes You Worthy?"

A guy went to heaven. He was real smug because he'd been a very good man. Peter met him at the pearly gates and asked, "Well, what makes you worthy to enter?"

He answered, "I'm a really good person."

"Okay. You need a hundred points to get into heaven. Tell me what you've done."

"I went to church every single Sunday. In fact, I had a church attendance award pin for never missing."

"Good! That's worth half a point."

"Half a point!"

"Yes, half a point."

"Well, I was faithful to my wife. I never cheated on her."

"Good! That's worth one point."

Starting to get desperate, he said, "I tithed to the church all my life and gave offerings a few times too!"

"That's worth one point."

This man listed four or five different things, but had only accumulated five points. So he threw up his arms in exasperation and exclaimed, "At this rate, I can't get in unless it's by the grace of God!"

"BINGO! That's worth one hundred points. Come on in."

That's the purpose of the Law. It's for people who were thinking, *I'm pretty good*. We can't get saved by trusting in ourselves and our own goodness. God had to take away this self-righteousness and get us to recognize we had to trust in His mercy and grace, not ourselves. How did He do it? He gave such a standard that we would despair of self-righteousness. It would get us out of thinking we could be good enough on our own. The Law made us guilty before God (Rom. 3:23). It shut our mouths and reveals how far we've missed the mark.

The Word of Reconciliation

Religion has made the Law out to be something positive: "God loved us so much that He gave us step one through ten thousand to show us exactly what we must do to get right with Him." No! The Law was meant to kill (2 Cor. 3:7). It was meant to destroy. The Law was meant to shut you up—make you hopeless and helpless—so that you would cry out to God for mercy (Gal. 3:23). Yet most of the church has embraced it and wants to promote it. The Law was given to kill you. You need to get out from under the Law and start relating to God based on His mercy and grace.

So for those first 2,500 years, God dealt with mankind in mercy. But when people began to take His lack of judgment as approval, He needed to do something. They had lost their concept of right and wrong because they were comparing themselves among themselves. They were getting into self-righteousness, living ungodly, but thinking, *I'm wonderful even though I've done all of these things*. God had to bring an end to that, so He gave the Law and started judging and punishing people for their sin.

That put fear in people. It limited the amount of sin they did, but it caused the sin they committed to destroy them (Prov. 16:6). Instead of enjoying relationship with God, people were living under condemnation. Jesus came to redeem us from the Law and condemnation, and He has put us back into right relationship with the Father. Now we can just love God, and He's not imputing our sins unto us.

> **God was in Christ, reconciling the world unto himself, not imputing their trespasses unto them; and hath committed unto us the word of reconciliation. Now then we are ambassadors for Christ, as though God did beseech you by us: we pray you in Christ's stead, be ye reconciled to God.**
>
> 2 Corinthians 5:19-20

The Lord has given us this ministry of telling people, "God's not mad at you. He's not angry. He's not imputing your sins unto you." It's His goodness that leads us to repentance (Rom. 2:4).

Relate by Love

As believers, we need to have enough discernment to know what the Old Testament Law was and why He gave it. We need to recognize that under the New Testament, we have a better covenant. We aren't under the Old Testament Law anymore. We're under the law of loving God and loving people. Those are the two commandments Jesus gave. If you love God with all your heart, and love your neighbor as yourself, you'll fulfill all of the precepts and ordinances of the Old Testament Law (Matt. 22:37-39). In fact, you'll do it better than living out of fear and trying to pay it by debt and obligation.

When I first saw the grace and mercy of God in the New Testament and the wrath of God in the Old, I couldn't reconcile it. I thought, *Is God schizophrenic? Has He changed? What happened?* God has always been the same. He's always loved us, because He is love (1 John 4:8).

283

We had to correct our children for a period of time by spanking them. It wasn't because we hated them; it was because they didn't have full understanding, and we were trying to get them to do the right thing. However, it was just a temporary way of dealing with them. Now that they're adults, we have to release them and deal with them in a different manner. The parent doesn't change, but the child does. Therefore, the way the parent deals with the child changes as they grow up. But we've always loved them and had their best interests in mind.

Now that we're born again, God isn't imputing our sins unto us. God's not going to "get us." He's not punishing us. God isn't the one who's causing problems in our lives. Now we're free to relate to Him based on love. We have a New Covenant—a better covenant. Isn't that good news?

New Covenant Eyes

Christ redeemed us from the Law. We've been redeemed from the curse of the Law (Gal. 3:13). Thank You, Jesus!

Even though the emphasis of my preaching is God's love and grace, I spend most of my time studying the Old Testament. Now that I have this revelation of the New Covenant, I can look back at what I've been redeemed from. I can see how terrible it was when God put wrath and punishment upon people. Even though I deserve those things, God is extending mercy and grace toward me. This makes me love and appreciate Him that much more.

Most Christians have been looking at the New Testament through Old Testament glasses. However, once you understand these truths, you'll be able to look at the whole of God's Word in proper perspective. You'll start seeing the Old Covenant through New Covenant eyes.

As you see what we've been redeemed from, gratefulness will well up in your heart toward the Lord. You'll find yourself saying, "Thank You, Jesus, for the greater day we live in today!"

As the body of Christ, we haven't been taking advantage of our New Covenant. We've been living as Old Covenant people. We've been living as if Jesus hadn't come and set us free from all of these rituals and legalistic obligations. We need to recognize and receive a revelation of the New Covenant we've been given. We need to get into God's Word to discover what all of our benefits are and how we can take full advantage of them.

Old vs. New
LESSON 18 – OUTLINE

I. In the New Covenant, we aren't supposed to be serving God out of fear of punishment.

> **There is no fear in love; but perfect love casteth out fear: because fear hath torment. He that feareth is not made perfect in love.**
>
> 1 John 4:18

   A. Now that we're new creatures in Christ, we have an intuitive knowledge.

   B. God is inside us, informing us of right and wrong, and leading us in the way we should go.

   C. As a Christian, you don't have to fear the wrath and judgment of God.

   D. Now I do what's right, but with a totally different motivation.

II. The Old Testament Law was a brief period of time—until people could be born again—that God used fear, wrath, and punishment to motivate people.

   A. The negative side effect of fear is torment (1 John 4:18).

   B. Most people are tormented and aren't able to enter into the closeness and relationship God desires, which is the reason He didn't start imputing man's sins unto him from the very beginning.

   C. The Law was never God's best.

   D. God didn't want us to know the depths of our sin.

III. God extended mercy to people for 2,500 years, but they were taking His lack of judgment as approval.

   A. After Cain got by with murder, his great, great, great-grandson, Lamech, killed a man in self-defense.

> **If Cain shall be avenged sevenfold, truly Lamech seventy and sevenfold.**
>
> Genesis 4:24

   B. In other words, Lamech said, "I am more justified in my murder than Cain was. So if God protected Cain, then He has to protect me that much more."

   C. God had to do something to impose a standard on people because they didn't know what was right or wrong anymore.

IV. The Law was given to give you such a standard that it would condemn you.

The strength of sin is the law.

1 CORINTHIANS 15:56

The letter [of the Law] **killeth.**

2 CORINTHIANS 3:6, BRACKETS MINE

I had not known sin, but by the law...For without the law sin was dead. For I was alive without the law once: but when the commandment came, sin revived, and I died.

ROMANS 7:7-9

A. The Law was given to take away your self-righteousness, condemn you, and make you feel unworthy.

B. The purpose of the Law was to drive you to the mercy and grace of God.

C. The Law made all of us guilty before God (Rom. 3:23).

D. The Law was meant to kill and destroy (2 Cor. 3:7).

E. The Law was meant to shut you up—make you hopeless and helpless—so that you would cry out to God for mercy (Gal. 3:23).

V. We need to get out from under the Law and start relating to God based on His mercy and grace.

A. For those first 2,500 years, God dealt with mankind in mercy.

B. But when people began to take His lack of judgment as approval, He needed to do something.

C. They had lost their concept of right and wrong because they were comparing themselves among themselves.

D. They were getting into self-righteousness, living ungodly, but thinking, *I'm wonderful even though I've done all of these things*.

E. God had to bring an end to that, so He gave the Law and started judging and punishing people for their sin—which put fear in them.

   i. It limited the amount of sin they did, but it caused the sin they committed to destroy them (Prov. 16:6).

   ii. Instead of enjoying relationship with God, people were living under condemnation.

F. Jesus came to redeem us from the Law and condemnation, and He has put us back into right relationship with the Father.

G. Now we can just love God—and He's not imputing our sins unto us.

> **God was in Christ, reconciling the world unto himself, not imputing their trespasses unto them; and hath committed unto us the word of reconciliation. Now then we are ambassadors for Christ, as though God did beseech you by us: we pray you in Christ's stead, be ye reconciled to God.**
>
> 2 CORINTHIANS 5:19-20

VI. As believers, we need to have enough discernment to know what the Old Testament Law was and why He gave it. We need to recognize that under the New Testament, we have a better covenant.

A. Now that we're born again, God isn't imputing our sins unto us.

B. Christ redeemed us from the curse of the Law (Gal. 3:13).

C. Most Christians have been looking at the New Testament through Old Testament glasses.

D. However, once you understand these truths, you'll be able to look at the whole of God's Word in proper perspective—you'll start seeing the Old Covenant through New Covenant eyes.

E. We need to recognize and receive a revelation of the New Covenant we've been given.

Old vs. New
LESSON 18 – TEACHER'S GUIDE

1.   In the New Covenant, we aren't supposed to be serving God out of fear of punishment (1 John 4:18). Now that we're new creatures in Christ, we have an intuitive knowledge. God is inside us, informing us of right and wrong, and leading us in the way we should go. As Christians, we don't have to fear the wrath and judgment of God. Now we do what's right, but with a totally different motivation.

2.   The Old Testament Law was a brief period of time—until people could be born again—that God used fear, wrath, and punishment to motivate people. The negative side effect of fear is torment. Most people are tormented and aren't able to enter into the closeness and relationship God desires, which is the reason He didn't start imputing man's sins unto them from the very beginning. The Law was never God's best. God didn't want us to know the depths of our sin.

3.   God extended mercy to people for 2,500 years, but they were taking His lack of judgment as approval. After Cain got by with murder, his great, great, great-grandson, Lamech, killed a man in self-defense (Gen. 4:24). Basically, he said, "I am more justified in my murder than Cain was. So if God protected Cain, then He has to protect me that much more." God had to do something to impose a standard on people because they didn't know what was right or wrong anymore.

1. A. Read 1 John 4:18. In the New Covenant, are we supposed to be serving God out of fear of punishment? (No)
   B. Now that we're new creatures in Christ, where is God, and what is He doing? (God is inside us, informing us of right and wrong, and leading us in the way we should go)
2. A. How long did God use the Old Testament Law—to impose fear, wrath, and punishment on people—to motivate them? (A brief period of time—until people could be born again)
   B. Why didn't God start imputing man's sins unto them from the very beginning? (Because He didn't want people to be tormented. He wanted them to be able to enter into a close relationship with Him)
3. A. Read Genesis 4:24. As God extended mercy to people for 2,500 years, how did they take His lack of judgment? (As approval)
   B. What did God have to do because people didn't know what was right or wrong anymore? (He imposed a standard on them)

4. The Law was given to give us such a standard that it would condemn us (1 Cor. 15:56, 2 Cor. 3:6, and Rom. 7:7-9). The Law was given to take away our self-righteousness, condemn us, and make us feel unworthy. The purpose of the Law was to drive us to the mercy and grace of God. The Law made all of us guilty before God (Rom. 3:23). The Law was meant to kill and destroy (2 Cor. 3:7). The Law was meant to shut us up—make us hopeless and helpless—so that we would cry out to God for mercy (Gal. 3:23).

5. We need to get out from under the Law and start relating to God based on His mercy and grace. For the first 2,500 years, God dealt with mankind in mercy. But when people began to take His lack of judgment as approval, He needed to do something. They had lost their concept of right and wrong because they were comparing themselves among themselves. They were getting into self-righteousness, living ungodly, but thinking, *I'm wonderful even though I've done all of these things*. God had to bring an end to that, so He gave the Law and started judging and punishing people for their sin, which put fear in them. It limited the amount of sin they did, but it caused the sin they committed to just destroy them (Prov. 16:6). Instead of enjoying relationship with God, people were living under condemnation. Jesus came to redeem us from that Law and condemnation, and He has put us back into right relationship with the Father. Now we can just love God, and He's not imputing our sins unto us (2 Cor. 5:19-20).

6. As believers, we need to have enough discernment to know what the Old Testament Law was and why He gave it. We need to recognize that under the New Testament, we have a better covenant. Now that we're born again, God isn't imputing our sins unto us. Christ redeemed us from the curse of the Law (Gal. 3:13). Most Christians have been looking at the New Testament through Old Testament glasses. However, once we understand these truths, we'll be able to look at the whole of God's Word in proper perspective—we'll start seeing the Old Covenant through New Covenant eyes. We need to recognize and receive a revelation of the New Covenant we've been given.

4. A. Read 1 Corinthians 15:56; 2 Corinthians 3:6; Romans 3:23; and 7:7-9. Why was the Law given? (To give us such a standard that it would condemn us, take away our self-righteousness, and make us feel unworthy)
   B. What was the Law meant to do? (Kill, destroy, and shut us up—make us hopeless and helpless—so that we would cry out to God for mercy)
5. A. We need to get out from under the Law and start relating to God how? (Based on His mercy and grace)
   B. Read Proverbs 16:6 and 2 Corinthians 5:19-20. What did Jesus come to do? (Redeem us from the Law and condemnation and put us back into right relationship with the Father)
6. A. Read Galatians 3:13. As born-again believers who understand these truths, how should we see the whole of God's Word? (In proper perspective—through New Covenant eyes)
   B. What do we need to recognize and receive a revelation of? (The New Covenant we've been given)

Old vs. New
LESSON 18 – DISCIPLESHIP QUESTIONS

1. According to 1 John 4:18, what does fear produce?

2. Who is not made perfect in love?

3. What does perfect love do to fear?

4. According to Genesis 4:24, how much more did Lamech presume God would protect and avenge him than Cain?

5. When we measure and compare ourselves with other people, what does 2 Corinthians 10:12 say we are?

6. According to Leviticus 19:19, what were people under the Law not allowed to do?
   A. Wear a garment mingled of linen and wool.
   B. Sow their fields with mingled seed.
   C. Allow their cattle to gender with a diverse kind.
   D. All of the above.
   E. None of the above.

7. The Law gives instruction in Deuteronomy 23:12-14 on what?

8. According to 2 Corinthians 3:6-7, what has God made us?

9. The letter of the Law does what?

10. What does the spirit of the New Testament (Covenant) do?

11. What was written and engraved on stones?

12. Was it glorious?

13. Was it permanent?

14. Who does the Word reveal that the Pharisee in Luke 18:11-12 was really praying with?

15. According to 1 Corinthians 15:56, what is the sting of death?

16. What is the strength of sin?

17. According to Romans 3:19-20, we know that what things the Law says, it says to whom?

18. This causes every mouth to be stopped and the whole world to what?

19. Shall anyone be justified—made righteous—in God's sight by the deeds of the Law?

20. What knowledge comes to us by the Law?

21. According to Romans 4:15, can there be transgression where there is no Law?

22. What does the Law work?

23. According to Romans 6:14, the Law gives sin _____ over us?

24. Are we under the Law, or under grace?

25. According to Romans 7:7-9, how did we know sin?

26. Without the Law, what was sin?

27. What happened when the commandment came?

28. According to Romans 3:23, sinners come short of what?

29. According to Galatians 3:23, when were we kept under the Law?

30. What were we shut up unto?

31. Even though fear limits sin, Proverbs 16:6 reveals that it takes mercy and truth to purge what?

32. By what do men depart from evil?

33. According to 2 Corinthians 5:19-20, what has been committed unto us?

34. As ambassadors for Christ, what do we beseech and pray people in Christ's stead?

35. According to Romans 2:4, what should we be careful not to despise?
    A. God's forbearance.
    B. God's longsuffering.
    C. The riches of His goodness.
    D. All of the above.
    E. None of the above.

36. What should we know?
    A. That the goodness of God leads us to repentance.
    B. That the judgment of God leads us to fear.
    C. That the holiness of God leads us to condemnation.
    D. All of the above.
    E. None of the above.

37. According to Matthew 22:37-39, what did Jesus say was the first and greatest commandment?

38. How should we love God?
    A. With all our minds.
    B. With all our souls.
    C. With all our hearts.
    D. All of the above.
    E. None of the above.

39. Who else are we commanded to love?

40. How?

41. According to 1 John 4:8, what can we tell about someone who doesn't love others?

42. What is God's very nature?

43. According to Galatians 3:13, what has Christ done for us?

44. What was He made in order to accomplish this?

45. What is everyone who hangs (is crucified) on a tree?

Old vs. New
LESSON 18 – ANSWER KEY

1. Torment.

2. Those who fear.

3. Casts it out.

4. Seventy more (sevenfold vs. seventy and sevenfold).

5. Not wise.

6. A. Wear a garment mingled of linen and wool.
   B. Sow their fields with mingled seed.
   C. Allow their cattle to gender with a diverse kind.
   D. All of the above.

7. How to ease ourselves (use the bathroom) properly.

8. Able ministers of the New Testament (Covenant).

9. Kills.

10. Gives life.

11. The ministration of death—Ten Commandments.

12. Yes.

13. No, it was to be done away with.

14. Himself.

15. Sin.

16. The Law.

17. Those who are under the Law.

18. Become guilty before God.

19. No.

20. The knowledge of sin.

21. No.

22. Wrath.

23. Dominion.

24. Under grace.

25. By the Law.

26. Dead.

27. Sin revived and I died.

28. The glory of God.

29. Before faith came.

30. The faith which should afterward be revealed.

31. Iniquity.

32. The fear of the Lord.

33. The word of reconciliation.

34. To be reconciled to God.

35. A. God's forbearance.
    B. God's longsuffering.
    C. The riches of His goodness.
    D. All of the above.

36. A. That the goodness of God leads us to repentance.

37. To love the Lord your God.

38. A. With all our minds.
    B. With all our souls.
    C. With all our hearts.
    D. All of the above.

39. Our neighbors.

40. As ourselves.

41. They don't know God.

42. Love.

43. He redeemed us from the curse of the Law.

44. A curse.

45. They are cursed.

There is no fear in love; but perfect love casteth out fear: because fear hath torment. He that feareth is not made perfect in love.

1 John 4:18

If Cain shall be avenged sevenfold, truly Lamech seventy and sevenfold.

Genesis 4:24

For we dare not make ourselves of the number, or compare ourselves with some that commend themselves: but they measuring themselves by themselves, and comparing themselves among themselves, are not wise.

2 Corinthians 10:12

Ye shall keep my statutes. Thou shalt not let thy cattle gender with a diverse kind: thou shalt not sow thy field with mingled seed: neither shall a garment mingled of linen and woollen come upon thee.

Leviticus 19:19

Thou shalt have a place also without the camp, whither thou shalt go forth abroad: And thou shalt have a paddle upon thy weapon; and it shall be when thou wilt ease thyself abroad, thou shalt dig therewith, and shalt turn back and cover that which cometh from thee: For the LORD thy God walketh in the midst of thy camp, to deliver thee, and to give up thine enemies before thee; therefore shall thy camp be holy: that he see no unclean thing in thee, and turn away from thee.

Deuteronomy 23:12-14

Who also hath made us able ministers of the new testament; not of the letter, but of the spirit: for the letter killeth, but the spirit giveth life. But if the ministration of death, written and engraven in stones, was glorious, so that the children of Israel could not stedfastly behold the face of Moses for the glory of his countenance; which glory was to be done away.

2 Corinthians 3:6-7

The Pharisee stood and prayed thus with himself, God, I thank thee, that I am not as other men are, extortioners, unjust, adulterers, or even as this publican. I fast twice in the week, I give tithes of all that I possess.

Luke 18:11-12

The sting of death is sin; and the strength of sin is the law.

1 Corinthians 15:56

Now we know that what things soever the law saith, it saith to them who are under the law: that every mouth may be stopped, and all the world may become guilty before God. Therefore by the deeds of the law there shall no flesh be justified in his sight: for by the law is the knowledge of sin.

ROMANS 3:19-20

Because the law worketh wrath: for where no law is, there is no transgression.

ROMANS 4:15

For sin shall not have dominion over you: for ye are not under the law, but under grace.

ROMANS 6:14

What shall we say then? Is the law sin? God forbid. Nay, I had no known sin, but by the law: for I had not known lust, except the law had said, Thou shalt not covet. But sin, taking occasion by the commandment, wrought in me all manner of concupiscence. For without the law sin was dead. For I was alive without the law once: but when the commandment came, sin revived, and I died.

ROMANS 7:7-9

For all have sinned, and come short of the glory of God.

ROMANS 3:23

But before faith came, we were kept under the law, shut up unto the faith which should afterwards be revealed.

GALATIANS 3:23

By mercy and truth iniquity is purged: and by the fear of the LORD men depart from evil.

PROVERBS 16:6

To wit, that God was in Christ, reconciling the world unto himself, not imputing their trespasses unto them; and hath committed unto us the word of reconciliation. Now then we are ambassadors for Christ, as though God did beseech you by us: we pray you in Christ's stead, be ye reconciled to God.

2 CORINTHIANS 5:19-20

Or despisest thou the riches of his goodness and forbearance and longsuffering; not knowing that the goodness of God leadeth thee to repentance?

ROMANS 2:4

Jesus said unto him, Thou shalt love the Lord thy God with all thy heart, and with all thy soul, and with all thy mind. This is the first and great commandment. And the second is like unto it, Thou shalt love thy neighbour as thyself.

MATTHEW 22:37-39

He that loveth not knoweth not God; for God is love.

1 John 4:8

Christ hath redeemed us from the curse of the law, being made a curse for us: for it is written, Cursed is every one that hangeth on a tree.

Galatians 3:13

Spiritual Dyslexia
LESSON 19

God has already placed all of our sin upon Jesus. He not only paid for all the sins of believers, but of unbelievers too. Christ paid for all the sins—past, present, and even future sins—of the entire world. Sins have been paid for!

God isn't angry. He's not judging us for our sin. Jesus drew all judgment to Himself at the cross. God is really just dealing with people today based on whether or not they've made Jesus their Lord. It's all a matter of what we do with Jesus.

People go to hell not because of their individual sins but because they rejected Jesus. If you've accepted Christ, then you have a relationship with God. All sins—past, present, and even future sins—have been paid for. You're not going to do anything that will surprise the Lord or that hasn't already been dealt with. Every time you sin, you don't have to go and get the blood "reapplied." You don't have to get that sin confessed and "back under the blood," or you're out of fellowship and relationship with God until you do so. Those things are being taught, but they're not what the Scripture reveals at all.

Understanding that Jesus has suffered for us and paid for all our sin, and that He's not angry with us and He'll never rebuke us again, enables us to enjoy God's love in a much deeper way. When we comprehend how much the Lord loves us, our faith shoots through the roof, because faith works by love (Gal. 5:6). Every area of our lives is affected. Basically, this is what the book of 1 John is about.

Relationship with God

That which was from the beginning, which we have heard, which we have seen with our eyes, which we have looked upon, and our hands have handled, of the Word of life; (For the life was manifested, and we have seen it, and bear witness, and shew unto you that eternal life, which was with the Father, and was manifested unto us;) That which we have seen and heard declare we unto you, that ye also may have fellowship with us: and truly our fellowship is with the Father, and with his Son Jesus Christ. And these things write we unto you, that your joy may be full.

1 JOHN 1:1-4

John was saying, "We're writing this so you can receive a revelation of Jesus. Then you can have fellowship with both the Father and us. We're writing this so you can have fellowship with God." This close, intimate relationship with God is actually the true goal and aim of Christianity.

If you really understood how much God loves you, it would just increase your relationship with Him. Then, as you come to know Him more, He'll reveal things to you. Everything in the Christian life flows out of this.

John said, "I'm writing this so you will come into a deeper revelation of God, have fellowship with Him, and so your joy would be made full." In both the world and the church, people are trying to find joy in every possible way apart from intimacy with God. However, it's through a vital, growing, daily relationship with God that joy—and everything else we need—comes. It all boils down to relationship with God.

Seeing Things Backwards

Then John said some things that appear, on the surface, to be contrary to some of these truths I've been emphasizing.

And hereby we do know that we know him, if we keep his commandments.

1 John 2:3

There is a condition that exists in the body of Christ called *spiritual dyslexia*. Dyslexia causes people to see things backwards. To a dyslexic person, the word G-O-D is seen as D-O-G. There's a huge difference between *God* and *dog*! But for the spiritual dyslexic, everything is reversed in their minds.

Spiritual dyslexia is contagious. You get it through close contact with religion. It's amazing how people turn these verses in 1 John around and see them as performance-based scriptures.

Hereby we do know that we know him, if we keep his commandments.

1 John 2:3

People read this and think, *I want to know God, so what do I have to do? I have to keep His commandments. If I keep His commandments, that's how I'll know Him.* That's not what this verse is saying. It's saying the exact opposite. It's not saying that keeping God's commandments will cause you to know Him. It's saying that you can tell if you really know Him, because knowing God will cause you to keep His commandments. If you're truly in fellowship with God—loving Him and having His love flow through you—you'll know because you'll start loving other people.

Communication Isn't the Problem

Most marriage seminars today have totally missed the boat. They emphasize communication, sharing your feelings, and so on. Now don't get me wrong; communication is important. If you never talk to your mate, it'll definitely hinder your relationship. You do need to talk, but that's just dealing with a byproduct of the true problem. Communication itself isn't the problem.

People go to marriage seminars and are taught how to communicate. They're told, "Vent it, let it out, don't hold anything in, talk about it, and get it out." They're even instructed on how to write notes and letters, but all that happens is they now can communicate their anger and hatred that much better. Many people who have attended my marriage seminars have told me, "Communication nearly killed my marriage!"

Communication isn't the problem; it's just a symptom of the problem. The real problem is that people haven't first of all received the love of God for themselves. They don't know an unconditional love. They think God is just giving them what they deserve and that every time they mess up, He rejects them. Therefore, people tend to turn around and give others, especially their spouses, what they have inside of them.

You can't give away what you don't have. You can't love other people unconditionally if you haven't first of all received the unconditional love of God. If you ever experience God's unconditional—not-based-on-your-performance—love, you'll be able to love your mate unconditionally. If you ever receive a true revelation of God's kind of love, it'll enable you to love your spouse the same way. And when you do love your mate unconditionally, you'll wind up communicating it. Whenever you truly love someone, you communicate it. It's that simple!

However, we're teaching communication techniques instead of going to the root of the problem. There is a place for these things, but they aren't affecting the root of the problem.

Can You See the Difference?

This is what 1 John 2:3 is talking about. If you want to know "Do I truly love God? Do I really have His love in me?" you need to check the fruit. God's love in you will cause you to live right and to treat other people right.

However, for people who suffer from spiritual dyslexia, religion has come in and caused them to think, *Well, I want to know God, so I'm going to try to keep His commandments*. They try to do everything right, thinking that doing so will cause them to love God. But it's just the opposite. If you aren't loving God, you don't need to start trying to love God and love people better. Instead, you need to say, "God, it's evident that I really don't know Your love for me. If I truly understood how much You love me, I wouldn't treat people like this. If I was in a close relationship with You, I wouldn't be doing these things. Lord, forgive me for not knowing You. Please, reveal Yourself to me. Help me understand, know, and experience Your unconditional love." If you ever get filled with the love of God, I guarantee you'll treat other people better. If you aren't keeping the commandment of loving other people, it's because you don't know God.

> **He that saith, I know him, and keepeth not his commandments, is a liar, and the truth is not in him.**
>
> 1 JOHN 2:4

People say, "I don't want to be a liar—I want to operate in the truth—so what do I have to do? I have to keep the commandments." No, that's not what this is saying. This is saying that if you profess to know God but that knowledge isn't being manifest through your actions toward other people, you're just deceiving yourself. Why? Because knowing God—having an intimate relationship with Him—will cause you to love other people. Can you see the difference?

3D Image

But whoso keepeth his word, in him verily is the love of God perfected: hereby know we that we are in him.

1 John 2:5

People say, "I want God's love perfected, so what I have to do is keep His Word. If I just keep His Word, then the love of God will be perfected in me." No, it's saying just the opposite. If God's love is perfected in you, that will cause you to keep His Word.

If you can see it, this is very simple; if you can't, it's like one of those 3D pictures you hang on the wall. On the surface, it just looks like some pattern. But if you stare at it, all of a sudden a 3D image comes out. Then, once you see it, you can't miss it. But until you see it, you can look at it and miss the true picture.

That's the way it is with these verses. People look at them and they just can't understand. They think 1 John 2:3-5 is saying we have to keep the commandments so that we can have the love of God. No! It's saying that if we understood the love of God and had a relationship with Him, that would cause us to keep the commandments. Living holy is a fruit, not a root, of relationship with God. It's a byproduct of knowing Him.

Therefore, we must receive a revelation of how God loves us unconditionally before we can keep His commandments. Teaching people "Keep the commandments and then God will love you, accept you, and answer your prayers" is trying to get people to do something they're incapable of doing. You can't give away what you don't have.

Be honest with yourself. Are you suffering from spiritual dyslexia? Have you received a revelation of the unconditional love of God?

Spiritual Dyslexia
LESSON 19 – OUTLINE

I. When we comprehend how much the Lord loves us, our faith shoots through the roof, because faith works by love (Gal. 5:6).

> **That which was from the beginning, which we have heard, which we have seen with our eyes, which we have looked upon, and our hands have handled, of the Word of life; (For the life was manifested, and we have seen it, and bear witness, and shew unto you that eternal life, which was with the Father, and was manifested unto us;) That which we have seen and heard declare we unto you, that ye also may have fellowship with us: and truly our fellowship is with the Father, and with his Son Jesus Christ. And these things write we unto you, that your joy may be full.**
>
> 1 JOHN 1:1-4

   A. This close, intimate relationship with God is actually the true goal and aim of Christianity.

   B. If you really understood how much God loves you, it would just increase your relationship with Him.

   C. Everything in the Christian life flows out of this.

II. There is a condition in the body of Christ called *spiritual dyslexia*.

   A. Dyslexia causes people to see things backwards.

   B. Spiritual dyslexia is contagious—you get it through close contact with religion.

   C. It's amazing how people turn these verses in 1 John around and see them as performance-based scriptures.

> **And hereby we do know that we know him, if we keep his commandments.**
>
> 1 JOHN 2:3

   D. This verse isn't saying that keeping God's commandments will cause you to know Him.

   E. It's saying that you can tell if you really know Him, because knowing God will cause you to keep His commandments.

   F. If you're truly in fellowship with God—loving Him and having His love flow through you—you'll know because you'll start loving other people.

III. You can't give away what you don't have.

    A. You can't love other people unconditionally if you haven't first of all received the unconditional love of God.

    B. If you ever experience God's unconditional—not based on your performance—love, you'll be able to love your mate unconditionally.

    C. And when you do love your mate unconditionally, you'll wind up communicating it.

IV. God's love in you will cause you to live right and to treat other people right.

    A. But for people who suffer from spiritual dyslexia, religion has come in and caused them to think, *Well, I want to know God, so I'm going to try to keep His commandments.*

    B. They try to do everything right, thinking that doing so will cause them to love God.

    C. If you aren't keeping the commandment of loving other people, it's because you don't know God.

> **He that saith, I know him, and keepeth not his commandments, is a liar, and the truth is not in him.**
>
> 1 JOHN 2:4

    D. This is saying that if you profess to know God but that knowledge isn't being manifest through your actions toward other people, you're just deceiving yourself.

    E. Knowing God—having an intimate relationship with Him—will cause you to love other people.

V. If God's love is perfected in you, that will cause you to keep His Word.

> **But whoso keepeth his word, in him verily is the love of God perfected: hereby know we that we are in him.**
>
> 1 JOHN 2:5

    A. If we understood the love of God and had a relationship with Him, that would cause us to keep the commandments.

    B. Living holy is a fruit, not a root, of relationship with God.

    C. It's a byproduct of knowing Him.

    D. Therefore, we must receive a revelation of how God loves us unconditionally before we can keep His commandments.

    E. Have you received a revelation of the unconditional love of God?

Spiritual Dyslexia
LESSON 19 – TEACHER'S GUIDE

1.   When we comprehend how much the Lord loves us, our faith shoots through the roof, because faith works by love (Gal. 5:6). This close, intimate relationship with God is actually the true goal and aim of Christianity (1 John 1:1-4). If we really understood how much God loves us, it would just increase our relationship with Him. Everything in the Christian life flows out of this.

2.   There is a condition in the body of Christ called *spiritual dyslexia*. Dyslexia causes people to see things backwards. Spiritual dyslexia is contagious—we get it through close contact with religion. It's amazing how people turn these verses in 1 John around and see them as performance-based scriptures. First John 2:3 isn't saying that keeping God's commandments will cause us to know Him; it's saying that we can tell if we really know Him, because knowing God will cause us to keep His commandments. If we're truly in fellowship with God—loving Him and having His love flow through us—we'll know because we'll start loving other people.

3.   We can't give away what we don't have. We can't love other people unconditionally if we haven't first of all received the unconditional love of God. If we ever experience God's unconditional—not based on our performance—love, we'll be able to love our mates unconditionally. And when we do love our mates unconditionally, we'll wind up communicating it.

1. A. Read Galatians 5:6 and 1 John 1:1-4. What will cause our faith to shoot through the roof? (Comprehending how much the Lord loves us)
   B. What is the true goal and aim of Christianity? (A close, intimate relationship with God)
   C. What does everything in the Christian life flow out of? (Relationship with God)
2. A. What is 1 John 2:3 not saying? (Keeping God's commandments will cause us to know Him)
   B. What is 1 John 2:3 saying? (We can tell if we really know God, because knowing Him will cause us to keep His commandments)
3. A. Can we give away what we don't have? (No)
   B. In order to love other people unconditionally, what must we first of all receive? (The unconditional—not based on our performance—love of God)

4.   God's love in us will cause us to live right and to treat other people right. But for people who suffer from spiritual dyslexia, religion has come in and caused them to think, *Well, I want to know God, so I'm going to try to keep His commandments.* They try to do everything right, thinking that doing so will cause them to love God. If we aren't keeping the commandment of loving other people, it's because we don't know God. First John 2:4 says that if we profess to know God but that knowledge isn't being manifest through our actions toward other people, we're just deceiving ourselves. Knowing God—having an intimate relationship with Him—will cause us to love other people.

5.   If God's love is perfected in us, that will cause us to keep His Word (1 John 2:5). If we understood the love of God and had a relationship with Him, that would cause us to keep His commandments. Living holy is a fruit, not a root, of relationship with God. It's a byproduct of knowing Him. Therefore, we must receive a revelation of how God loves us unconditionally before we can keep His commandments.

4. A. What does 1 John 2:4 say? (If we profess to know God but that knowledge isn't being manifest
          through our actions toward other people, we're just deceiving ourselves)
    B. What does knowing God—having an intimate relationship with Him—produce? (It causes us to love
          other people)
5. A. Read 1 John 2:5. What will cause us to keep God's Word? (His love being perfected in us)
    B. Is living holy a fruit or a root of relationship with God? (A fruit—it's a byproduct of knowing Him)
    C. What must we receive before we can keep God's commandments? (A revelation of how He loves
          us unconditionally)

Spiritual Dyslexia
LESSON 19 – ADDITIONAL INFORMATION

My teaching entitled "Eternal Life" addresses this very topic. If I only had one chance to minister to someone, I'd share this message with them.

Spiritual Dyslexia
LESSON 19 – DISCIPLESHIP QUESTIONS

1. According to Galatians 5:6, does circumcision or uncircumcision avail anything in Jesus Christ?

2. What avails in Jesus Christ?

3. How does faith work?

4. According to 1 John 1:1-4, what has he seen with his eyes, and what have his hands handled?

5. What did he declare unto you?

6. Why did he declare it?

7. Truly, his fellowship is with whom?

8. Why did he write these things unto you?

9. According to 1 John 2:3-5, how do we know—what evidence or fruit do we have—that we know Him?

10. Is it possible to truly know Him and not keep His commandments?

11. What does the Bible call someone who says they know God but doesn't keep His commandments?

12. Is the truth in them?

13. What evidence, or fruit, is produced in those in whom the love of God is perfected?

14. If this same fruit is evident in our lives, what can we know?

Spiritual Dyslexia
LESSON 19 – ANSWER KEY

1. No.

2. Faith.

3. By love.

4. The Word of life.

5. That which he has seen and heard.

6. That you also may have fellowship with him.

7. The Father and His Son, Jesus Christ.

8. That your joy may be full.

9. If we keep His commandments.

10. No.

11. A liar.

12. No.

13. They keep His Word.

14. That we are in Him.

Spiritual Dyslexia
LESSON 19 – SCRIPTURES

For in Jesus Christ neither circumcision availeth any thing, nor uncircumcision; but faith which worketh by love.

GALATIANS 5:6

That which was from the beginning, which we have heard, which we have seen with our eyes, which we have looked upon, and our hands have handled, of the Word of life; (For the life was manifested, and we have seen it, and bear witness, and shew unto you that eternal life, which was with the Father, and was manifested unto us;) That which we have seen and heard declare we unto you, that ye also may have fellowship with us: and truly our fellowship is with the Father, and with his Son Jesus Christ. And these things write we unto you, that your joy may be full.

1 JOHN 1:1-4

And hereby we do know that we know him, if we keep his commandments. He that saith, I know him, and keepeth not his commandments, is a liar, and the truth is not in him. But whoso keepeth his word, in him verily is the love of God perfected: hereby know we that we are in him.

1 JOHN 2:3-5

Motivated by Love
LESSON 20

The Christian life isn't difficult—it's impossible! It is absolutely, physically, humanly impossible.

> **But I [Jesus] say unto you, That ye resist not evil: but whosoever shall smite thee on thy right cheek, turn to him the other also. And if any man will sue thee at the law, and take away thy coat, let him have thy cloke also. And whosoever shall compel thee to go a mile, go with him twain [two].**
>
> MATTHEW 5:39-41, BRACKETS MINE

That's not just hard to do—it's impossible! Human nature doesn't respond that way. The flesh wants to fight, hurt somebody, or do whatever else it has to do to defend itself. But God has asked us to do things that are absolutely impossible to do.

So, first of all, we must have a relationship with God. Then, it's not us living, but Christ living in and through us (Gal. 2:20).

When you have a relationship with God and you understand His perfect love, then you're able to forgive someone else, because you understand that you've been forgiven. When you've received His unconditional love, you're able to love people who don't deserve it, because you understand that God has loved you that way. However, by and large, people haven't been doing this.

Deep Ruts

We've been telling people to start doing what's right, "and if you'll do enough good stuff, then God will love you, accept you, and all these things will work." That's impossible! People can't live up to that standard. It drives them away.

I talked with a lady recently whose father had raised her in a Pentecostal church. She remembers hearing him speak in tongues. When she received the baptism in the Holy Spirit recently, he was so excited, he cried. He had fallen back into drinking, was having problems, and wasn't serving the Lord. She asked me if I knew what to do about it. I don't know all of the reasons, but part of the problem is that he's been trying to do what's right all of his life and he's failed. It's impossible to do right all the time. Everyone fails sometimes, but now he has all of this guilt and condemnation. He's still sensitive to God though. When his daughter received the baptism in the Holy Spirit, tears rolled down his cheek. He loves God, but he just can't live up to "the standard." So all of that condemnation is just beating him down.

That's not the way the Word of God was intended to operate. The Lord wants us to come into a relationship with Him and receive His love. Then the love of Christ constrains us (2 Cor. 5:14). God's love will just flow through us.

I wish I had a better way of making people understand what I'm saying, because it's backwards from the way everyone has thought for so long. We've been taught this so often and so much, that it's like going down a dirt road that has ruts so deep you just can't miss them. Every time you go down the road, you just fall into the same old ruts. People just automatically fall into the same thought patterns because it's been said so often, so loud, and so much, but the truth is different than the way most people are thinking today.

"Great Service"

I was genuinely converted as an eight-year-old. The very next day, without me telling them, my classmates discerned the change, and they made fun of me. So there was immediate fruit of my newfound life in Christ. I know I was genuinely saved. But even though I loved the Lord with all my heart, I fell into the trap of thinking I had to do something to get God to love me. Therefore, I was always doing things. I didn't really have a revelation of God's love for me. I would have said "God loves me," but I didn't truly understand it. I didn't realize God's love was unconditional, or I wouldn't have always been trying to do something to get Him to love me more.

I "rededicated" myself every time our church had a service. It didn't matter if we had special meetings every night for a week; I'd go forward. If I would've had a "re-dedicator," I would have worn it out! I was always seeking after God, but I thought I had to do something to get Him to love me.

An introvert by nature, I couldn't look people in the face and talk to them. When I was a senior in high school, people would walk down the street and say, "Good morning." I'd be two blocks away before I could respond. I just couldn't talk to people.

However, even though I was an introvert and had all of these problems, I was told, "You have to do all of these things, and if you'll do enough good things, then God will accept you." So I took the soul-winning courses, psyched myself up, and went out and knocked on doors every Thursday night for "Adult Visitation." On top of that, I became so zealous, that I started a special Tuesday night visitation for the youth. At the age of fourteen, I had trained others in soul-winning and was "leading" three or four people "to the Lord" every week. I'd have them repeat a prayer after me. Then I'd go back to church with their "scalp" and show everybody what I did, trying to gain acceptance and approval. I was doing all of this stuff—Tuesday nights, Thursday nights, reading my Bible every day, never missing a church meeting, and so forth—thinking I was doing this "great service," trying to get God to love me.

Daylight to Dark

Then on March 23, 1968 I had an experience where God revealed His love to me. First of all, He showed me that my self-righteousness and all the things I was taking pride in were an offense to Him. He showed me I was trusting in myself and my own goodness. I honestly thought God was going to kill me. For an hour and a half, I turned myself inside out confessing all my sins and saying, "God, I'm sorry!" I didn't know how bad and how much of a religious Pharisee I was. So I repented of all that and honestly expected God to kill me that night.

When I saw how bad I was, I thought it was the first time God knew about it. Under the logic I had at the time—that He deals with people based on performance—I deserved to be killed. So I just confessed everything, hoping that if He killed me, I wouldn't go to hell but to heaven. To my great surprise, after confessing all of that, the love of God just poured out in my life for about four and a half months. I was just gone somewhere—caught up in the love of God. Tangibly, I knew that God loved me. It was awesome!

I knew that God's love for me was unconditional. I knew that there was nothing I did to deserve it. I knew there was nothing I could ever do to make God not love me. His love for me was totally disconnected from me, separate from anything I deserved. The only thing I had to do was either receive it or reject it, but God loved me passionately, completely separate from anything I deserved.

When I saw that, it didn't make me want to serve God less. I did quit both the Tuesday and Thursday night visitations. However, that was because I realized that even though I was making three to six, maybe eight, visits a week inviting people to church, I was still letting hundreds of people pass me by every day. So I stopped going out on Tuesday and Thursday nights, and I just started talking to everything that moved. I witnessed daylight to dark. I was knocking on a hundred doors a day!

At one time, I actually made a commitment that I would never see a person who I wouldn't talk to about Jesus. I kept that for nearly a year. Finally, I was drafted into the army during Vietnam. I remember standing at attention and seeing hundreds of people march by, and I couldn't talk to them. I thought, *God, I'm going to have to renege on this because I just can't feasibly do it*. But for nearly a year, I talked to everyone.

We'd go into a restaurant, and I'd stand up and pray over everybody's food at the top of my lungs. They'd look at me, and I'd say, "You need your food blessed too!" I was obnoxious, but I led people to the Lord after doing that. I'd see them coming out of a convenience store with a pack of cigarettes or some booze, and I'd tell them, "You're going to hell. You need to repent!" It was legalism, but it was motivated by love. I just didn't know any other way to do it. That's the way everybody I was exposed to did it.

Same Action, Different Motive

Instead of feeling like I had to try to do something to get God's love, now I understood that He loved me. So, instantly I started sharing with people. I began witnessing to folks. I just gave my life trying to share this love with other people. If you truly fall in love with God, nobody will have to preach to you about sharing your faith.

If you're a pastor, do you have trouble motivating the people in your church to evangelize? Do you say, "Why don't you share your faith? Why don't you talk to people at work? Why don't you tell others about God?" That's just a symptom of a problem. The problem is they really haven't received the love of God. They don't truly know how much He loves them. If they knew, they wouldn't be able to keep their mouths shut!

Do you use condemnation, saying, "If you don't witness, someday you'll stand before God without any stars in your crown, and you'll be embarrassed"? If so, people will go out and start knocking on doors, not because they love others, but because they love themselves. They don't want to be embarrassed. Since they're doing it out of fear and condemnation, their "witness" comes across like a sounding brass and a tinkling cymbal (1 Cor. 13:1). There's no love in it. People get offended and turned off because of "fanatics" who say, "Repent or else. Turn or burn!" The problem is that they aren't "witnessing" motivated by love. They're doing it trying to obtain God's love and earn His favor.

We need to tell people about the love of God. We need to let them know how good He is. If they ever received a revelation of that, they'd tell everyone about God's love. The issue is motivation. We're trying to get people to do the same action, but from totally different motivations.

Old or New?

Brethren, I write no new commandment unto you, but an old commandment which ye had from the beginning. The old commandment is the word which ye have heard from the beginning. Again, a new commandment I write unto you, which thing is true in him and in you: because the darkness is past, and the true light now shineth.

1 John 2:7-8

This sounds a little bit confusing. John said, "This isn't a new commandment. It's the old commandment—the same thing you've heard from the beginning." Then he said, "It's a new commandment." Which is it? Is it an old commandment, or a new one? It's both.

What he meant is, none of the rules have changed. It's not that you aren't supposed to love the Lord, worship God, study the Word, pray, and seek Him. It's not that you aren't supposed to love people and treat them right. It's the same thing the Old Testament said, but now it's to be done with a different motivation. Therefore, it's a brand-new commandment because, instead of commanding you to do all these things, God is saying to love Him and love people. As you do, you'll automatically do these other things.

You'd never lie to someone you truly loved. When you lie, you are manipulating that person. You are changing the facts and taking advantage of them. You would never lie to someone you truly loved, because it's making that person act on false information. It'll make a fool out of them. You're taking advantage of them. When you lie, you are operating in nothing but self-love. You don't care about the other person. You're just going to do what it takes to take advantage of them.

If you really loved someone else, you wouldn't steal from them. If you ever steal from somebody—whether it's your boss or your parents, your friend or a stranger—you don't give a rip about them. You don't know what their situation is, and you don't care. You just want something, and you're going to take it. All you're doing is thinking about yourself. All thievery is total self-love. It's based on not loving other people.

Receive God's Love

If you truly loved other people, you'd never gossip about them. You'd never say things behind their backs that could hurt them. If they find out what you said, would you be ashamed all of a sudden and not want to say it anymore? That's not because you care anything about them. All you care about is yourself, and you'd say anything that would promote yourself, anything you feel like. You just don't care about other people. The only time it would bother you is if it's going to cost you something or make you look bad.

If we really loved people, we wouldn't gossip, steal, lie, or treat them the way we do. If we truly loved God, church leaders wouldn't have to force us to study the Word, meet with other believers, or anything else. The bottom line is that we're still telling people, "You need to love God and do all of these other things."

However, we have a brand-new motivation. I'm not telling people that we shouldn't be serving God and sharing Jesus with others; I'm just saying that first of all, we need to receive the love of God for ourselves. We need to understand that the Lord isn't going to love us more if we do everything right, and He's not going to love us less if we do everything wrong. If we could ever get a revelation of that and receive the love of God, His love would cause us to live holy.

Motivated by Love
LESSON 20 – OUTLINE

I. The Christian life isn't difficult—it's impossible!

> **But I [Jesus] say unto you, That ye resist not evil: but whosoever shall smite thee on thy right cheek, turn to him the other also. And if any man will sue thee at the law, and take away thy coat, let him have thy cloke also. And whosoever shall compel thee to go a mile, go with him twain [two].**
>
> MATTHEW 5:39-41, BRACKETS MINE

    A. The flesh wants to fight, hurt somebody, or do whatever else it has to do to defend itself—but God has asked us to do things that are absolutely impossible to do.

    B. So, first of all, we must have a relationship with God.

    C. Then it's not us living, but Christ living in and through us (Gal. 2:20).

    D. When you have a relationship with God and you understand His perfect love, then you're able to forgive someone else, because you understand that you've been forgiven.

    E. The Lord wants us to come into a relationship with Him and receive His love.

    F. Then the love of Christ constrains us (2 Cor. 5:14). God's love will just flow through us.

II. I was genuinely converted as an eight-year-old.

    A. Even though I loved the Lord with all my heart, I fell into the trap of thinking I had to do something to get God to love me.

    B. Therefore, I was always doing things.

    C. I was doing all of this stuff—Tuesday and Thursday night visitations, reading my Bible every day, never missing a church meeting, and so forth, thinking I was doing this "great service," trying to get God to love me.

III. Then on March 23, 1968 I had an experience where God revealed His love to me.

    A. First of all, He showed me that my self-righteousness and all the things I was taking pride in were an offense to Him.

    B. I honestly thought God was going to kill me.

    C. To my great surprise, after confessing all of that, the love of God just poured out in my life for about four and a half months.

D. Tangibly, I knew that God loved me.

E. When I saw that, it didn't make me want to serve God less.

F. I just gave my life trying to share this love with other people.

IV. We need to tell people about the love of God.

A. We need to let them know how good He is.

B. If they ever received a revelation of that, they'd go tell everyone about God's love.

C. The issue is motivation.

V. We're trying to get people to do the same action, but from totally different motivations.

> **Brethren, I write no new commandment unto you, but an old commandment which ye had from the beginning. The old commandment is the word which ye have heard from the beginning. Again, a new commandment I write unto you, which thing is true in him and in you: because the darkness is past, and the true light now shineth.**
>
> 1 JOHN 2:7-8

A. Is it an old commandment, or a new one? It's both.

B. It's the same thing the Old Testament said, but now it's to be done with a different motivation.

C. Therefore, it's a brand-new commandment now because, instead of commanding you to do all these things, God is saying to love Him and love people—as you do, you'll automatically do these other things.

D. If we really loved people, we wouldn't gossip, steal, lie, or treat them the way we do.

E. If we truly loved God, church leaders wouldn't have to force us to study the Word, meet with other believers, or anything else.

VI. First of all, you need to receive the love of God for yourself.

A. You need to understand that the Lord isn't going to love you more if you do everything right, and He's not going to love you less if you do everything wrong.

B. If you could ever get a revelation of that and receive the love of God, His love would cause you to live holy.

Motivated by Love

1.   The Christian life isn't difficult—it's impossible (Matt. 5:39-41). The flesh wants to fight, hurt somebody, or do whatever else it has to do to defend itself. But God has asked us to do things that are absolutely impossible to do. So, first of all, we must have a relationship with God. Then, it's not us living, but Christ living in and through us (Gal. 2:20). When we have relationship with God and we understand His perfect love, we're able to forgive someone else, because we understand that we've been forgiven. The Lord wants us to come into a relationship with Him and receive His love. Then the love of Christ constrains us (2 Cor. 5:14). God's love will just flow through us.

2.   Andrew was genuinely converted as an eight-year-old. Even though he loved the Lord with all his heart, he fell into a trap of thinking he had to do something to get God to love him. Therefore, he was always doing things. Andrew was doing all of this stuff—Tuesday and Thursday night visitations, reading his Bible every day, never missing a church meeting, and so forth—thinking he was doing this "great service," trying to get God to love him.

3.   Then on March 23, 1968 Andrew had an experience where God revealed His love to him. First of all, He showed him that his self-righteousness and all the things he was taking pride in were an offense to Him. Andrew honestly thought God was going to kill him. To his great surprise, after confessing all of that, the love of God just poured out in his life for about four and a half months. Tangibly, he knew that God loved him. When Andrew saw that, it didn't make him want to serve God less; he just gave his life trying to share this love with other people.

1. A. Read Matthew 5:39-41, Galatians 2:20, and 2 Corinthians 5:14. What does the Lord want us to do? (Come into a relationship with Him and receive His love)
   B. What happens then? (The love of Christ constrains us. God's love will just flow through us)
2. A. What trap did Andrew fall into as a young believer? (A trap of thinking he had to do something to get God to love him)
   B. What did this produce? (He was always doing things trying to get God to love him)
3. A. What happened on March 23, 1968? (Andrew had an experience where God revealed His love to him)
   B. Once he knew God loved him, did it make him want to serve God less? (No, Andrew just gave his life trying to share this love with other people)

4.   We need to tell people about the love of God. We need to let them know how good He is. If they ever received a revelation of that, they'd go tell everyone about His love. The issue is motivation.

5.   We're trying to get people to do the same action, but from totally different motivations (1 John 2:7-8). Is it an old commandment, or a new one? It's both. It's the same thing the Old Testament said, but now it's to be done with a different motivation. Therefore, it's a brand-new commandment because, instead of commanding us to do all these things, God is saying to love Him and love people—as we do, we'll automatically do these other things. If we really loved people, we wouldn't gossip, steal, lie, or treat them the way we do. If we truly loved God, church leaders wouldn't have to force us to study the Word, meet with other believers, or anything else.

6.   First of all, we need to receive the love of God for ourselves. We need to understand that the Lord isn't going to love us more if we do everything right, and He's not going to love us less if we do everything wrong. If we could ever get a revelation of that and receive His love, His love would cause us to live holy.

4. A. What do we need to tell people about? (The love of God and how good He is)
   B. If they ever received a revelation of that, what would they do? (They'd go tell everyone about His love)
5. A. Read 1 John 2:7-8. What's different between the old commandment and the new, the action or the motivation? (We're trying to get people to do the same action, but from a totally different motivation)
   B. What happens when we love God and love people? (We automatically do these other things—live holy, keep the commandments)
6. A. Is the Lord going to love us more if we do everything right? (No)
   B. Is the Lord going to love us less if we do everything wrong? (No)
   C. What would happen if we ever got a revelation of and received the love of God? (His love would cause us to live holy)

Motivated by Love
LESSON 20 – DISCIPLESHIP QUESTIONS

1. Who was speaking in Matthew 5:39-41?

2. What are we not to resist?

3. What are we to do when we're smitten on the right cheek?

4. What are we to do if someone sues us and takes away our coats?

5. What are we to do if someone compels us to go a mile?

6. According to Galatians 2:20, who is crucified with Christ?

7. If you're a believer, who lives in you?

8. How do I now live in the flesh?

9. Fill in the blank. The faith of the _____ of God.
   A. Disciple.
   B. Son.
   C. Follower.
   D. All of the above.
   E. None of the above.

10. Whose faith is it?

11. In addition to giving every believer His faith, what has He done for them?

12. According to 1 Corinthians 5:14, what constrains a believer?

13. If one died for all, then what?

14. According to 1 Corinthians 13:1, what kinds of tongues can we speak in?
    A. The tongues of angels.
    B. The tongues of animals.
    C. The tongues of men.
    D. All of the above.
    E. None of the above.

15. What heart motivation must be present when I speak?

16. If that's not motivating me, what do I come across as?
    A. Soothing music.
    B. Tinkling cymbal.
    C. Sounding brass.
    D. All of the above.
    E. None of the above.

17. To whom is 1 John 2:7-8 written?

18. Did the author write a new commandment, or an old commandment to the brethren?

19. How long have they had the old commandment?

20. What is the old commandment?

21. The new commandment is true where?
    A. In you.
    B. On earth.
    C. In Him.
    D. All of the above.
    E. None of the above.

22. What has happened to the darkness?

23. What now shines?

Motivated by Love
LESSON 20 – ANSWER KEY

1. Jesus.

2. Evil.

3. We are to turn the other cheek to the person also.

4. We are to let them have our cloaks also.

5. We are to go with them two miles.

6. Every believer.

7. Christ.

8. By the faith of the Son of God.

9. B. Son.

10. The Son of God's faith.

11. Loved them and gave Himself for them.

12. The love of God.

13. All were dead.

14. A. The tongues of angels.
    C. The tongues of men.

15. Charity (God's kind of love).

16. B. Tinkling cymbal.
    C. Sounding brass.

17. The brethren.

18. Both.

19. From the beginning.

20. The Word which you have heard from the beginning.

21. A. In you.
    C. In Him.

22. It's past.

23. The true light.

Motivated by Love

But I say unto you, That ye resist not evil: but whosoever shall smite thee on thy right cheek, turn to him the other also. And if any man will sue thee at the law, and take away thy coat, let him have thy cloks also. And whosoever shall compel thee to go a mile, go with him twain.

MATTHEW 5:39-41

I am crucified with Christ: nevertheless I live; yet not I, but Christ liveth in me: and the life which I now live in the flesh I live by the faith of the Son of God, who loved me, and gave himself for me.

GALATIANS 2:20

For the love of Christ constraineth us; because we thus judge, that if one died for all, then were all dead.

2 CORINTHIANS 5:14

Though I speak with the tongues of men and of angels, and have not charity, I am become as sounding brass, or a tinkling cymbal.

1 CORINTHIANS 13:1

Brethren, I write no new commandment unto you, but an old commandment which ye had from the beginning. The old commandment is the word which ye have heard from the beginning. Again, a new commandment I write unto you, which thing is true in him and in you: because the darkness is past, and the true light now shineth.

1 JOHN 2:7-8

God Looks at the Heart
LESSON 21

Beloved, let us love one another: for love is of God; and every one that loveth is born of God, and knoweth God.

1 John 4:7

People say, "Well, I want to be born of God and know God, so what do I have to do? I have to love everybody else." No, this is saying the opposite. It's saying that if you know God, then you'll be born of God, and you will love other people. Keeping the commandments and doing these things is the byproduct of—not the way to—a relationship with God.

He that loveth not knoweth not God; for God is love.

1 John 4:8

People say, "Well, I want to know God, so what do I have to do? I have to love other people." No, this is saying the opposite. It's saying that if you would just understand God's love for you and come to know Him, then you would wind up loving other people, because God is love. If you're filled with God, you'll be filled with love. Isn't that simple?

Receive First, Then Give

In this was manifested the love of God toward us, because that God sent his only begotten Son into the world, that we might live through him. Herein is love, not that we loved God, but that he loved us, and sent his Son to be the propitiation for our sins.

1 John 4:9-10

What a great truth! You don't love God first, and then He loves you back. God loved us first! You must first of all receive the love of God. Then you can love God and love others.

You can't give away what you don't have. You can't treat other people right if you think God is treating you wrong. If you think God is dealing with you based on your performance, you'll wind up reproducing that same thing and give other people what they deserve. You'll be as mean as a snake.

I heard about someone recently who had gone through some kind of religious school. The person turned from being sweet to be being a mean person. That's what religion does, because that's what they're teaching about God: "God is a harsh God!"

At some Bible colleges, if men don't wear sleeves down to their wrists, they're "going to hell." One school I know of would kick a person out for wearing a crimson shirt, because it's "the color of the beast." That's just legalism. God isn't mad at you because of the way you dress.

Hair, Jewelry, and Makeup

Other people say, "You can't wear any makeup or put on any jewelry." They base it on 1 Peter 3, which says:

> **Whose adorning let it not be that outward adorning of plaiting the hair, and of wearing of gold.**
>
> 1 Peter 3:3

They say, "You shouldn't fix your hair fancy or wear any gold." Well, if they would just keep reading, this verse goes on to say…

> **Or of putting on of apparel.**
>
> 1 Peter 3:3

Does that mean we aren't supposed to wear clothes? Of course not! This whole passage is simply emphasizing, "Don't put your focus on the outward part."

I've seen Pentecostal women who put on five layers of powder so it wouldn't look like they had rosy cheeks. Since their cheeks were naturally rosy, they went to all of this effort just to look bland and ugly. Personally, I believe that if your "barn" needs painting, paint it. If it needs two coats, give it two coats! But that's not what this passage is talking about.

A Holy Life

> **Beloved, if God so loved us, we ought also to love one another. No man hath seen God at any time. If we love one another, God dwelleth in us, and his love is perfected in us.**
>
> 1 John 4:11-12

People say, "Well, I want God to dwell in me and His love to be perfected, so what do I have to do? I have to love others!" No, this is saying just the opposite. If you would receive the unconditional love of God and let that love dwell in you, you'll wind up loving other people.

> **Hereby know we that we dwell in him, and he in us, because he hath given us of his Spirit. And we have seen and do testify that the Father sent the Son to be the Saviour of the world. Whosoever shall confess that Jesus is the Son of God, God dwelleth in him, and he in God. And we have known and believed the love that God hath to us. God is love; and he that dwelleth in love dwelleth in God, and God in him.**
>
> 1 John 4:13-16

I could just go on and on with this. If you don't understand what I'm talking about, the book of 1 John will seem to say you have to do these things for God to respond. But it's actually saying just the opposite. It's saying that if you truly knew God, you would wind up living a holy life.

Actions Are Evidence

Living holy doesn't earn us favor with God, but it does evidence His presence in our lives. If someone comes to me and says, "Oh, yeah, I know God. He and I are tight. I fellowship with Him and love Him with all of my heart. We're best friends!" If they don't trust God in their giving, if they are lying, stealing, and committing adultery (I'm not talking about an isolated instance, but it's their lifestyle) then they can say whatever they want; I don't believe it. Those things don't reflect God in a person's life.

"But, Andrew, isn't that undoing everything you've said?" No, it's a perfect balance. Our holiness doesn't make God love us. But if God's love is dwelling in us and we're dwelling in it, His love will cause us to live holy. "Living holy" doesn't mean you'll live by all the principles and standards of some religious sect. Everything people say is "holy" isn't necessarily holy. But God's love will cause you to love Him and love people.

If you say "I really do know God. We have a great relationship," yet you're as mean as a snake—you don't love others, you never do anything for anyone, you don't think about anybody besides yourself, you can see people in need and not even care—confess what you will, but the Word of God says:

> **But whoso hath this world's good, and seeth his brother have need, and shutteth up his bowels of compassion from him, how dwelleth the love of God in him?**
>
> 1 John 3:17

You can say you love God, but the truth is you can tell by your actions whether His love is really dwelling in you or not.

Religion or True Christianity?

Instead of thinking you have to earn the blessing of God by doing these things, you need to recognize that living properly, treating other people right, loving your mate, and so forth are all byproducts of a relationship with God. If you have a temper and you fly off the handle, don't say "O God, help me quit this!" and start trying to treat other people right so God will love you. Instead, reverse it and say, "Father, I recognize that the reason I'm like this is because I don't really know You. I haven't really received Your love. I'm just treating people the way I think You are treating me. Lord, I need a revelation of Your love for me!"

If you would take the truths I've talked about in this study—that all of your sins have been paid for, that God's not angry with you, and so on—and meditate on them, the Lord would reveal His love to you. Once you fall in love with God and His love begins to flow in your life, it'll cause you to live holy. You will have your...

> **Fruit unto holiness, and the end everlasting life.**
>
> Romans 6:22

Holiness is the fruit, not the root, of salvation. This is where religion has gone wrong.

Man looketh on the outward appearance, but the LORD looketh on the heart.

1 Samuel 16:7

This is one way you can tell if it's religion or true Christianity. Religion always focuses on the external person. It's always trying to get you to clean up the outside—fix this and quit doing that—because that's what mankind looks at and deals with. Religious people don't really care about the heart. As long as you come to church, pay your tithes, and dress the way they want when you're there, they don't care what you do during the week. It doesn't matter if your heart is right or not. Religion just deals with the external, but God deals with the heart.

Short Shorts and Halter Tops

The Lord wants to come in, touch your heart, and reveal His love to you. If that ever happens, the rest will be taken care of.

Jamie and I pastored this little church in Childress, Texas. One day we took a small group out to the park for a picnic. While there, we came across this family—a husband, wife, and their two-year-old daughter—who had been living out of the back of their pickup. It turned out that they had just left the nudist colony where they had been living for the past three years. They were totally broke and had run out of gas in this city park where we were having our picnic. They came over and begged us for some food.

We gave them something to eat and shared the Gospel with them. They hadn't taken a bath in days, so some of our people opened up their homes, helped them get cleaned up, gave them some clothes, and other things. Anyway, we led this couple to the Lord, and they started coming to church.

This woman was well built and nice looking. Since they'd been in a nudist colony for so long, all she had was short shorts and halter tops. So that's what she came to church in. We all sat in a semicircle. No one could avoid looking at her, because we were all facing each other. During praise and worship, she'd go to bouncing, jumping, and praising God. It just left little to the imagination.

"Cover Up!"

This was causing some problems with other people in the church, so several of them came to me, demanding, "Aren't you going to tell her she needs to put some clothes on?" I answered, "We didn't tell her that before she became born again. We didn't throw a sheet over her and tell her that God wouldn't save her if she didn't put some clothes on. Give her some time. She just became born again. Let her enjoy the fact that God loves her. He'll show her some things. But in the meantime, I'm not going to condemn her."

So we allowed this woman to keep coming to church. Not too long after that, she came to one of Jamie's Bible studies. She stood up and told these women, "I have never owned a dress in all of my life. I would really like to have a dress. Would you all pray with me?" They not only prayed with her, but within an hour after that Bible study, she had a dozen dresses that were all up to her neck and all the way down to the floor. She came to church that night showing off one of her new dresses and just praising God. "Look what the Lord did!" She never had anyone tell her, "God's angry with you. He doesn't love you because of the way you dress." It worked out.

However, most people would say "Cover up!" instead of just letting God love her and speak to her over time. She and her husband had just been miraculously saved. Although great things were happening, it takes a little while for a person to turn their whole life around. Religious people just want to deal with the external. They want to put people in their clothes, make them as drab as they are, and do all of these kinds of things so they will feel better. But they don't care what's going on in a person's heart. The Lord isn't like that.

God was more pleased with that woman coming to church in her short shorts and halter top than many Christians who have never dressed that way. Why? Her heart was right. She was in love with Jesus and worshiping Him. God looked at her heart and said, "Awesome!"

"God Is the Best Blankety-Blank!"

One time while I was preaching in Phoenix, this woman was so excited, she was literally bouncing up and down on the front row. Between sessions, I went over and talked to her. She'd just been born again a little over a month, so I asked her to come up and give her testimony.

She stood up in front of the group, and every third or fourth word was profanity. She blasted, cursed, and damned everything. She said words I didn't even know! She was saying, "God is the best blankety-blank thing that's ever happened to me. This beats sex! This beats drugs!" She was saying things that would make a sailor turn red.

When the people started reacting, she looked at me and asked, "Am I saying something wrong?"

I answered, "Nope. You're doing great!" So she finished her testimony.

People came up to me afterward and said, "Why didn't you tell her to stop and not do that?" Again, that's just religion. I'm not saying that we should use profanity, but God was looking at her heart, and she didn't realize that Christians didn't talk that way. I went back the next year. This woman came up to me and said, "I'm so sorry! I was just born again. I didn't know Christians didn't talk that way. I thought everybody talked that way!" She had learned.

God was more pleased with that woman, who used profanity in her testimony about how good He is, than He was with many Christians who would never use those kinds of words. They may have the right religious form, but they don't know Him. They aren't excited about Him. God looks at your heart!

God Looks at the Heart
LESSON 21 – OUTLINE

I. Keeping the commandments and doing these things is the byproduct of—not the way to—a relationship with God.

> **Beloved, let us love one another: for love is of God; and every one that loveth is born of God, and knoweth God.**
>
> 1 JOHN 4:7

    A. This is saying that if you would just understand God's love for you and come to know Him, you would wind up loving other people, because God is love.

> **He that loveth not knoweth not God; for God is love.**
>
> 1 JOHN 4:8

    B. If you're filled with God, you'll be filled with love.

II. God loved us first!

> **In this was manifested the love of God toward us, because that God sent his only begotten Son into the world, that we might live through him. Herein is love, not that we loved God, but that he loved us, and sent his Son to be the propitiation for our sins.**
>
> 1 JOHN 4:9-10

    A. You don't love God first, and then He loves you back.

    B. You must first of all receive the love of God. Then you can love God and love others.

    C. You can't give away what you don't have.

    D. You can't treat other people right if you think God is treating you wrong.

    E. God isn't mad at you because of the way you dress.

> **Whose adorning let it not be that outward adorning of plaiting the hair, and of wearing of gold, or of putting on of apparel.**
>
> 1 PETER 3:3

III. If you would receive the unconditional love of God, and let that love dwell in you, you'll wind up loving other people.

Beloved, if God so loved us, we ought also to love one another. No man hath seen God at any time. If we love one another, God dwelleth in us, and his love is perfected in us.

1 John 4:11-12

A. If you don't understand what I'm talking about, the book of 1 John will seem to say you have to do these things for God to respond.

Hereby know we that we dwell in him, and he in us, because he hath given us of his Spirit. And we have seen and do testify that the Father sent the Son to be the Saviour of the world. Whosoever shall confess that Jesus is the Son of God, God dwelleth in him, and he in God. And we have known and believed the love that God hath to us. God is love; and he that dwelleth in love dwelleth in God, and God in him.

1 John 4:13-16

B. This is saying that if you truly knew God, you would wind up living a holy life.

C. Living holy doesn't earn us favor with God, but it does evidence His presence in our lives.

IV. God's love will cause you to love Him and love people.

A. You can say that you love God, but the truth is you can tell by your actions whether His love is really dwelling in you or not.

But whoso hath this world's good, and seeth his brother have need, and shutteth up his bowels of compassion from him, how dwelleth the love of God in him?

1 John 3:17

B. Instead of thinking you have to earn the blessing of God by doing these things, you need to recognize that living properly, treating other people right, loving your mate, and so forth are all byproducts of a relationship with God.

C. If you would take the truths I've talked about in this study—that all of your sins have been paid for, that God's not angry with you, and so on—and meditate on them, the Lord would reveal His love to you.

D. Once you fall in love with God and His love begins to flow in your life, it'll cause you to live holy. You will have your...

Fruit unto holiness, and the end everlasting life.

Romans 6:22

E. Holiness is the fruit, not the root, of salvation.

V. Religion always focuses on the external person.

Man looketh on the outward appearance, but the LORD looketh on the heart.

1 SAMUEL 16:7

A. Religion is always trying to get you to clean up the outside—fix this and quit doing that—because that's what mankind looks at and deals with.

B. As long as you come to church, pay your tithes, and dress the way they want you to when you're there, religious people don't care what you do during the week.

C. Religion just deals with the external, but God deals with the heart.

D. The Lord wants to come in, touch your heart, and reveal His love to you.

E. If that ever happens, the rest will be taken care of.

F. God looks at your heart!

God Looks at the Heart
LESSON 21 – TEACHER'S GUIDE

1.   Keeping the commandments and doing these things is the byproduct of—not the way to—a relationship with God. First John 4:7 is saying that if we would just understand God's love for us and come to know Him, we would wind up loving other people, because God is love (1 John 4:8). If we're filled with God, we'll be filled with love.

2.   God loved us first (1 John 4:9-10). We don't love God first, and then He loves us back. We must first of all receive the love of God—then we can love God and love others. We can't give away what we don't have. We can't treat other people right if we think God is treating us wrong. God isn't mad at us because of the way we dress (1 Pet. 3:3).

3.   If we would receive the unconditional love of God, and let that love dwell in us, we'll wind up loving other people (1 John 4:11-12). If we don't understand these truths, the book of 1 John will seem to say we have to do these things for God to respond. First John 4:13-16 is saying that if we truly knew God, we would wind up living holy lives. Living holy doesn't earn us favor with God, but it does evidence His presence in our lives.

1. A. Read 1 John 4:7-8. Is keeping the commandments the way to or the byproduct of a relationship with God? (The byproduct of)
   B. If we're filled with God, what will we be filled with? (Love)
2. A. Read 1 John 4:9-10. What must we first of all receive before we can love God and love others? (The love of God)
   B. Can we treat other people right if we think God is treating us wrong? (No)
3. A. Read 1 John 4:11-16. If we don't understand these truths concerning the unconditional love of God, what will the book of 1 John seem like it's saying to us? (We have to do all these things for God to respond)
   B. What is 1 John 4:13-16 really saying? (If we truly knew God, we would wind up living holy lives)
   C. Since living holy doesn't earn us favor with God, what does it do? (It evidences His presence in our lives)

4. God's love will cause us to love Him and love people. We can say that we love God, but the truth is we can tell by our actions whether His love is really dwelling in us or not (1 John 3:17). Instead of thinking we have to earn the blessing of God by doing these things, we need to recognize that living properly, treating other people right, loving our mates, and so forth are all byproducts of a relationship with God. If we would take the truths Andrew's talked about in this study—that all of our sins have been paid for, that God's not angry with us, and so on—and meditate on them, the Lord would reveal His love to us. Once we fall in love with God and His love begins to flow in our lives, it'll cause us to live holy. We will have our **"fruit unto holiness, and the end everlasting life"** (Rom. 6:22). Holiness is the fruit, not the root, of salvation.

5. Religion always focuses on the external person (1 Sam. 16:7). It's always trying to get us to clean up the outside—fix this and quit doing that—because that's what mankind looks at and deals with. As long as we come to church, pay our tithes, and dress the way religious people want us to when we're there, they don't care what we do during the week. Religion just deals with the external, but God deals with the heart. The Lord wants to come in, touch our hearts, and reveal His love to us. If that ever happens, the rest will be taken care of. God looks at our hearts!

4. A. Read 1 John 3:17 and Romans 6:22. How can we tell if God's love is really dwelling in us or not? (By our actions)
   B. Is holiness the fruit or the root of salvation? (The fruit)
5. A. Read 1 Samuel 16:7. What does religion always focus on and deal with? (The external person)
   B. What does God look at and deal with? (Our hearts)

God Looks at the Heart
LESSON 21 – DISCIPLESHIP QUESTIONS

1. To whom was 1 John 4:7-10 written?

2. How should we treat one another?

3. Why?

4. If someone is born of God and knows Him, what fruit will be evident in their life?

5. Someone who doesn't know God cannot what?

6. Why?

7. How was the love of God manifested toward us?

8. Why did He come?

9. How?

10. Since God loved us, whom did He send?

11. Why did He come?

12. According to 1 Peter 3:3, should our outward adorning be of the utmost importance to us?

13. To whom was 1 John 4:11-16 written?

14. What ought we to do since God so loved us?

15. Has anyone seen God at any time?

16. When God dwells in us and His love is perfected in us, what will we do?

17. Why did the Father send the Son?

18. If God dwells in someone and they dwell in God, what will they confess?

19. What have John and the believers he's writing known and believed?

20. Who is love?

21. Someone who dwells in love dwells in whom?

22. And who in them?

23. According to 1 John 3:17, what causes the author to ask, "How does the love of God dwell in them?"
    A. Someone sees their brother in need.
    B. They have this world's goods.
    C. They shut up their bowels of compassion from them.
    D. All of the above.
    E. None of the above.

24. According to Romans 6:22, what have we been made free from?

25. What have we become?

26. What kind of fruit have we?

27. The end of which is what?

28. In 1 Samuel 16:7, who was speaking to Samuel?

29. Who looks on the outward appearance?

30. Who looks on the heart?

God Looks at the Heart

LESSON 21 – ANSWER KEY

1. The beloved.

2. With love.

3. Because love is of God.

4. Love.

5. Love.

6. Because God is love.

7. God sent His only begotten Son into the world.

8. That we might live.

9. Through Him.

10. His Son.

11. To be the propitiation for our sins.

12. No.

13. The beloved.

14. We ought also to love one another.

15. No.

16. Love one another.

17. To be the Savior of the world.

18. That Jesus is the Son of God.

19. The love that God has toward them.

20. God.

21. God.

22. God.

23. A. Someone sees their brother in need.
    B. They have this world's goods.
    C. They shut up their bowels of compassion from them.
    D. All of the above.

24. Sin.

25. Servants to God.

26. Holiness.

27. Everlasting life.

28. The Lord.

29. Man.

30. The Lord.

God Looks at the Heart

Beloved, let us love one another: for love is of God; and every one that loveth is born of God, and knoweth God. He that loveth not knoweth not God; for God is love. In this was manifested the love of God toward us, because that God sent his only begotten Son into the world, that we might live through him. Herein is love, not that we loved God, but that he loved us, and sent his Son to be the propitiation for our sins.

1 JOHN 4:7-10

Whose adorning let it not be that outward adorning of plaiting the hair, and of wearing of gold, or of putting on of apparel.

1 PETER 3:3

Beloved, if God so loved us, we ought also to love one another. No man hath seen God at any time. If we love one another, God dwelleth in us, and his love is perfected in us. Hereby know we that we dwell in him, and he in us, because he hath given us of his Spirit. And we have seen and do testify that the Father sent the Son to be the Saviour of the world. Whosoever shall confess that Jesus is the Son of God, God dwelleth in him, and he in God. And we have known and believed the love that God hath to us. God is love; and he that dwelleth in love dwelleth in God, and God in him.

1 JOHN 4:11-16

But whoso hath this world's good, and seeth his brother have need, and shutteth up his bowels of compassion from him, how dwelleth the love of God in him?

1 JOHN 3:17

But now being made free from sin, and become servants to God, ye have your fruit unto holiness, and the end everlasting life.

ROMANS 6:22

But the LORD said unto Samuel, Look not on his countenance, or on the height of his stature; because I have refused him: for the LORD seeth not as man seeth; for man looketh on the outward appearance, but the LORD looketh on the heart.

1 SAMUEL 16:7

Receive His Love
LESSON 22

(See *Note to Teacher* in **Additional Information**.)

When you see someone fall in love with God, don't try to squelch that and put them into your religious form. Just encourage them in the love of God! His love will cause them to start keeping the commandments.

If you're sinning, it's because the love of God isn't flowing through you. If you're committing adultery, don't just say, "O God, help me do this so I'll quit operating in lust, and then I can start getting my prayers answered." That's totally wrong. If you're operating in lust, it's because you don't love God with all of your heart, and you aren't loving your mate. If you were, then you'd never do anything to hurt them. You aren't receiving and giving God's love.

Certain segments of the body of Christ are really big into these so-called "accountability groups." You meet together with other people for the purpose of holding each other "accountable." Basically, somebody's checking up on you. If you would lie to God, if you were going to sneak around and try to do something behind His back, you'll find a way to beat that accountability group. It may be a factor—something in your line of defense—but it shouldn't be your first line of defense.

What ought to keep you on the straight and narrow is your own personal relationship with God. It ought to be the fact that He loves you.

Joseph

When Potiphar's wife pressed Joseph to commit adultery with her, he said:

How then can I do this great wickedness, and sin against God?

GENESIS 39:9

Joseph didn't consider whether he'd get caught or not. He didn't think about how much he had suffered. After all he'd been through, it would have been easy for him to rationalize and say "I deserve to indulge myself this time," but he didn't. Joseph had a personal relationship with God. That's what kept him straight.

This is what's missing in many people's lives. They have a system of rules, and they're doing all kinds of things. They're practicing "behavior modification."

You may be trying to quit smoking, drinking, or some other bad habit, thinking that doing so will make you accepted with God. Yet the problem is that in your heart, you just haven't understood how much God loves you. You haven't been enjoying Him. If you truly fell in love with God, you'd find that these other things would just fall by the wayside.

God loves you independent of your performance. If you ever really received a revelation of that, and knew it, you'd be so thankful that God Almighty—the only one who really has a right to hate you—loves you. If you received a revelation of His unconditional love, you would fall so head over heels in love with Him that you'd give up bubble gum if you thought that would please Him. You'd do anything. It wouldn't matter. Instead of saying "How little do I have to do to get God to answer my prayer?" it'd be just the opposite. You'd be serving the Lord with your whole heart.

The First Step

God loves us! If we were preaching the love of God, people would be laying down their lives because of love. Love is a greater motivation than fear. You don't need to be afraid, wondering, *What's going to happen if I just start loving God? Will I just go out and commit sin?* No. You'll wind up serving God more accidentally than you ever have on purpose.

A friend of mine in Chicago started preaching on God's love and grace, saying, "You just need to love God. He's not mad at you. You don't go to hell for smoking." Some of the elders in the church became really upset. Within a week or two, some of the people in the congregation began standing on the doorstep smoking as people came in and out of church. So the elders came to the pastor and said, "See what your preaching has done! Now they're standing out there smoking because you're saying that God loves them whether they smoke or not." Wisely, he answered, "Go ask if any of them have started smoking since I began preaching this." Not a single one of them had! What happened was they just quit being hypocritical about it. They stopped trying to hide it behind breath mints, hoping nobody could tell they were smoking. This was their first step toward getting free.

I'm not advocating that we change the standards. It's not a new commandment; it's the same thing. But it's a new method. Instead of telling people to quit those things so God will love them, tell them, "God loves you in spite of who you are, not because of who you are." Let them know about the love of God, and the love of God will cause them to start living holy. It will inspire and empower them to begin doing the right things.

That's what Jesus did. He embraced people who were harlots, tax collectors, and thieves—people who were rejected by the religious system. If Jesus were here today, I believe He would do just like He did in Bible times. The religious leaders would persecute Him, and the religious people would crucify Him. Jesus wouldn't last three years in today's religious system. They'd crucify Him in a much shorter period of time. Why? Because Jesus loved people totally independent of their performance. Then He made covenant with them not based on their actions but on whether or not they received His love.

The church has been preaching the wrong message. Mankind tends to look on the flesh and judge people by their actions and outward appearance. We need to start operating in the Spirit and loving people unconditionally. However, we can't give away what we don't have. First of all, we need to receive God's unconditional love for ourselves.

He Wants to Set You Free

Have you been suffering from spiritual dyslexia? Are you trying to overcome some specific problem so God will love you? Or are you saying in your heart, "Lord, I need to know Your love for me. I need a spiritual revelation—not just a goose bump or a feeling. God, I want to see Your love for me"?

Once you see that love, it'll transform your life. That's how it happened for me.

Are you saying, "Lord, I've been going about this all wrong. I've been trying to change from the outside in, instead of the inside out"? Is the Holy Spirit showing you that you need a revelation of the love of God? If so, it's because He wants to set you free.

Be honest with yourself. Are you saying, "I don't have a revelation of God's love. I need a total transformation. I need to be healed of this spiritual dyslexia and receive a revelation of God's love"? If that's you, I want to lead you in a prayer. God wants to do a miracle in your heart right now. He wants to transform you from the inside out.

When you receive a spiritual revelation of God's unconditional love, and start walking in it, your actions will change. God's love will set you free from things. Perfect love always casts out fear.

Open Your Heart

God touched my life and transformed me. Since He's no respecter of persons, He wants to reveal to you the same unconditional love that He's revealed to me. You just have to open your heart and receive.

Pray out loud right now:

"Father, my focus has been on the outside. I've been trying to stop all of these actions and clean myself up in order for You to love me. But now I see that it's not this way at all. It's just a matter of receiving Your love. Father, I want to know You. I desire to receive a spiritual revelation of Your love. Your Word says that the Holy Spirit will teach me all things, lead me into all truth, and bring all things to my remembrance that Jesus has spoken to me. Right now, I believe that You are revealing Yourself to me through the Holy Spirit. By faith, I receive Your unconditional love.

"Father, I ask You to break these feelings of guilt, shame, confusion, and condemnation that a works mentality has produced on the inside of me. Thank You for showing me Your supernatural love. Right now, I believe that a seed is being planted in me that will grow. As I meditate on these truths from Your Word, they are going to become a deeper conviction, a deeper revelation of Your unconditional love for me. I thank You that it's Your love that will cause me to start living right. It's Your love that will break these bondages in my life. I receive Your love. Thank You, Jesus!"

Have other people hurt you? Have you been abused? Are you transposing those things onto God, thinking that He treats you the same way these people have? That's wrong. It's irrational for you to be mad at God for the way other people have treated you. God isn't like that. He doesn't control all of those things. God is a good God. He's been faithful to you. God has never failed you!

Pray:

"Father, You've been faithful to me. You've been good to me. Please forgive me for swallowing the devil's lie that You love me only when I'm lovely, only when I've done things right. Forgive me for not searching this out in Your Word and allowing myself to be deceived. I believe that You are setting me free from all religious bondage. I am beginning to experience Your unconditional love right now. I break these religious strongholds that have exalted themselves against the knowledge of You in my life. I release my spiritual weapons and cast that junk down. I take every thought captive and bring them under obedience to Christ."

Progressive Revelation

"Father, I thank You that these truths will be brought back to my remembrance by the Holy Spirit. Your Word is going to burn on the inside of me until it cleans out all of this wrong thinking and I come to know You intimately as a good, merciful, kind heavenly Father. You placed all of the judgment I deserved upon Jesus. You aren't angry with me. You aren't disappointed with me. The war is over. Your anger against my sin is satisfied. You rejected Your own Son so that You would never reject me. Thank You for loving me! I receive Your love!"

I encourage you to spend some time right now just praising and worshiping Him. Let His unconditional love overwhelm you. Enjoy His awesome presence. Relationship with God is what you were created for. Hallelujah!

What you're receiving is a progressive revelation. Although I had that encounter with the Lord on March 23, 1968, I've grown tremendously in what God has done since then. I had an emotional experience, but emotions don't last forever. If I hadn't received the truth, begun to meditate on it, and learned these things, I would have long since lost that experience. It's the truth you know and have established in your heart that sets you free (John 8:32). It doesn't matter how you feel; you could minister this truth to yourself and control your emotions. You can learn to enjoy the presence of God even without a goose bump. The love of God isn't a feeling; it's a revelation. That revelation can produce feelings, but feelings come and go. The revelation doesn't. Praise God!

If you prayed these prayers in faith, something has definitely begun. Go to the Word of God. Start praying and seeking Him. Meditate on these truths, and the Lord will continue revealing His love to you. He's promised that when you seek Him with all your heart, you will find (Jer. 29:13). God is love (1 John 4:8). He longs to reveal Himself to you and draw you into a deeper relationship with Him. Praise God, the war is over!

Receive His Love
LESSON 22 – OUTLINE

I. If you're sinning, it's because the love of God isn't flowing through you.

    A. You aren't receiving and giving God's love.

    B. What ought to keep you on the straight and narrow is your own personal relationship with God.

    C. It ought to be the fact that He loves you.

    D. Joseph had a personal relationship with God—that's what kept him straight.

> **How then can I do this great wickedness, and sin against God?**
>
> Genesis 39:9

    E. If you truly fell in love with God, you'd find that these other things would just fall by the wayside.

II. God loves you independent of your performance.

    A. Love is a greater motivation than fear.

    B. Let people know about the love of God, and the love of God will cause them to start living holy.

    C. It will inspire and empower them to begin doing the right things.

    D. Jesus loved people totally independent of their performance.

    E. Then He made covenant with them not based on their actions but on whether or not they received His love.

III. First of all, you need to receive God's unconditional love for yourself.

    A. When you receive a spiritual revelation of God's unconditional love, and start walking in it, your actions will change.

    B. You just have to open your heart and receive.

"Father, my focus has been on the outside. I've been trying to stop all of these actions and clean myself up in order for You to love me. But now I see that it's not this way at all. It's just a matter of receiving Your love. Father, I want to know You. I desire to receive a spiritual revelation of Your love. Your Word says that the Holy Spirit will teach me all things, lead me

into all truth, and bring all things to my remembrance that Jesus has spoken to me. Right now, I believe that You are revealing Yourself to me through the Holy Spirit. By faith, I receive Your unconditional love.

"Father, I ask You to break these feelings of guilt, shame, confusion, and condemnation that a works mentality has produced on the inside of me. Thank You for showing me Your supernatural love. Right now, I believe that a seed is being planted in me that will grow. As I meditate on these truths from Your Word, they are going to become a deeper conviction, a deeper revelation of Your unconditional love for me. I thank You that it's Your love that will cause me to start living right. It's Your love that will break these bondages in my life. I receive Your love. Thank You, Jesus!"

    C. It's irrational for you to be mad at God for the way other people have treated you.

"Father, You've been faithful to me. You've been good to me. Please forgive me for swallowing the devil's lie that You love me only when I'm lovely, only when I've done things right. Forgive me for not searching this out in Your Word and allowing myself to be deceived. I believe that You are setting me free from all religious bondage. I am beginning to experience Your unconditional love right now. I break these religious strongholds that have exalted themselves against the knowledge of You in my life. I release my spiritual weapons and cast that junk down. I take every thought captive and bring them under obedience to Christ."

"Father, I thank You that these truths will be brought back to my remembrance by the Holy Spirit. Your Word is going to burn on the inside of me until it cleans out all of this wrong thinking and I come to know You intimately as a good, merciful, kind heavenly Father. You placed all of the judgment I deserved upon Jesus. You aren't angry with me. You aren't disappointed with me. The war is over. Your anger against my sin is satisfied. You rejected Your own Son so that You would never reject me. Thank You for loving me! I receive Your love!"

    D. Spend some time right now just praising and worshiping Him.

    E. Let His unconditional love overwhelm you—enjoy His awesome presence.

    F. Relationship with God is what you were created for.

IV. What you're receiving is a progressive revelation.

    A. If I hadn't received the truth, begun to meditate on it, and learned these things, I would have long since lost that experience of God revealing His love to me.

    B. It's the truth you know and have established in your heart that sets you free (John 8:32).

    C. The love of God isn't a feeling—it's a revelation.

    D. That revelation can produce feelings, but feelings come and go—the revelation doesn't.

V. If you prayed these prayers in faith, something has definitely begun.

A. Go to the Word of God.

B. Start praying and seeking Him (Jer. 29:13).

C. Meditate on these truths, and the Lord will continue revealing His love to you.

D. He longs to reveal Himself to you and draw you into a deeper relationship with Him (1 John 4:8).

E. Praise God, the war is over!

Receive His Love

1.   If we're sinning, it's because the love of God isn't flowing through us. We aren't receiving and giving God's love. What ought to keep us on the straight and narrow is our own personal relationship with God. It ought to be the fact that He loves us. Joseph had a personal relationship with God—that's what kept him straight (Gen. 39:9). If we truly fell in love with God, we'd find that these other things would just fall by the wayside.

2.   God loves us independent of our performance. Love is a greater motivation than fear. Let people know about the love of God, and the love of God will cause them to start living holy. It will inspire and empower them to begin doing the right things. Jesus loved people totally independent of their performance. Then He made covenant with them not based on their actions but on whether or not they received His love.

3.   First of all, we need to receive God's unconditional love for ourselves. When we receive a spiritual revelation of God's unconditional love, and start walking in it, our actions will change. We just have to open our hearts and receive.

1. A. Why do we sin? (Because the love of God isn't flowing through us—we are aren't receiving and giving God's love)
   B. Read Genesis 39:9. What is it that ought to keep us on the straight and narrow? (Our own personal relationship with God)
2. A. Is God's love for us dependent upon our performance? (No)
   B. How are people inspired and empowered to live holy and do the right things? (Through knowing the love of God)
   C. How did Jesus make covenant with people? (Based on whether or not they received His love)
3. A. First of all, what do we need to receive for ourselves? (God's unconditional love)
   B. How will our actions change? (By receiving and starting to walk in a spiritual revelation of God's unconditional love)
   C. What must we do? (Open our hearts and receive)

4.   What we're receiving is a progressive revelation. If Andrew hadn't received the truth, begun to meditate on it, and learned these things, he would have long since lost that experience of God revealing His love to him. It's the truth we know and have established in our hearts that sets us free (John 8:32). The love of God isn't a feeling—it's a revelation. That revelation can produce feelings, but feelings come and go—the revelation doesn't.

5.   Let's go to the Word of God. Let's start praying and seeking Him (Jer. 29:13). As we meditate on these truths, the Lord will continue revealing His love to us. He longs to reveal Himself to us and draw us into a deeper relationship with Him (1 John 4:8). Praise God, the war is over!

4. A. Is this a one-time or a progressive revelation? (Progressive)
   B. Read John 8:32. What is it that sets us free? (The truth we know and have established in our hearts)
   C. Is the love of God a feeling or a revelation? (A revelation)
5. A. Read Jeremiah 29:13 and 1 John 4:8. As we go to the Word of God—praying, seeking Him, and meditating on these truths—what will the Lord do? (He will continue revealing His love to us)
   B. What does Jesus long to do? (He longs to reveal Himself to us and draw us into a deeper relationship with Him)

Receive His Love

Note to Teacher: As you read through this final **Lesson** aloud, take time to minister to the individual or group that you are leading through this study. Pray with them through the prayers included in this **Lesson**. This is your opportunity to respond to God and what He's saying to you individually and as a group. Don't rush this time, but give the Holy Spirit room to work in each person's heart. Then, be sure to discuss with each other what the Lord has said and done.

My teachings entitled, *God's Kind of Love: The Cure for What Ails Ya!*, *God's Kind of Love To You*, and *God's Kind of Love Though You* will help you continue to meditate on the love of God. I encourage you to get these materials and water the seed that's been planted in your heart.

And remember, these audio teachings—and many more—are available free as MP3 downloads at our website: www.awmi.net.

Receive His Love
LESSON 22 – DISCIPLESHIP QUESTIONS

1. Who was speaking in Genesis 39:9?

2. To whom was he speaking?

3. Besides Potiphar himself, was there anyone greater in his house than Joseph?

4. Other than his wife, had Potiphar kept anything back from Joseph?

5. What did Joseph call this opportunity he was being offered?

6. Joseph recognized that if he were to yield to this temptation, he would sin against whom?

7. Joseph had received God's love and maintained a close relationship with Him, which kept him walking in what?

8. According to John 8:32, what shall we know?

9. What shall the truth make us?

10. According to Jeremiah 29:13, when will we find Him?

11. According to 1 John 4:8, what fruit does knowing God produce in us?

12. God is what?

Receive His Love
LESSON 22 – ANSWER KEY

1. Joseph.

2. Potiphar's wife.

3. No.

4. No.

5. Great wickedness.

6. God.

7. Holiness.

8. The truth.

9. Free.

10. When we search for Him with all our hearts.

11. Love.

12. Love.

Receive His Love

There is none greater in this house than I; neither hath he kept back any thing from me but thee, because thou art his wife: how then can I do this great wickedness, and sin against God?

GENESIS 39:9

And ye shall know the truth, and the truth shall make you free.

JOHN 8:32

And ye shall seek me, and find me, when ye shall search for me with all your heart.

JEREMIAH 29:13

He that loveth not knoweth not God; for God is love.

1 JOHN 4:8

Receive Jesus as Your Savior

Choosing to receive Jesus Christ as your Lord and Savior is the most important decision you'll ever make!

God's Word promises,

> **That if thou shalt confess with thy mouth the Lord Jesus, and shalt believe in thine heart that God hath raised him from the dead, thou shalt be saved. For with the heart man believeth unto righteousness; and with the mouth confession is made unto salvation.**
>
> ROMANS 10:9-10

And,

> **For whosoever shall call upon the name of the Lord shall be saved.**
>
> ROMANS 10:13

By His grace, God has already done everything to provide salvation. Your part is simply to believe and receive.

Pray out loud, *"Jesus, I confess that You are my Lord and Savior. I believe in my heart that God raised You from the dead. By faith in Your Word, I receive salvation now. Thank You for saving me!"*

The very moment you commit your life to Jesus Christ, the truth of His Word instantly comes to pass in your spirit. Now that you're born again, there's a brand-new you!

Receive the Holy Spirit

As His child, your loving heavenly Father wants to give you the supernatural power you need to live this new life.

> **For every one that asketh receiveth; and he that seeketh findeth; and to him that knocketh it shall be opened...If ye...know how to give good gifts unto your children: how much more shall your heavenly Father give the Holy Spirit to them that ask him?**
>
> LUKE 11:10 AND 13

All you have to do is ask, believe, and receive!

Pray, *"Father, I recognize my need for Your power to live this new life. Please fill me with Your Holy Spirit. By faith, I receive it right now! Thank You for baptizing me. Holy Spirit, You are welcome in my life."*

Congratulations! Now you're filled with God's supernatural power. Some syllables from a language you don't recognize will rise up from your heart to your mouth (1 Cor. 14:14). As you speak them out loud by faith, you're releasing God's power from within and building yourself up in the spirit. (1 Cor. 14:4.) You can do this whenever and wherever you like.

It doesn't really matter whether you felt anything or not when you prayed to receive the Lord and His Spirit. If you believed in your heart that you received, then God's Word promises you did. **"Therefore I say unto you, What things soever ye desire, when ye pray, believe that ye receive them, and ye shall have them"** (Mark 11:24). God always honors His Word; believe it!

Please contact me and let me know that you've prayed to receive Jesus as your Savior or to be filled with the Holy Spirit. I would like to rejoice with you and help you understand more fully what has taken place in your life. I'll send you a free gift that will help you understand and grow in your new relationship with the Lord. Welcome to your new life!

About the Author

For over three decades, Andrew Wommack has traveled America and the world teaching the truth of the Gospel. His profound revelation of the Word of God is taught with clarity and simplicity, emphasizing God's unconditional love and the balance between grace and faith. He reaches millions of people through the daily *Gospel Truth* radio and television programs, broadcast both domestically and internationally. He founded Charis Bible College in 1994 and has since established CBC extension schools in other major cities of America and around the world. Andrew has produced a library of teaching materials, available in print, audio, and visual formats. And, as it has been from the beginning, his ministry continues to distribute free audio materials to those who cannot afford them.

Other Teachings by Andrew Wommack

Discover the Keys to Staying Full of God

Do you feel as if your Christian life is full of highs and lows? Perhaps you attend a special church service that draws you close to God or even experience a healing. In those moments your heart is filled with the presence of God, but within a few days or weeks, you once again feel empty or sick. You are not alone. Even though many believers experience this, it is not what the Lord intended.

The keys to staying full of God are not a secret and they are not mysterious; they are simple. For that very reason, few people recognize their value and even less practice it! In this amazingly practical message, Andrew reveals the essentials to a strong, close relationship with God. Learn what they are and how to put them into practice. It will keep your heart sensitive toward God, and your relationship will grow like never before!

Item Code: 1029-C   4-CD album
Item Code: 324   Paperback
Item Code: 424   Study Guide

Grace, the Power of the Gospel

Recent surveys indicate that the vast majority of Christians, those claiming to be born again, believe their salvation is at least in part dependent upon their behavior and actions. Yes, they believe Jesus died for their sin, but once they accept Him as their Savior, they believe they must still meet a certain standard to be "good" enough.

If that is true, then what is that standard, and how do you know when you have met it? The church has tried to answer these questions for centuries, and it always results in religious and legalistic bondage.

So, what is the answer? It begins by asking the right question. It is not "What must I do?" but rather "What did Jesus do?" By understanding the Apostle Paul's revelation from the book of Romans of what Jesus did, you will never again wonder if you're meeting the standard.

Item Code: 1014-C   4-CD album
Item Code: 322   Paperback
Item Code: 422   Study Guide

Spirit, Soul & Body

Understanding the relationship of your spirit, soul, and body is foundational to your Christian life. You will never truly know how much God loves you or believe what His Word says about you until you do. In this series, learn how they're related and how that knowledge will release the life of your spirit into your body and soul. It may even explain why many things are not working the way you had hoped.

Item Code: 1027   4-Tape album
Item Code: 1027-C   4-CD album
Item Code: 1027-D   DVD album
Item Code: 318   Paperback
Item Code: 418   Study Guide

The True Nature of God

Are you confused about the nature of God? Is He the God of judgment found in the Old Testament or the God of mercy and grace found in the New Testament? Andrew's revelation on this subject will set you free and give you a confidence in your relationship with God like never before. This is truly nearly-too-good-to-be-true news.

Item Code: 1002   5-Tape album
Item Code: 1002-C   5-CD album
Item Code: 308   Paperback

Living in the Balance of Grace and Faith

This book explains one of the biggest controversies in the church today. Is it grace or faith that releases the power of God? Does God save people in His sovereignty, or does your faith move Him? You may be surprised by the answers as Andrew reveals what the Bible has to say concerning these important questions and more. This will help you receive from God in a greater way and will change the way you relate to Him.

Item Code: 301B   Paperback

The Believer's Authority

Like it or not, every one of us is in a spiritual war. You can't be discharged from service, and ignorance of the battlefield only aids the enemy. In war, God is always for us, and the devil is against us. Whichever one we cooperate with will win. And there's only one way the enemy can get your cooperation—that's through deception. In this teaching, Andrew exposes this war and the enemy for what he is.

Item Code: 1045   6-Tape album
Item Code: 1045-C   6-CD album
Item Code: 1045-D   DVD album (as recorded from television)

The Effects of Praise

Every Christian wants a stronger walk with the Lord. But how do you get there? Many don't know the true power of praise. It's essential. Listen as Andrew teaches biblical truths that will not only spark understanding but will help promote spiritual growth so you will experience victory.

Item Code: 1004   3-Tape album
Item Code: 1004-C   3-CD album
Item Code: 309   Paperback

God Wants You Well

Health is something everyone wants. Billions of dollars are spent each year trying to retain or restore health. So why does religion tell us God uses sickness to teach us something? It even tries to make us believe that sickness is a blessing. That's just not true. God wants you well!

Item Code: 1036   4-Tape album
Item Code: 1036-C   4-CD album
Item Code: 1036-D   DVD album